AN INTRODUCTION TO THE COMPARATIVE GRAMMAR
OF THE SEMITIC LANGUAGES

PORTA LINGUARUM ORIENTALIUM

HERAUSGEGEBEN VON BERTOLD SPULER UND HANS WEHR

NEUE SERIE

VI

AN INTRODUCTION
TO
THE COMPARATIVE GRAMMAR
OF
THE SEMITIC LANGUAGES

PHONOLOGY AND MORPHOLOGY

SECOND PRINTING

1969

OTTO HARRASSOWITZ · WIESBADEN

AN INTRODUCTION
TO
THE COMPARATIVE GRAMMAR
OF
THE SEMITIC LANGUAGES
PHONOLOGY AND MORPHOLOGY

BY

SABATINO MOSCATI
ANTON SPITALER   EDWARD ULLENDORFF
WOLFRAM VON SODEN

EDITED BY
SABATINO MOSCATI

SECOND PRINTING

1969

OTTO HARRASSOWITZ · WIESBADEN

Table of Contents

Preface

The nature of this book and the principles which guided its composition depend in the first place on the series to which it belongs. It is thus an elementary introduction to the comparative grammar of the Semitic languages, intended primarily as a textbook and limited in its scope so as to serve for a beginners' course. Such an introduction must be clear in expression while respecting scientific terminology; it must concentrate upon the essential facts while mentioning various particular questions of special importance; it must avoid doubtful and disputed hypotheses while indicating certain of the lines of research being pursued and certain more important divergences of opinion, so as to give an adequate notion of present-day scientific trends.

To these general principles dependent upon the present series, others must be added, adopted in view of the particular situation of Semitic linguistics. The limits in time and space of the material to be taken into consideration, the classification of the various languages, the manner for reconstructing the presumed common forms and tracing their development in the various languages, the reasons for abstaining from a systematic treatment of syntax and of vocabulary, the choice of a system of transliteration, the solution of the problem of a conventional root for schemes and for paradigms, the dates up to which the bibliography can be taken into account: these questions, and others too, called for decisions, and these decisions are set forth in the course of the exposition (cf. in particular §§ 1.1—9, 6.1—15, 8.66—96, 12.3, introduction to the Bibliography etc.). It must be admitted that many of these decisions are but imperfect ones, but one may well doubt whether different decisions would have been any more felicitous, or even equally so.

As is well known, an introduction to the comparative grammar of the Semitic languages has been a *desideratum* for several decades, and the need for such an introduction as a textbook was urgent. Hence, when the directors of *Porta Linguarum Orientalium* did me the honour of inviting me to write this book (an honour for which I offer them my sincere thanks), I was of two minds. On the one hand, I was but too well aware of the need for someone at long last to undertake the task; but on the other hand, it was equally clear to me that the accomplishment of this task, involving as it did the digestion of an immense linguistic and bibliographical material and its condensation into an exposition which by reason of its brevity could not but be partial and simplified, would inevitably be open to criticism from all sides. When the author is obliged to sift his matter, to make selections, to confine his exposition within strict limits, then any one can make a running criticism of the result and easily cite imperfections and omissions; furthermore, not everyone is ready to recognize the sacrifice represented by the undertaking of a thankless task whose accomplishment is, after all, indispensable for the common good.

If, however, I was thus able from the start to foresee the endless difficulties and the inevitable deficiencies connected with such an enterprise, I was likewise able to endeavour to reduce those difficulties and deficiencies to a minimum. The procedure which I adopted was the following: I first composed as best I could a preliminary and summary draft (*Lezioni di linguistica semitica*, Rome 1960), and I then requested certain eminently qualified colleagues to lend me their aid by suggesting, with particular but not exclusive regard for each one's speciality, an abundance of additions and alterations. These colleagues, who most generously responded to my appeal for their collaboration, are Professors A. Spitaler, E. Ullendorff and W. von Soden; and to them I express my heartfelt gratitude. Having assembled the list of additions and alterations thus proposed, I proceeded to a new and fuller redaction of the book, bearing in mind the material thus furnished. It is, of course, clear that not in every single case was it possible to bring my views into harmony with those of my three collaborators; this obliged me to make a certain selection, and I have not always been able to accord full weight to their proposals; it is therefore only just that I bear the entire responsibility for this work. However, I must add that I have very largely taken their proposals into account, even in not a few cases in which I was not in agreement with them, so that the work is truly the result of a collaboration.

Other eminently qualified colleagues have likewise read my preliminary draft and favoured me with their suggestions and opinions, namely Professors K. Petráček, C. Rabin and S. Segert, to whom I offer my sincere gratitude. I owe a like debt of gratitude to Professor B. Migliorini, for his advice in the area of general linguistics, and to Professor T. de Mauro, who has likewise advised me in this respect. Finally, I owe a special gratitude to the Publishers, for having so willingly undertaken the not inconsiderable labour involved in a work composed with the collaboration of several persons.

Now that the book is written, I can in all frankness declare that I find it unsatisfactory; and I think that my collaborators would agree with me. Each one of us could, if he wished, write dozens of pages of criticism of the book, for the reasons already given. We trust, however, that our colleagues, in reading this book, instead of dwelling upon the admitted manifold defects will duly reflect upon the fact that in a work such as this these defects, were almost inevitable, and that different solutions of the problems involved would in all probability have been equally unsatisfactory. We trust, indeed, that our colleagues will take into consideration the fact that at last, after so many decades, they have at their disposal an elementary textbook — although necessarily defective — of the comparative grammar of the Semitic languages.

October 1962   Sabatino Moscati

I. The Semitic Languages

A. *Scope of the Survey*

1. Definition

1.1. The name "Semitic" is conventionally applied to a group of languages spoken in western Asia, or generally originating from that area, and characterized by a large number of common elements in their phonology, morphology, vocabulary, and syntax; they also share certain common tendencies in their evolution. These elements, preserved despite lapse of time and change of place, suggest the idea of a common origin; at all events, they characterize and set apart a linguistic group possessed of a remarkable degree of internal unity.

1.2. The adjective "Semitic" was brought into use by A. L. Schlözer (1781) as a designation of the languages spoken by the Aramaeans, the Hebrews, the Arabs, and other peoples, on the basis of *Gen.* 10, 21—31; 11, 10—26. Once introduced, the adjective "Semitic" was applied to all the languages of the group, including those subsequently discovered. The affinities existing between the various languages had, of course, been recognized long before Schlözer's time; but the group itself had not as such been identified and marked out: these languages, like others in Asia, had generally been referred to as "Oriental languages".

2. Classification

1.3. The Semitic languages occupied in ancient times the following regions of western Asia (from east to west): Mesopotamia, Syria-Palestine, Arabia. On the coast that lies opposite southwestern Arabia, waves of migration led to the occupation by Semitic populations (and thus by Semitic languages) of another region: Ethiopia. Mesopotamia, Syria-Palestine, Arabia, and Ethiopia constitute, therefore, the ancient habitat of the Semitic

1*

languages. Beyond this area they have spread only as a result of secondary developments, i.e. migration, colonization, or conquest.

1.4. The grouping of the Semitic languages is usually based on their geographical distribution: North-East Semitic (Mesopotamia), North-West Semitic (Syria-Palestine), and South-West Semitic (Arabia and Ethiopia). It is obvious that this division is closely connected with that of the peoples who spoke those Semitic languages; for the purposes of linguistic inquiry, however, a division which simply projects ethnical entities on to the linguistic plane is bound to be imprecise. Schemes of classification which identify and distinguish groupings within the Semitic area on the basis of specific bundles of isoglosses may derive support from structural, functional, and genetic criteria. The position of certain languages in these classification schemes has been, and still is, the object of controversy; this applies to the position of Ugaritic (cf. § 3.9) and of Amorite (cf. § 3.8) as between the western and the eastern languages; to Nabataean and Palmyrene within Aramaic (cf. § 3.16); to South Arabian as between Arabic and Ethiopic (cf. §4.1), etc. Particular connexions have repeatedly been postulated between individual languages of different areas; but the problem remains as to how such affinities can be tested on the statistical, typological, or historical plane. Of some interest in this respect are certain common elements as well as points of contrast which have been observed between, for instance, Akkadian and Ethiopic: such relationships may be explained in accordance with the principles of linguistic geography. Similar interest, on the general Hamito-Semitic level, would attach to the connexions which have been claimed to exist between Akkadian and Libyco-Berber (cf. § 5.5). On the whole, it may however be said that the geographical division indicated above corresponds tolerably well (though not without certain exceptions) to the distribution of gross linguistic features. East Semitic exhibits from the outset certain independent characteristics as compared with West Semitic (cf. § 3.2); and these features become further accentuated in the course of time. In the western area, the distinction between the northern and the southern languages is more evident in their fully developed form than at the archaic stage (but it must be borne in mind that our knowledge of the archaic phase is fairly limited).

3. Nature and Extent of the Survey

1.5. The present survey has as its object the whole body of the classical Semitic languages. Data drawn from modern dialects will only be taken into consideration when they have a contribution to make to an examination of the earlier phases of the classical languages, either by reason of archaic elements which these modern tongues may have preserved or by virtue of any other relevant characteristics.

1.6. Within these limits the linguistic material of the present survey extends in time over some four thousand years: from the third millennium B.C., when we encounter the earliest manifestations of a Semitic language (Akkadian), until the first millennium A.D., when some of the great literary languages (Syriac, Arabic, Ethiopic) begin to flourish and to exert an influence well beyond those limits.

1.7. Geographically, the bulk of the material originates from the region indicated above (§ 1.3), while a limited portion of it comes from outside that area as a result of the spread of Semitic populations (Assyrians in Anatolia, Phoenicians on the coasts and islands of the Mediterranean—even as far as the Atlantic, Arabs in Africa and on the islands of the Indian Ocean, etc.).

1.8. Within the limits of time and space already described, the present study aims at a reconstruction of the earliest phonological and morphological units (Proto-Semitic, for which see § 5.1) as well as their historical development in the principal languages of the group. From this limitation the following consequences will inevitably result: in the first place, the exclusion of modern dialects and especially of secondary developments due to them; and, secondly, the relegation of a specific treatment of syntax and vocabulary, partly because of the elementary nature of this treatise and partly on account of the somewhat backward state of studies in those fields. Moreover, the present work does not aim at exhaustiveness and, while it places its main emphasis on the position in the great literary languages (Akkadian, Hebrew, Syriac, Arabic, Ethiopic), it adduces evidence from other Semitic languages and modern dialects only when of particular relevance—as is indeed appropriate to a survey of an essentially elementary character.

1.9. For a detailed description of the Semitic languages (which is outside the scope of this study) the reader is referred to the standard introductory works. The following observations are restricted to what is necessary for the clarification of the concepts and nomenclature adopted in this inquiry—especially in view of changing notions and terminological fluctuations current at the present time.

B. North-East Semitic

2.1. North-East Semitic is represented by Akkadian, spoken in Mesopotamia in the pre-Christian era. This language, which in the civilization of that region prevailed over, and eventually replaced, the non-Semitic Sumerian, derives its name from that of the city of Akkade, the capital of the empire of Sargon the Great (2350—2294 B.C., according to the "short" chronology). The principal phases of Akkadian are:

2.2. a) Old Akkadian may be dated between 2500 and 2000 B.C. approximately; owing to the limited extent of our documentation (very few texts from Assyria are extant) it is at present impossible to establish clearly defined differentiations of dialect. About 2000 B.C. the following principal dialects can be distinguished:

2.3. b) Babylonian, the dialect of the southern part of the region, is divided into Old Babylonian (about 2000—1500 B.C.) with several dialectal variations, Middle Babylonian (about 1500 to 1000 B.C.), and New Babylonian (about 1000 B.C. till the beginning of the Christian era). The most recent phase of New Babylonian (from about 600 B.C.), characterized by the infiltration of Aramaic words and linguistic peculiarities (cf. § 3.18), is more specifically called Late Babylonian ("Spätbabylonisch"), while the literary language used between about 1400 and 500 B.C. in Babylonia as well as in Assyria (and differing considerably from the spoken language) may be referred to as Later Babylonian ("Jungbabylonisch").

2.4. c) Assyrian, the dialect of the northern part of the region, is divided into Old Assyrian (about 2000—1500 B.C.), with texts principally of Cappadocian origin, Middle Assyrian (about 1500 to 1000 B.C.), and New Assyrian (about 1000—600 B.C.); the last-named is strongly aramaicized in its final phase.

2.5. In Old Akkadian and Old Babylonian texts (ca. 2400 to 1700 B.C.) occur hundreds of Semitic names which cannot be explained either on the basis of Akkadian or of "East Canaanite" (Amorite, cf. § 3.8). These names as well as other linguistic phenomena led von Soden (WZKM 56 [1960], pp. 185—91) to the conclusion that in the second half of the third millennium B.C. there must have existed a further Semitic language for which he proposed the name "Old-Amorite". A grammatical sketch of Old Amorite (from which certain peculiarities of Ugaritic might possibly be explained) has not yet been produced.

C. North-West Semitic

1. General Characteristics

3.1. North-West Semitic displays notable internal variations which reflect the rather chequered history of Syria and Palestine. It is the custom of grammars and works of introduction to the Semitic languages to divide the languages of this area into two main groups, i.e. the Canaanite and the Aramaic languages. But recent studies tend to show that this division is not in accord with the most ancient phase of Syro-Palestinian linguistic history (second millennium B.C.), because in that phase some of the isoglosses which distinguish the two groups had not yet been clearly drawn. This does not mean, of course, that in the second millennium B.C. there existed a lesser degree of variation in the local speech-forms of the North-West Semitic area, but merely that such distinctions manifested themselves in forms different from those current in the following millennium (Garbini, SNO). The division into Canaanite and Aramaic can be assessed only from the time when Aramaic made its historically and epigraphically attested appearance, i.e. from the first millennium B.C.; and even then the homogeneity of Aramaic is not matched by a comparable measure of uniformity in the languages grouped under the general heading of "Canaanite" (cf. § 3.12).

3.2. In the earliest historically attested phase of North-West Semitic many of the distinctive features that were later to contrast it with South-West Semitic had not yet been clearly realized—at least so far as our limited knowledge goes. Hence it may be surmised that in its first historical manifestations West Semitic displayed a greater degree of unity than can be discerned in its subsequent development when it was subjected to powerful disintegrating tendencies (cf. § 1.4). East Semitic was at every stage notably differentiated from its western neighbour.

2. The Languages of the Second Millennium B.C.

3.3. The most ancient form of North-West Semitic may be placed in the second millennium B.C. It embraces, in the first place, a group of texts of doubtful date and interpretation which, precisely for that reason, will not normally be discussed in this treatise. These texts include:

3.4. a) The pseudo-hieroglyphic inscriptions of Byblos, originally assigned by Dunand to the end of the third millennium B.C. but more recently dated by some scholars several centuries later and regarded linguistically as the most ancient manifestation of Phoenician.

3.5. b) The Proto-Sinaitic inscriptions, previously assigned to about 1800 B.C. but more recently dated by Albright about 1500. They are considered (but this is a matter of pure hypothesis which reflects the uncertainty of all schemes of classification) by Albright as North-West Semitic and by van den Branden as Proto-Arabic (representing a linguistic stage prior to the diffcrentiation between North and South Semitic).

3.6. c) A series of short inscriptions originating for the most part from Lachish and attributable to various dates in the second millennium (between 1800 and 1300 B.C. approx.).

3.7. Along with the group of texts just mentioned there exists another one (also belonging to the second millennium B.C.) whose interpretation and dating may be said to be generally established. The languages of these texts are:

3.8. a) Amorite (also called "East Canaanite", an inappropriate term used to designate the North-West Semitic tongues of the first half of the second millennium), which is reflected in the proper names and in certain linguistic peculiarities of the Akkadian texts of the period of the First Babylonian Dynasty, and in particular in the Mari texts (speech-forms not lacking in internal variegation which our inadequate knowledge does not as yet allow us to appreciate fully). The data drawn from the Akkadian texts are corroborated by transcriptions of North-West Semitic names of persons and places in Egyptian execration-texts (cf. also § 2.5).

3.9. b) Ugaritic, the language of the texts discovered at Ugarit (Rās Šamra) and belonging to the fourteenth and thirteenth centuries B.C. There has been much discussion as to the typological placing of this language within the framework of the Semitic languages (cf. § 1.4).

3.10. c) The language of the glosses (usually called "Canaanite") in the Tell Amarna letters (14th cent. B.C.) which are written in an Akkadian showing many Canaanite peculiarities. Similar considerations apply to the Akkadian texts from Ugarit (14th—13th cent.). The data drawn from this material are supplemented by a further group of Egyptian transcriptions belonging to the second half of the second millennium.

3.11. Towards the end of the second millennium B.C. we can discern the onset of other North-West Semitic languages which, since their full development belongs almost entirely to the first millennium, will be dealt with in the following paragraphs. With these languages, and within the limits set forth above (cf. § 3.1), the distinction between Canaanite and Aramaic may properly be introduced.

3. Canaanite

3.12. Canaanite represents the non-Aramaic linguistic manifestations of the Syro-Palestinian area, from the end of the second millennium B.C. onwards. The coherence or independence of Canaanite (except in so far as it is clearly distinguished from Aramaic) appears somewhat limited; so much so, in fact, that the very individuality of the group has been questioned by some scholars (Friedrich). This may, however, be largely attributable to our deficient means of ready linguistic identification. The Canaanite languages are:

3.13. a) Hebrew—including: the Biblical period whose literature may be dated approximately between 1200 and 200 B.C. and which is supplemented by a number of short inscriptions; the post-Biblical period, beginning with the apocryphal literature and the documents recently discovered near the Dead Sea (second and first centuries B.C.) and continuing with the rabbinical writings of the first centuries of the Christian era (Mišnā, Tōseftā, Midrāš); the poetical, philosophical, and exegetical literature of the Middle Ages and of modern times; and finally Modern Hebrew, nowadays spoken in Israel.

3.14. b) Phoenician and Punic, represented by the inscriptions of the ancient Phoenician cities (to be dated between the tenth and the first centuries B.C.) and by those of their Mediterranean colonies (between the ninth century B.C. and the second century A.D.).

3.15. c) Moabite, represented by the inscription of King Mẹša' of Moab of the ninth century B.C.; this inscription, according to the latest study (Segert), might however be regarded as a Hebrew text, belonging to the central Palestinian dialect, having possibly been drawn up by an Israelite in the service of the King of Moab.

4. Aramaic

3.16. Aramaic forms a considerable and wide-spread linguistic group whose earliest manifestation goes back to the beginning of the first millennium B.C. and which survives, in a few remnants, to the present day. We distinguish between an ancient phase, up to the first century B.C., and a subsequent division into two branches, West Aramaic (which appears to be a more direct continuation of Old Aramaic) and East Aramaic. Some scholars are inclined to ascribe the division into two branches to the second or the third century A.D. and include, under the name of Old Aramaic, Nabataean and Palmyrene; in the present survey these languages will, however, be subsumed under "West Aramaic".

a. Old Aramaic

3.17. a) Old Aramaic is the language (with some dialectal variants) of the most ancient inscriptions originating from Da-

mascus, Hama, Arpad, Šam'al, and Assyria, and belonging to the
period between the tenth and the eighth centuries B.C. Of these
inscriptions two from Šam'al (one of Panamuwa I and one of
Bar-Rakib) are of special importance, owing to their independent
characteristics, and represent the type of Aramaic known as
Ya'udic (derived from the name of the state of Šam'al Ya'udi).

3.18. b) Classical or Imperial Aramaic is the language used under
the Assyrian, Babylonian, and Persian empires (seventh to fourth
centuries B.C.) and continued by certain offshoots into the period
which followed. Evidence of this comes from Mesopotamia (Aramaic inscriptions and proper names, words and constructions in
New Assyrian and New Babylonian texts), Persia, western India,
Anatolia, Arabia, and Egypt. The papyri and ostraca from Egypt,
of the fifth and fourth centuries B.C., are of particular importance
and constitute what has been termed Egyptian Aramaic.

3.19. c) A type of Classical or Imperial Aramaic is represented by
Biblical Aramaic, found in certain parts of the Old Testament
(*Gen.* 31,47 [two words]; *Jer.* 10,11; *Ezra* 4,8—6,18; 7,22—26;
Dan. 2,4—7,28); the age of these documents ranges probably
from the fifth to the second centuries B.C.

b. West Aramaic

3.20. a) Nabataean is the language of an (ethnically) Arab
population which established a state at Petra and flourished between the first century B.C. and the third century A.D.; Nabataean
papyri have been discovered among the Dead Sea documents, and
Nabataean inscriptions have been identified as far afield as Greece
and Italy.

3.21. b) Palmyrene is the language of an (ethnically) Arab
population which established a state at Palmyra and flourished
between the first century B.C. and the third century A.D.; Palmyrene
inscriptions have been found as far afield as England.

3.22. c) Jewish Palestinian Aramaic is the language that was
spoken in Palestine at the time of Christ and during the first centuries of the Christian era. In literary sources it is found in the
Genesis Apocryphon (discovered among the Dead Sea documents)
and the Palestinian Targūm (of which a complete manuscript has

been identified in the Vatican Library by Díez Macho). Jewish
Palestinian Aramaic survives above all in a sizable body of Jewish
post-Biblical texts of the second to the fifth centuries A.D.; these
may be divided into two groups, one being represented by the
Targūmīm of Onkelos and of Jonathan, and the other by the Galilean variety (some Midrāšīm and the Jerusalem Talmūd).

3.23. d) Samaritan Aramaic is the language of the Samaritan
Targūm to the Pentateuch (probably of the fourth century A.D.)
and of some later writings.

3.24. e) Christian Palestinian Aramaic is the language used by
the Melkites between the fifth and the eighth centuries A.D.; it is
written in Syriac characters and is attested in several Old Testament
passages, Gospel Lectionaries, and liturgical writings.

3.25. Limited and gradually disappearing survivals of West
Aramaic can still be heard in the villages of Maʻlūla, Ǧubbʻadīn
and Baḫʻa, in the neighbourhood of Damascus.

c. East Aramaic

3.26. a) Syriac, originally the language of Edessa, later developed
a rich Christian literature extending from the third to the thirteenth
century A.D., although it was generally replaced, as a spoken
language, by Arabic during the great Islamic conquests of the
8th cent.

3.27. b) Babylonian Aramaic is the language of the Babylonian
Jews, prominently represented in the Babylonian Talmūd (fourth
to sixth centuries A.D.) and in a series of magical texts composed
in the fifth and sixth centuries A.D.

3.28. c) Mandaean is the language of the Gnostic sect of the
Mandaeans who flourished in Mesopotamia; their writings extend
from the third to the eighth century A.D.

3.29. Survivals of East Aramaic can still be found in the neighbourhood of Lake Urmia, at Ṭūr ʻAbdīn, and near Mosul. It should
be mentioned that the "Assyrians" (as these Aramaic-speaking
populations are referred to) were displaced, as a result of the first
world war, and now live in scattered communities in the United

States and in Russia. The Aramaic of Georgia, in particular, has been the subject of several recent studies (Tsereteli).

D. South-West Semitic

1. General Characteristics

4.1. South-West Semitic is, in grammars and introductions to Semitic languages, usually divided into two groups: (1) North Arabic and (2) South Arabian together with Ethiopic. It has, however, recently been pointed out by some scholars that (at least within the limits of the ancient period) the separation of South Arabian from North Arabic, if intended to contrast the former with the latter and to place it alongside Ethiopic, is not entirely justified. It is true that historically Ethiopic makes its appearance as a successor tongue of South Arabian, but such a genetic relationship differs to some extent from the requirements of a descriptive classification which is based on the convergence of isoglosses. From the descriptive point of view it has been noted that ancient South Arabian is in several respects in agreement with North Arabic and at variance with Ethiopic (and *vice versa*). Ethiopic, laid as it was upon a non-Semitic substratum, has undergone certain developments not to be found in South Arabian. The present exposition, based on *geographical* principles, will present South Arabian within the area of the Arabian peninsula—without thereby implying an undervaluation of its independent characteristics or of its agreements with Ethiopic.

4.2. As regards the relationship between South-West and North-West Semitic, cf. § 3.2.

2. Arabic (incl. South Arabian)

4.3. For the reasons explained in § 4.1, we have chosen to take the term "Arabic" as a linguistic complex embracing all the tongues of the Arabian peninsula—with the exception of some Aramaic infiltrations (Nabataean and Palmyrene) in the extreme north. This complex, containing many dialectal divergences, may be subdivided as follows:

4.4. a) Ancient or Epigraphic South Arabian (ESA—for whose independent position cf. the remarks in § 4.1) is the language of the inscriptions of the ancient South-West Arabian city-states. Their dates range from the eighth century B.C. (this is subject to considerable current controversy; cf. the studies of J. Pirenne) to the sixth century A.D.; the following dialects, corresponding to the regions of the principal states, are being distinguished: (1) Sabaean, (2) Minaean, (3) Qatabanian, (4) Ḥaḍramī, (5) Awsanian.

4.5. b) Pre-classical North Arabic is the language embodied in a series of inscriptions which may be dated between the fifth century B.C. and the fourth century A.D. (approximately) and be divided into the following regional and dialectal groups: (1) Tamūdic (a conventional term which lacks precision and covers, in fact, many of the tongues over a wide area of pre-Islamic central and northern Arabia), (2) Liḥyānite, (3) Ṣafāitic.

4.6. c) Classical North Arabic, the "Arabic" *par excellence*, is attested from the fourth century A.D. in a few inscriptions and in some dialectal samples preserved by Islamic writers. It attains its full realization in pre-Islamic Arabic poetry and later in the Qur'ān (seventh century A.D.); it owes its diffusion and survival to Islam which turned Arabic into a great literary language as a result of the Arab conquests and the enormous expansion of this dynamic religion. The generally attested form of classical Arabic is the result of a process of systematization by Arab grammarians; this linguistic material is represented by the pre-Islamic standard speech ("Hochsprache") and was nurtured by the ample flow of Arabian dialects. This process has concealed original dialectal divergences as well as other elements of subsequent evolution (Fück).

4.7. The modern Arabic dialects are numerous and will only be dealt with peripherally in this treatise (cf. § 1.5). In the South Arabian area there exists a separate group of languages which, according to some scholars, represent the continuation and development of the ancient speech-forms: the principal ones among these are Meḥrī, Šḥawrī, and Soqotrī. The large number of dialects developed from classical Arabic are most appropriately classified according to regional groupings: Central-Asian, Iraqi, Arabian,

Syro-Lebanese and Palestinian, Egyptian, North African or Maghrebi. A separately developed form, owing to its long historical severance and its exposure to non-Semitic influences, is Maltese.

3. Ethiopic

4.8. Ancient Ethiopic (or Gǝ'ǝz) is first attested in epigraphic material of the first few centuries A.D. and, above all, in the great Aksum inscriptions of the fourth century. It later developed an extensive, predominantly religious, literature reaching up to modern times.

4.9. The modern Semitic languages of Ethiopia are represented by Tigriña, Tigre, Amharic, Harari, and Gurage; Gafat and Argobba are now virtually extinct.

E. Proto-Semitic, Hamito-Semitic, Indo-European

1. Proto-Semitic

5.1. By Proto-Semitic (or Common Semitic or simply Semitic) we refer to the *ensemble* of elements which an examination of the historically documented Semitic languages leads us to regard as common property of the Semitic group in its most ancient phase (Semitic isoglosses); hence we discover here the starting-points for developments peculiar to each individual language. Whether such postulated reconstructions invariably possessed historical reality it is difficult to determine, but this uncertainty is not necessarily an obstacle to comparative inquiry. It is reasonable to suppose that the dialectal fluctuations with which we are confronted by the existing historical evidence formed part also of the pre-historic phase (in contrast to the concept of the genealogical tree). It must not be forgotten that 'Proto-Semitic' is merely a linguistic convention or postulate, but such a convention is a necessary pre-requisite for an understanding and reconstruction of linguistic history.

5.2. The concept of Proto-Semitic would seem comparable to that of Proto-Indo-European. The problems of the former do, however, appear more manageable owing to the lesser degree of geographical dispersion of the Semitic languages and the greater measure of affinity between them. It would, therefore, be more appropriate to compare Hamito-Semitic with Indo-European, on the one hand, and Semitic with the Romance, Slavonic, or Germanic languages, on the other.

5.3. The value and importance of individual Semitic languages to a reconstruction of Proto-Semitic has been variously estimated at different periods in the history of our studies. Account has to be taken of archaizing tendencies in some languages in contrast to genuinely old material which may at times appear in strangely disguised forms. The central position long occupied by Arabic as either the proto-type or true image of primitive Semitic has come to be challenged in recent times. The rich phonological structure of Arabic is now paralleled by that of Ugaritic and South Arabian, and its highly developed verbal system is regarded as the result of systematization rather than archaism. A more profound knowledge of Akkadian, of some of the North-West Semitic languages, of the modern Ethiopian and South Arabian languages, etc., has to some extent modified our ideas about Proto-Semitic and those of the classical tongues which were alleged to resemble it most closely.

2. Hamito-Semitic

5.4. It has long been held that Semitic is not an isolated group but forms part of a larger complex of languages, conventionally called Hamito-Semitic. In addition to Semitic, this larger grouping comprises Egyptian, Libyco-Berber, and Cushitic; thus Hamito-Semitic is also sometimes referred to in purely geographical terms as Afro-Asiatic. There is no "Hamitic" unit comparable to the Semitic one: Semitic possesses a much greater measure of structural uniformity than can be detected among the "Hamitic" languages. The relationship between the various units of the Hamito-Semitic group cannot be explained as a secondary development, and this makes the concept of an original Hamito-Semitic linguistic body one of great cogency. We have to aim at the reconstruction of Proto-Hamito-Semitic forms; though naturally with all the reservations called for by such a conjectural reconstruction. Semitic is, of course, the group that is more fully attested and generally also the most replete with ancient forms.

5.5. Certain studies (Rössler) have asserted that Libyco-Berber is possessed of an essentially Semitic character and have claimed a particular affinity with Akkadian; this is based on correspondences of a phonological, morphological, and lexical nature. If this theory were shown to be correct, the independence of Semitic would, to some extent, be impaired. However, the similarities adduced in support of the thesis seem to be in part open to question and in part inconclusive, for most of the parallels can much more readily be explained within the framework of the long-established general Hamito-Semitic affinity (Cohen). Consequently, there is at present no cogent reason to question the independence of Semitic within the larger Hamito-Semitic complex.

3. Hamito-Semitic and Indo-European

5.6. A few points of contact have long been noticed between Hamito-Semitic and Indo-European languages. These are generally concerned with relations of a phonological and especially lexical character and have given rise to the so-called "Aryo-Semitic" (Ascoli) or "Nostratic" (Pedersen, Cuny) hypothesis which is claimed as common ancestor of Hamito-Semitic and Indo-European. Such conjectures are, however, very highly speculative, especially on account of deep-seated morphological divergences between those groups, although the inflexional structure appears to be common to both. A more reliable explanation is to be sought in the common Mediterranean environment (especially as regards lexical elements) and consequent historical contacts and influences (particularly marked in Anatolia and the Eastern Mediterranean). Such limited links as may exist between Indo-European and Hamito-Semitic should not, therefore, be regarded as a heritage from a 'parent' language, but rather as a haphazard collection of isoglosses not unconnected with the geographical proximity of the two groups and certain historical contacts between them.

F. Language and Script

6.1. A treatment of Semitic writing lies outside the scope of the present work. However, since systems of writing may condition and at times even influence linguistic elements, it is well to recall certain essential facts.

6.2. North-East Semitic (Akkadian) is written in cuneiform characters, inscribed with a pointed instrument on tablets of clay or more rarely on stone or metal; this form of writing was taken over from the non-Semitic Sumerians who preceded the Semites in Mesopotamia. The cuneiform system possesses many hundreds of signs which have ideographic or syllabic value and are often multivalent, so that their reading offers considerable difficulties (quite apart from the fact that the tablets are not always in a good state of preservation and that there existed notable divergences in orthography in different areas and times). The script indicates both consonants and vowels which (in contrast to the majority of Semitic alphabets denoting consonants only) is of considerable assistance to our knowledge of the language. On the other hand, the consonantal inventory of Sumerian (for which this form of writing was originally devised) differed materially from the Semitic sound system, so that the graphic representation of Akkadian consonants by means of Sumerian writing exhibits many imperfections and difficulties. In the transliteration of Akkadian (for the purposes of this comparative study) syllables which are separately represented in cuneiform will, as a rule, be joined together in the same word (e.g., *inaddin* "he gives", instead of *i-na-ad-di-in*). It is important to realize that length of vowels and doubling of consonants are not consistently expressed in cuneiform. It is, therefore, difficult to reach satisfactory conclusions; at times data drawn from comparative Semitic grammar will prove useful for the reconstruction of relevant features.

6.3. West Semitic, both northern and southern, is represented in consonantal alphabetic scripts with a limited number of signs (generally less than thirty). The origins of this alphabetic form of writing are to be sought in the Syro-Palestinian area in the first half of the second millennium B.C. After the first attempts (their interpretation is still in doubt: cf. §§ 3.3—6) we witness, in the second half of the same millennium, the appearance of the Ugaritic alphabet, the only one in the Semitic west to use characters of cuneiform type—though alphabetic in structure. From about the same period dates the formation of the so-called Phoenician alphabet which was carved on stone and was not of the cuneiform type. This alphabet has a long history connected with the emergence of the ancient Hebrew as well as the Moabite and Samaritan alphabets. The Aramaic script, too, is derived from the Phoenician, but its independent evolution gave rise, in its turn, not only to the various alphabets of the Aramaic languages but also to the Hebrew "square" script and the classical Arabic alphabet.

6.4. Another alphabet whose origin has probably to be sought in the Syro-Palestinian area is that which makes its appearance in the ancient South Arabian inscriptions. Closely connected with the latter are, on the one hand, the pre-classical Arabic scripts (Tamūdic, Liḥyānite, and Ṣafāitic) and, on the other, the Ethiopic syllabary (see § 6.9).

6.5. The West Semitic alphabets are, as has been said, purely consonantal in character. From this fact arise some of the principal difficulties in the study of the Semitic languages as well as many of the obscure points in our understanding of their comparative grammar. However, the principle of not denoting vowels was in practice subjected to certain subsequent modifications (cf. §§ 8.69 to 96). Among these are the following:

6.6. a) In Ugaritic the consonant ' has three forms, according to its vocalization with *a, i, u*.

6.7. b) In some alphabets the use of *matres lectionis* is developed, i.e. of the consonant-signs *w, y, ', h*. This device, limited at first to final vowels, is later extended to internal long vowels and sometimes, though rarely, even to short ones (East Aramaic).

6.8. c) In some writing-systems additional signs were later introduced to indicate vowels: this applies to Syriac, Hebrew, and Arabic, where these signs are, however, used only for certain texts of particular importance (the Bible, the Qur'ān, etc.).

6.9. d) In Ethiopic the script has been adapted to denote seven vowels by a variety of changes in the structure of the consonantal symbol. Vowels have thus become an integral part of Ethiopic writing which now assumes a quasi-syllabic character—yet without sacrificing the general Semitic concept of the predominance of consonants over vowels.

6.10. Vowel notation by means of the methods just described still leaves certain deficiencies and problems (cf. §§ 8.73—96).

We shall here limit ourselves to mentioning the artificial character of seemingly very precise vocalizations, such as those of Hebrew and Biblical Aramaic; or the ambiguity in Hebrew of the sign which indicates either a vowel of the *ə* type or the absence of a vowel (and the similar ambiguity of the sixth order in Ethiopic); and, finally, the situation in Syriac which possesses no symbol either for *ə* or zero vowel.

6.11. Another notable deficiency in most of the Semitic writing-systems concerns the marking of gemination or consonant-doubling —even though this may be a feature of phonemic significance. Such doubling (inconsistently expressed already in cuneiform— § 6.2) lacks specific symbols in the West Semitic alphabets, though Hebrew, Biblical Aramaic, and Arabic have developed a gemination mark along with their general vowel system.

6.12. The transliteration of the Semitic languages which is employed in this book is based on certain principles which it seems well to explain beforehand. It is obvious that these principles are open to a great deal of argument and are not exempt from certain disadvantages, but it appears to be beyond doubt that any other set of principles would be subject to an equal measure of ambiguity:

6.13. a) Our mode of graphic representation is, in fact, a trans-literation rather than a transcription, for it aims at reproducing, as far as possible, each symbol by one sign, in order to permit the reconstruction of the original orthography. It need hardly be mentioned that proper transcription has not been abandoned without regret, but in the case of many of the ancient Semitic languages the conjectural element involved in such a course seemed unjustifiably prominent.

6.14. b) The system of transliteration has been kept as simple as possible—in accordance with the requirements of an elementary grammar; it eschews the notation of sub-phonemic variants (allophones)—except where this is called for by special circumstances. Non-distinctive variants can generally be determined in accordance with grammatical rules (for example, the fricative articulation of consonants in postvocalic position [cf. § 8.10] or the not always consistently employed *matres lectionis* [cf. §§ 8.81, 8.87]).

6.15. c) The choice of transliteration symbols takes into consideration the usual conventions (which it is well not to alter in an elementary grammar, unless there are compelling reasons) as well as phonetic and (especially) etymological data which are of considerable importance in a comparative study: thus, for example, in Ethiopic the transliterations *ḍ* and *ś* will be used, although in their pronunciation these consonants became early identified with *ṣ* and *s*, respectively (cf. §§ 8.20, 8.37); for Ethiopic vowels the quantitative indications derived from etymological comparison will be retained—in preference to the purely qualitative distinctions on which the Ethiopic vowel system appears to be based (cf. §§ 8.95 to 96).

II. Phonology

A. *Preliminaries*

7.1. A phonological study of the Semitic languages must be based on the clear distinction, now generally accepted in linguistic work, between phonetics and phonemics: on the one hand, the articulatory, acoustic, and auditory characteristics of actual speech (phonetics) and, on the other, phonemes, i.e. minimal distinctive sound units relevant to meaning (phonemics). For ancient languages reconstruction is of necessity phonemic, i.e. the analysis of data obtained by means of a study of distinctive oppositions (cf. especially Cantineau's studies).

7.2. The pronunciation—or, more exactly, the complex of phonetic expressions—of the ancient Semitic languages is reconstructed and assessed on the basis of indications of various kinds: a) traditional pronunciation—in the case of languages which have been transmitted (living or otherwise) up to the present time (Hebrew, Aramaic, Arabic, Ethiopic); b) testimony of grammarians—for languages in which a grammatical tradition exists (Hebrew, Syriac, Arabic); c) transcriptions of Semitic words and phrases in other languages (Greek, Egyptian, Aramaic and Hebrew for Akkadian; Greek and Latin for Hebrew and Phoenician-Punic, etc.) and *vice versa*; d) orthographic peculiarities indicative of phonetic characteristics not otherwise expressed; e) comparative Semitic linguistics (reconstruction of Akkadian, Ugaritic, or ancient South Arabian pronunciations based on parallels in Arabic, Hebrew, etc.).

7.3. This body of evidence is neither complete nor sufficient. There remain, consequently, doubts and uncertainties, and our reconstructions are by and large schematic and conventional. Sometimes, moreover, tradition proves to be an obstacle rather than a help—as in the case of classical Ethiopic whose pronunciation has been preserved by speakers of languages derived from it, with the result that that pronunciation embodies developments peculiar to these modern languages. Similar considerations apply to Hebrew whose transmission is affected not only by differences between the Sephardi and Ashkenazi pronunciations but also by influences due to the substratum-languages of those who have gone back to the use of Hebrew as a spoken tongue.

B. The Phonological System

1. Classification

8.1. The Semitic phonological system is made up of consonants, semivowels, and vowels as well as certain stress patterns. Their classification may be based either on the musical principles of acoustic phonetics or on the physiological elements of articulatory phonetics. In the latter case, classification is related to the place and the manner of articulation. According to the place of articulation we have: bilabials, interdentals, dentals, palato-alveolars, velars, pharyngals, and laryngals; according to the manner of articulation: plosives (or stops), fricatives, laterals (and lateralized consonants ?), rolled consonants, and nasals.

8.2. Within the groups so classified a further distinction may be made according to the voiced or "emphatic" character of some consonants. As regards sonority, doubts have been raised as to its nature in Proto-Semitic and it has been termed a "correlation of tenseness or pressure" (Cantineau). It is, however, difficult to arrive at concrete results beyond the indications furnished by the historically attested languages. As regards "emphasis", this term is used, not altogether properly, to denote a quality characteristic of the Semitic (and Hamito-Semitic) languages: velarization in Arabic, glottalization in Ethiopic. It is uncertain which of these types is primary. According to some scholars, the fact that glottalization is not found in Semitic outside Ethiopic, yet occurs in certain Cushitic languages, would point to its being a secondary feature. In favour of this thesis one might refer to the phenomenon of labialization which is probably also due to Cushitic influence (cf. § 8.43). According to others, there are reasons for maintaining, on the contrary, that the Ethiopic glottalized ejectives are primary, because: a) the Ethiopic "emphatics" are voiceless

and, apart from Arabic, so the Semitic "emphatics"—almost
without exception; b) the Ethiopic "emphatics" do not appear to
influence the timbre of neighbouring vowels and, again apart from
Arabic, this seems to be the norm in the Semitic languages (cf. however for certain facts in Akkadian von Soden, GAG, p. 12); c) the
phenomenon $q > $ ' in some Arabic dialects can only be explained
by way of glottalization.

2. The Proto-Semitic Consonantal System

8.3. The Proto-Semitic consonantal system may be hypothetically
reconstructed as follows (with such reservations as will be expressed
below):

	Plosive	*Fricative*	*Lateral*	*Lateralized?*	*Rolled*	*Nasal*
Bilabial	p, b					m
Interdental		ṯ, ḏ, ṱ		ḏ̣		
Dental	t, d, ṭ	s, z, ṣ	l	ś	r	n
Palato-alveolar		š				
Velar	k, q, g	ḫ, ġ				
Pharyngal		ḥ, '				
Laryngal	'	h				

8.4. Following the distinctions of voice and of "emphasis", we
may note, in certain positions of the classification-chart, the
juxtaposition of "triadic" groups, i.e. voiceless-voiced-emphatic.
Such "triads" exist: a) for the interdentals; b) for the dental
plosives and the dental fricatives; c) for the velar plosives.

3. Bilabials

8.5. Proto-Semitic has two bilabial plosives, voiceless p and
voiced b; it has further a bilabial nasal m. In the South Semitic
languages p is replaced by the voiceless labiodental fricative f:
e.g. Akk.Heb.Syr. *pqd* "to seek", Ar.Eth. *fqd*.

8.6. Ethiopic possesses a p in addition to the f (probably derived
from Proto-Semitic p); and in Egyptian and Cushitic likewise
both p and f occur. The problem therefore arises whether these two
consonants did not co-exist already in Proto-Semitic. As regards
Ethiopic p, it is rare and usually confined to transcriptions of

Greek words (e.g. *pisā* = πίσσα). Its shape, too, is borrowed from
Greek *p*, and its late appearance in the Ethiopic alphabet is corroborated by its place at the tail of the Ethiopic syllabary. As regards
Egyptian and Cushitic, the correspondences tend to show that the
two phonemes of these languages had as their Semitic counterpart
the single phoneme *p* (southern *f*): hence the differentiation in these
languages seems to be of a secondary character; and in any case,
for Proto-Semitic one single phoneme may be posited. This is
likely to have been *p* rather than *f*, for it is easier to suppose an
evolution *p* > *f* than one in the opposite direction (there are, moreover, signs pointing to a similar development—not conditioned by
the position of the consonant—in the northern Semitic area, e.g.
in the language manifested in the Egyptian transcriptions of the
second millennium).

8.7. Ethiopic possesses also a voiceless bilabial plosive *p* which is
emphatic (or ejective) and, like *p*, of rare occurrence. This consonant may well be of Cushitic origin, and it is worthy of note that,
for the purposes of its graphic expression, the form of another
ejective sound (though quite different in its basis of articulation)
was slightly modified: *p* was then placed, in the order of the alphabet, next to the character (*ṣ*) whose *shape* it had imitated. The new
consonant seems soon to have overstepped its original function,
for, like *p*, it is usually employed to transcribe Greek words (e.g.
parāqliṭōs = παράκλητος). However, since Semitic counterparts
are lacking, it should probably be regarded as secondary. Likewise
secondary, and similarly used for transcriptions from Greek, is
the special *p* which is to be found in Syriac (James of Edessa) and
in Christian Palestinian Aramaic. A secondary development in
the sphere of emphatic labials may be encountered in some modern
Arabic dialects which have emphatic *ḅ*, *f̣*, and *ṃ*, influenced by the
proximity of other emphatic consonants or of back vowels (positional variants).

8.8. Interchanges between consonants of the bilabial group, as
well as between them and the bilabial semivowel *w*, take place in
several languages, but we are not always in a position to ascribe
these interchanges to clearly identifiable linguistic reasons. Thus
we find in Ugaritic *p*:*b*:*m*: e.g. *npk* "well" from Sem. *nbk*, *špš*
"sun" from Sem. *šmš*. In Ya'udic the change *p* > *b* is attested:

e.g. *nbš* "soul" from Sem. *npš*. In several Aramaic dialects we find the change *b* > *w*, evidently by way of the fricative articulation of *b*: e.g. Syr. *rabrəbānē "great ones" > *rawrəbānē* (dissimilation may conceivably have been an additional factor in this process); Mand. *'wd* "to perish" from Sem. *'bd*. The transition *b* > *ḇ* > *w* (cf. Ullendorff, SLE, p. 106) is well represented in modern Aramaic (*zabna* > *zawna > *zōna* "time"; *gabra* > *gawra > *gōra* "husband"), modern South Arabian (*lbn > *lūn* "white"), modern Ethiopic (**sb'* > Amharic *saw* "man"; *nbr* > Amh. *nōra* "he stayed"). The change to *w* affects also other labials, though to a lesser extent: cf. Syr. *qwz* "to leap" compared with Aram. Ar. *qpz* and Heb. *qpṣ*. The transition *m* > *b* would account for the ESA *bn* "from" corresponding to Sem. *mn*. Ethiopic, too, has alternations *b*:*m*:*w*, e.g. *ṣabsa* and *ṣawasa*, "to be weak", etc. Akkadian is in a peculiar situation: the use of *m* and *b* for *w* is frequent, but owing to the absence of *w* in Sumerian this is often due to purely graphic reasons rather than phonetic causes. A change of intervocalic *m* to *w* is, however, attested soon after the earliest period of Akkadian (cf. von Soden, GAG, pp. 21—22, 31—32).

8.9. As regards the development of the bilabials in the various languages, the situation in Akkadian is of particular interest, for the cuneiform system of writing does not adequately distinguish between *p* and *b* (or between voiced and voiceless consonants generally): never in final position nor in other positions as far as Old Akkadian and Old Assyrian are concerned; in Babylonian and in the later phases of Assyrian special symbols are often employed for syllables with *p* and with *b*. New Assyrian appears to have lost any consistent distinction between *p* and *b* in pronunciation; this, in turn, has led to considerable graphic fluctuations. Some consonantal interchanges (e.g. *awīlum* and *abīlum* "man" in Old Akkadian) suggest the possibility of spirantization, i.e. fricative articulation (cf. § 8.10).

8.10. In North-West Semitic (or more precisely in Biblical Hebrew and in the Aramaic of the Christian era) spirantization of *p* > *f*, *b* > *v* occurs as a regular positional variant (the traditional pronunciation represents the resultant consonants as labiodental fricatives, like [f, v] in I.P.A. symbols, but this does not exclude their having been originally bilabial fricatives, [φ, β] in I.P.A.

symbols). This change affects the non-emphatic plosives (p b t d k g) which in postvocalic position come to be articulated as fricatives, i.e. I.P.A. [f v ϑ ð x γ]. This is, of course, a conditioned phonetic phenomenon (partial assimilation of consonant to vowel: cf. § 9.5) and of non-phonemic character (a sub-phonemic positional variant). As regards the period when spirantization became operative, there is no certain proof that it pre-dates the Christian era: neither the Egyptian transcriptions of North-West Semitic names nor Greek and Latin transcriptions of elements in the pre-Masoretic text furnish sufficient indications of the existence of this distinction (cf. Garbini, SNO, *passim*). At any rate, it would appear that such signs of non-plosive articulation as we encounter (cf. § 8.6) are not necessarily connected with post-vocalic position.

4. Interdentals

8.11. Proto-Semitic has two non-emphatic interdental consonants, voiceless $\underline{t}$ and voiced $\underline{d}$, i.e. I.P.A. [ϑ] and [ð], respectively. These consonants are, in fact, attested in certain languages only, but their proto-Semitic status appears to be vouchsafed by the *ensemble* of correspondences which can be satisfactorily explained on this assumption only.

8.12. Proto-Semitic had in addition an emphatic interdental, probably voiceless ($\underline{t}$). This consonant is represented in Arabic (where it is usually, but rather inappropriately, transliterated z), in South Arabian, and in Ugaritic by a graphic symbol of its own. The phonetic and phonological correspondences in the other languages can be explained only by accepting the consonant as Proto-Semitic.

8.13. Finally, Proto-Semitic appears to have possessed a consonant which Brockelmann and those who follow his system transcribe $\underline{d}$, i.e. regarding it as a voiced emphatic interdental; others (Cohen, Cantineau etc.) transcribe it $\underline{d}$, i.e. as a lateralized (or lateral ?—Martinet) voiced emphatic interdental. Apart from the question of its precise articulation (which it is difficult to determine with certainty), this consonant retains its independent status in the South Semitic languages only: phonological correspondences would nevertheless suggest its existence in Proto-Semitic. It is probable that it was voiced, for this is the position in the languages which have retained this sound. Its lateralization appears to be borne out by indications furnished by Arab grammarians and by the evidence of certain modern South Arabian languages. There are further indications in the more ancient languages: cf. Akk. *Ruldā'u* or *Rulṭā'u* for the Arabic name of the god *Ruḍā'*.

8.14. The following table (subject, of course, to certain additional explanations and reservations to be set forth below) displays the development of the Proto-Semitic interdentals in the principal Semitic languages:

Proto-Semitic	Akkadian	Ugaritic	Hebrew	Syriac	Arabic	ESA	Ethiopic
ṯ	*š*	*ṯ*	*š*	*t*	*ṯ*	*ṯ*	*s*
ḏ	*z*	*d* or *ḏ*	*z*	*d*	*ḏ*	*ḏ*	*z*
ṭ	*ṣ*	*ṭ*	*ṣ*	*ṭ*	*ẓ* (=*ṭ*)	*ẓ* (*ṭ*)	*ṣ*
ḍ	*ṣ*	*ṣ*	*ṣ*	ʿ	*ḍ* (=*ḏ*̣ ?)	*ḍ* (*ḍ*)	*ḍ*

Examples: *ṯ*: Akk. *šūru* "bull", Ug. *ṯr*, Heb. *šōr*, Syr. *tawrā*, Ar. *ṯawr*, ESA *ṯwr*, Eth. *sōr*; — *ḏ*: Akk. *'ḫz* "to take", Ug. *'ḫd (ḏ)*, Heb. *'ḫz*, Syr. *'ḫd*, Ar. *'ḫḏ*, ESA *'ḫd*, Eth. *'ḫz*; — *ṭ*: Akk. *ṣillu* "shadow", Ug. *ṭl*, Heb. *ṣēl*, Syr. *ṭellālā*, Ar. *ẓill*, (cf. ESA *ẓll* "to cover"), Eth. *ṣəlālōt*; — *ḍ*: Ug. Heb. *ṣrr* "to be hostile", Syr. *'rr*, Ar. ESA Eth. *ḍrr*; Akk. *erṣetu* "earth", Ug. *ảrṣ*, Heb. *'ereṣ*, Syr. *'ar'ā*, Ar. *'arḍ*, ESA *'rḍ*.

8.15. In Old Akkadian *ṯ* appears to remain independent, for it is written by means of the series of symbols for Sumerian *š*, while Proto-Semitic *š* is written with the series for *s*. Later on the change *ṯ* > *š* takes place. Certain orthographical divergences have been interpreted as traces of an independent *ḏ* in Old Akkadian (Gelb, OA, p. 38). The problem remains, however, unresolved.

8.16. In North-West Semitic, the most ancient phase probably reflects the situation in Proto-Semitic. In Ugaritic, *ṯ* and *ṭ* retain their independence (cf. Garbini, SNO, pp. 193—94); for a different opinion cf. Rössler, ZA 54 [1961], pp. 158—72); as regards *ṭ*, the fact that it is at times represented by the graphic symbol "*ġ*" suggests the possibility of a development analogous to that later found in Aramaic (cf. § 8.18). *ḏ* generally merges with *d*, but in some cases it is represented by another sign which we may hypothetically (cf. Gordon, UM, pp. 22—23) equate with *ḏ* (cf., for example, Ug. *ḏrʻ* "arm", Ar. *ḏirāʻ*, Heb. *zərōaʻ*, etc.); it may, therefore, be conjectured that either the evolutionary process was as yet fluid or that we have to envisage different orthographical phases, perhaps in documents of different dates. Proto-Semitic *ḍ* has developed into *ṣ*, but some spellings with *ṭ* have encouraged the assumption that this process passed through a prolonged indecisive stage. In North-West Semitic of the second millennium B.C. (as reflected in Egyptian transcriptions) we may note the survival of Proto-Semitic *ṭ*; the existence of *ḏ* (as an independent phoneme) is very doubtful, and *ṭ*, *ḍ* are seen to have merged with *ṣ*.

8.17. These developments—as indeed the process *ṯ* > *š* and *ḏ* > *z*—continue in Canaanite; for this we possess the evidence of Hebrew as well as that of Phoenician-Punic and Moabite. Some trace of an original differentiation in the Phoenician area has been claimed on the basis of Greek transcriptions (*Τύρος* and *Σιδών*) of two place-names which in Phoenician both begin with *ṣ*; but this phenomenon may conceivably have a different explanation altogether (cf. Garbini, SNO, pp. 32—33).

8.18. In the most ancient Aramaic inscriptions we find the symbols "š", "z", "ṣ" for *ṯ*, *ḏ*, *ṭ*, respectively, i.e. the same symbols as in Canaanite. Later, about the middle of the first millennium B.C., there takes place the change *ṯ* > *t*, *ḏ* > *d*, *ṭ* > *ṭ* (given in the table above for Syriac) which applies to other Aramaic languages. This state of affairs is to be explained, according to some scholars, as "Canaanisms" of a purely graphic type—at a time when the characteristic evolution of the Aramaic consonants had already taken place. According to others, however, the symbols employed in the most ancient phase are to be regarded as an attempt to represent, at least approximately, the Proto-Semitic interdentals— following upon the adoption of an alphabet (the Phoenician) which had no proper signs for them. The development might thus be exemplified as follows: Proto-Semitic **yṯb* "to sit" > Old Aram. *yṯb* (written "yšb") > common Aram. *ytb*; Proto-Semitic **ḏhb* "gold" > Old Aram. *ḏhb* (written "zhb") > common Aram. *dhb*; Proto-Semitic **nṭr* "to guard" > Old Aram. *nṭr* (written "nṣr") >

common Aram. *nṭr*. Proto-Semitic *ḏ* undergoes a peculiar development in Aramaic: the most ancient inscriptions employ the symbol
"q", while later " ' " takes its place (e.g. " 'rq' " "earth", later
" 'r' "; cf. Ar. *'arḏ*). Mandaean has preserved "q" in some cases.
The phonetic process reflected in these changes is far from being
clear: Nöldeke (*Mandäische Grammatik*, p. 73) considers the possibility that "q" might here be used to represent the articulation
of *ġ*, i.e. fricative *q* (as in fact happens extensively in modern
Ethiopian languages: cf. Ullendorff, SLE, pp. 64—65). *ġ* might
have been an intermediate stage in the transition *ḏ* > '.

8.19. In the Arabic sphere, classical Arabic maintains the four
interdental consonants as independent phonemes and also furnishes
some traditional indications as to their pronunciation. In this
tradition *ṯ* (conventionally transcribed *ẓ*) appears to have become
a voiced consonant; in some Arabic dialects it is pronounced as
a voiced emphatic interdental [ḏ̣], in others as a voiced emphatic
dental plosive [ḍ]. As for the fourth consonant of the series,
transliterated *ḍ*, indigenous grammarians have described its original
character as a voiced emphatic lateralized interdental. In modern
dialects its pronunciation is in general the same as that of the
previous consonant, i.e. [ḏ̣] or [ḍ]. South Arabian and pre-Islamic
North Arabic agree with classical Arabic as far as the retention of
the four interdentals is concerned. It would obviously be impossible
to say anything definite about their pronunciation, yet South
Arabian offers some interesting indications: the spelling of "s¹ṣy"
for *s¹ẓy* might connote, at a late period, a change *ṯ* > *ṣ* of the type
also found in other Semitic languages (including Ethiopic); "nz'"
for *nḍ'* suggests a fricative articulation of Proto-Semitic *ḍ*, since
the change *ḍ* > *z* is phonetically not improbable, while *ḍ* > *z* would
certainly be far less likely.

8.20. In Ethiopic the pronunciation of *ḍ* merges with that of *ṣ*,
soon after the early Aksum inscriptions, and the respective graphic
symbols become liable to arbitrary interchange. It may be noted
that the coalescence in pronunciation of *ḍ* and *ṣ* may suggest the
survival, in the early period, of a fricative articulation of Proto-
Semitic *ḍ* (as is also made probable by the spelling of "z" for *ḍ* in
South Arabian: cf. § 8.19).

5. Dental Plosives

8.21. Proto-Semitic has two non-emphatic dental plosives, voiceless *t* and voiced *d*, as well as an emphatic plosive which was probably voiceless and is for that reason transliterated *ṭ*. (The term "dental" is used to the exclusion of the interdentals which have already been dealt with.)

8.22. The voiceless nature of Proto-Semitic *ṭ* is corroborated by the traditional pronunciation of Arabic and Ethiopic. The fact that Old Babylonian *ṭ* is predominantly represented by the graphic element for *d* is probably due to the inconsistencies of the cuneiform system; yet it has to be observed that in northern Babylonia *ṭ* is generally expressed by *t* at that period. Also, Egyptian transcriptions of North-West Semitic names (second millennium B.C.) show *d* for *ṭ* (e.g. *dbḥ* = *Ṭebaḥ*). The weight to be attached to these considerations is nonetheless limited, and the balance of probabilities is clearly on the side of the voiceless character of *ṭ*.

8.23. Akkadian does not appear to distinguish between *t, d, ṭ* in final position. In other positions, Old Akkadian and Old Assyrian writing likewise lacks the distinction; on the other hand, it does exist in Babylonian and in later Assyrian for the majority of the syllabic symbols concerned. The lack of differentiation is due to the peculiarity of cuneiform (cf. § 8.9) which evolved some separate symbols for syllables with voiced and voiceless consonants or with emphatic and non-emphatic ones only after 2000 B.C. The reason for the latter deficiency is to be found in the absence in Sumerian (and hence in its writing system as taken over by the Akkadians) of emphatic phonemes. Some consonantal interchanges between *t* and *š* suggest the possibility of spirantization (cf. § 8.9): the available examples (*tit'āru* "glittering" and *šit'āru*, *tabsūtu* "midwife" and *šabsūtu*) are, however, substantially different from the postvocalic fricatives found in North-West Semitic in the first millennium B.C. (more relevant, perhaps, are instances of non-positional spirantization encountered in Egyptian transcriptions of North-West Semitic names in the second millennium B.C., §§ 8.6, 8.10).

6. Nasal, Lateral, and Rolled Dentals

8.24. Proto-Semitic has one nasal dental consonant *n*, one lateral dental *l*, and one rolled dental *r*. A non-phonemic variant

of *n* (the palatal nasal ŋ) seems to exist in Akkadian, while a variant
of *l* (the emphatic lateral *ḷ*), probably non-phonemic (for the contrary
view see Ferguson), is found in Arabic.

8.25. The dental basis of articulation of the consonants just
listed is suggested by their traditional as well as their modern
pronunciation. Certain reservations have however been expressed
(Cantineau) for *n* and *r*: *n* is frequently found contiguous to other
dentals, although Semitic languages generally shun homorganic
radicals in neighbouring position. *r* is pronounced as a uvular
(I.P.A. [R]) in certain spheres of the traditional pronunciation
of Hebrew and shares several of the characteristics peculiar to
pharyngals and laryngals—thus pointing to a uvular articulation.
A similar situation exists, though in a somewhat less systematic
form, in Syriac where it extends to *l* as well.

8.26. Interchanges between the consonants of this series occur
in various languages. Those involving *n* and *l* are especially frequent: Akk. *lamṣatu* and *namṣatu* "fly" (an occasional change
n > *l* may be observed in Old Assyrian: *kulkā* "seal!" for *kunkā*);
Phoen. *bl* "son" for *bn*; Nab. *ṣnm* "statue" for *ṣlm*; Eth. *sansal*
"chain" in contrast to Ar. *silsilat*. Interchanges between *n* and *r*
(a typical case is the Aramaic *br* "son" for *bn*) and between *l* and *r*
(e.g. Akk. *raqraqqu* and *laqlaqqu* "stork") are also fairly common.
In a modern Ethiopian language, Gurage, *n*, *l*, and *r* have become
positional variants and are thus members of the same phoneme
(H. J. Polotsky, BSLP 39 [1938], pp. 137—75).

8.27. Consonants of this group are sometimes dropped or reduced
to ʼ. A notable example of this is the surrender of nunation (or
mimation) in the course of the historical development of Arabic
(and Akkadian): cf. for Arabic (where the omission of nunation is
always connected with that of the case-endings) § 12.68, and for
Akkadian § 12.71. The consonant *n* is frequently dropped in Jewish
Aramaic and in Mandaean when it is the final element in plural
morphemes: hence nouns in the stat. absol. of the plural often have
the ending -*yʼ* instead of -*yn*, with the result that the construct and
emphatic states become formally identical. This may, however,
be a morphological phenomenon, i.e. an extension of the use of
-*yʼ* at the expense of -*yn*. Analogous cases of the shedding of final *n*

are found in modern Aramaic dialects: thus in the Ma'lūla dialect
*ḥablin "ropes" >ḥabli. Instances of the fall of final r occur in
Jewish Aramaic: e.g. 'm' for 'mr "to say" (in some forms of the
imperfect and of the imperative).

7. Dental and Palato-alveolar Fricatives

8.28. Proto-Semitic has two non-emphatic dental fricatives,
voiceless s and voiced z. It also possesses an emphatic dental
fricative ṣ, which, unlike some other emphatics, is always voiceless.
It has more than once been maintained that this consonant was
originally an affricate (of the type [ts]), largely on the basis of
the pronunciation of ṣ over a wide sector of the Jewish tradition,
but this pronunciation is probably secondary.

8.29. There is another consonant of this series whose attribution
to Proto-Semitic is debatable and whose character moreover has
hitherto defied precise definition: it is usually transliterated ś—but
at times also in other ways (in particular s̀). This consonant appears
in Hebrew and in Biblical Aramaic, but without a graphic sign of its
own (the symbol for š is used, and a diacritic mark was introduced
at a late date as part of the Masoretic pointing). Hence it may be
thought that it is merely a secondary differentiation of š; yet an
examination of the correspondences in the other languages suggests
its original autonomy (cf. the comparative table below). Old
South Arabian has three symbols for the non-emphatic voiceless
dental fricatives for which the following correspondences with
Proto-Semitic have been claimed: ⊓ (s¹) = š; ⟩ (s²) = ś; ⤬ (s³) = s.
At any rate, it may be inferred that the three symbols correspond to
three separate consonant phonemes. An independent ś with lateral
articulation is attested in modern South Arabian. North-West
Semitic in its most ancient phase shows traces of an autonomous ś:
at all events, the inferences drawn from Egyptian transcriptions
and from a gloss in the Tell Amarna letters (cf. § 8.33) seem to
point in this direction. On the other hand, the ś symbol often used
in the transliteration of Old Akkadian does not appear to connote
a phonemic distinction from š, and cannot, therefore, be regarded
as an independent consonant. The considerations adduced in the
foregoing would seem to be sufficient, at least cumulatively, to
claim ś as an independent consonant phoneme in Proto-Semitic.

As for the character of this consonant, it has been suggested (Cantineau) that it was lateralized and that its distinction from *s* lay in that peculiarity. This hypothesis is mainly based on the lateralized *ś* of modern South Arabian, where *ś* is held to correspond to Hebrew *ś*, Arabic *š*, and Proto-Semitic *ś* (e.g. *śbʿ* "to be sated", cf. Heb. *śbʿ*, Ar. *šbʿ*).

8.30. Finally, Proto-Semitic has a voiceless palato-alveolar *š* (i.e. I.P.A. [ʃ]). Yet another sibilant (s_x) has been proposed for Proto-Semitic by Goetze (RA 52 [1958], pp. 137—49) on the basis of certain correspondences adduced from Old Akkadian and Old South Babylonian; but this hypothesis has not been generally accepted.

8.31. Looking at the manifestation of the consonants of this series in the various languages, we notice that *s, z, ṣ* have regular correspondences, while *ś* and *š* have those indicated in the following table (the identification in this table of Proto-Semitic with Hebrew is, of course, purely conjectural):

Proto-Semitic	Akkadian	Ugaritic	Hebrew	Syriac	Arabic	ESA	Ethiopic
s	*s*	*s*	*s*	*s*	*s*	s^3	*s*
ś	*š*	*š*	*ś*	*s*	*š*	s^2	*š*
š	*š*	*š*	*š*	*š*	*s*	s^1	*s*

Examples: *s*: Akk. *kusītu* "garment", Ug. *kst*, Heb. *kəsūt*, Syr. *kussāyā*, Ar. *kuswat*, ESA *ks³w* — *ś*: Akk. *ešer* "ten", Ug. *ʿšr*, Heb. *ʿeśer*, Syr. *ʿəsar*, Ar. *ʿašr*, ESA *ʿs²r*, Eth. *ʿaśrū*; — *š*: Akk. *ḫameš* "five", Ug. *ḫmš*, Heb. *ḫāmēš*, Syr. *ḫammeš*, Ar. *ḫams*, ESA *ḫms¹*, Eth. *ḫaməs*.

8.32. In Akkadian the system of writing is, as usual, inadequate for indicating the difference between voiceless, voiced, and emphatic (*s, z, ṣ*). Where these occur at the end of syllables the same symbols are almost always used whatever the consonant, and the same is true at the beginning of syllables in Old Akkadian and Old Assyrian, and to a large extent in Old Babylonian. From the Middle Assyrian and Middle Babylonian period onwards, syllables beginning with *z* or *ṣ* are still, for the most part, written with the same symbols (the special symbols for *ṣi, ṣu, ṣir* are an exception), while *s* has either symbols of its own or shares them with *š* (e.g. *s/šar, s/šab*).

In Middle and New Assyrian original *š* often appears as *s*, especially before bilabials (e.g. *usbat* "she sits" in contrast to Bab. *wašbat*; *sapal* "under" as well as *šapal*). Hebrew transcriptions of Assyrian names confirm this fact: for Assyrian *Šarrukēn* we have Hebrew *Sargōn*. The change *š* > *s* occurs also in Amorite: e.g. *skn* "to put" for *škn*. In Assyrian (and less often in Babylonian) we have some instances of initial *s* for *z* (e.g. *siqqurratu* for *ziqqurratu* "temple tower"). Interchanges of *s* and *ṣ* may occur in the neighbourhood of *n* (e.g. *psn* and *pṣn* "to veil"). From the Middle Babylonian and Middle Assyrian period onwards the substitution of *l* for *š* before a dental has become a characteristic feature (e.g. New Babylonian *iktaldū* "they arrived" instead of *iktašdū*). The causes of this phenomenon are still not clear.

8.33. In the North-West Semitic of the second millennium B.C., Ugaritic has three symbols for the non-emphatic voiceless fricatives of this group. An examination of the correspondences shows that Proto-Semitic *s* remains, while *ś* and *š* coalesce in *š*. In Amorite, too, *ś*, *š* merge in *š* which, in its turn, develops into *s* (as has been pointed out in the preceding §). There are however indications of an autonomous *ś* in the Tell Amarna glosses and in the Egyptian transcriptions of North-West Semitic names. As for the glosses, letter 286,56 (of Jerusalem) shows *ša-te-e* (corresponding to Hebrew *ṣādē*): hence *ś* is rendered by *š*, whereas it would have been rendered by *s* if it had merged with *š* as in Ugaritic (but this is the only example, and the possibility of a purely graphic variant cannot be excluded). In the Egyptian transcriptions *ś* is rendered by *s*, whereas *š* remains unaltered: e.g. *s'r* = Heb. *Śēʿīr*; *šnm* = Heb. *Šūnēm* (but transcriptions vary at times even for the same name: *sk* and *šik* = Heb. *Śōkō*).

8.34. In the first millennium all the Canaanite languages, except Hebrew, show the merging of *ś* with *š* (the spelling *'sr* for *'šr* "ten" in Phoenician is an isolated case). In the late Phoenician inscriptions from Cyprus the use of the symbol "š" for *s* is a noteworthy feature (e.g. *ptlmyš* for "Ptolemaios"). In late Punic, interchange between dental and palato-alveolar fricatives is frequent (e.g. *sb'm* for *šb'm* "seventy", *š'w'r* for "Severus", etc.). As for Hebrew, it is, of course, well known that the Masoretes indicated a graphic distinction between *ś* and *š* by placing a point either above the

3*

left side of the letter (for *ś*) or its right (for *š*), the same symbol
having always served for both consonants. The distinction may
be based on ancient tradition, but we have no reliable evidence
for this: the indications furnished by the Tell Amarna letter from
Jerusalem are insufficient (§ 8.33), and the famous passage in
Judges 12,6, according to which the Ephraimites pronounced *š*
as *s*, probably points to a dialectal differentiation rather than to the
existence of an independent phoneme *ś*. In any case, the phenomenon which formed the basis of the Masoretic distinction must have
been of fairly limited extent, since by and large *ś* and *š* appear to
have coalesced in one single consonant (just as they possessed one
graphic symbol only). It has, therefore, been conjectured that the
Masoretes may have generalized a purely dialectal differentiation.
Indeed, the Akkadian, Greek, and Latin transcriptions of Hebrew
names do not distinguish between *ś* and *š*; and St. Jerome, in
a well-known passage (*Onomastica sacra*, p. 36), shows that he
knows of *s*, *ṣ* and *š*, but not of *ś*.

8.35. The most ancient Aramaic inscriptions show the symbol
"*š*" corresponding to Proto-Semitic *ś*; the Egyptian papyri likewise have "*š*"—except for a few doubtful cases. The development
to *s* takes place gradually during the second half of the first millennium B.C. and may be said to have been completed, save for rare
exceptions, about the beginning of the Christian era. The position
in the ancient inscriptions may be based either on a graphic
"Canaanism", at a time when the phonetic process characteristic
of Aramaic had already taken place, or on an approximate rendering of the Proto-Semitic consonant which still survived (cf. § 8.18).

8.36. It has already been mentioned that Old South Arabian
has three symbols, and their probable correspondences with
Proto-Semitic consonants have been listed (cf. § 8.29). Pre-
classical North Arabic has only two symbols which correspond
to *s* and *š*; the changes characteristic of classical Arabic (*ś* > *š*,
š > *s*) seem already to have been accomplished (e.g. Liḥyānite *sn*
"year" compared with Ar. *sanat*, Heb. *šānā*). It has been observed,
however, that these changes may not be very ancient, for in borrowings from Aramaic they are in part accomplished and in part not
(e.g. *śakkīn* "knife" > *sikkīn*).

8.37. In Ethiopic we encounter the same development as in classical Arabic. However, the distinctive articulation of *š* has been lost since the earliest time and has merged with that of *s*; consequently, the symbol for *s* has gradually extended its scope to cases where etymology would require the symbol for *š* (though there also exist many instances of *š* usurping the place of *s*), and spelling conventions have become quite arbitrary. It is interesting to note that modern Ethiopian languages have developed a new consonant *š* for which they do not use the ancient character for *š* but an adaptation of the symbol for *s* (Ullendorff, SLE, p. 111).

8. Velar Plosives

8.38. Proto-Semitic has two velar plosives, voiceless *k* and voiced *g*. It also possesses an emphatic velar plosive *q*, generally regarded as the emphatic consonant corresponding to *k* and therefore also transliterated *ḳ*.

8.39. The characterization of this last consonant as voiceless is not completely certain. The traditional Arabic articulation is indeed voiceless, but some indigenous grammarians and a few modern dialects support a voiced pronunciation. In Akkadian *q* is frequently written with the symbol for *g* (see, however, § 8.40); in Mandaean there are many cases of *g* for *q* (e.g. *g'yṭ'* "summer", Syr. *qayṭā*). Nevertheless, the voiceless correspondences in the other Semitic languages confirm the voiceless character of *q*; and from the phonemic point of view any uncertainty may be accounted for by the absence of a distinctive opposition.

8.40. In Akkadian, the writing system is, as usual, inadequate to indicate the distinction between voiceless, voiced, and emphatic. This differentiation is entirely lacking for consonants in final position, as well as for other positions in Old Akkadian and Old Assyrian. In Babylonian and later Assyrian initial *k* and *g* are consistently kept distinct in the majority of the symbols used, but not in all of them: e.g. *g/kir*, *g/kil*; as for *q*, a special symbol for *qa* occurs in Old Babylonian at Mari and Ešnunna, while for other syllables containing *q* separate symbols do not appear until a later period.

8.41. In the North-West Semitic languages of the second millennium B.C., certain interchanges between the consonants of this series are to be found in Amorite, in the Egyptian transcriptions of Semitic names, in the Tell Amarna glosses, and in Ugaritic. The series seems to attain stability later, in the first millennium: in the Canaanite area it is not until Neo-Punic times that inter-changes between the voiceless and the emphatic members are attested; in the Aramaic area interchanges between the voiceless and the voiced members are found in transcriptions of Assyrian names, but this phenomenon is due to Assyrian (cf. § 8.40) rather than to Aramaic factors.

8.42. In Classical Arabic g develops into $\check{g}$ (affricate and palato-alveolarized). The pronunciation as g is, however, attested by Arab grammarians (although regarded as faulty) and also occurs in some modern dialects of Egypt and Arabia. An analogous tendency $k > \check{c}$ (though again considered "faulty") is noted by Arab grammarians and appears in ancient and modern dialects (in the neighbourhood, it is true, of palatal vowels and thus as an aspect of assimilation: cf. § 9.5). A similar process of assimilation (under the influence of front vowels) underlies the transition $k > \check{s}$ which occurs in modern South Arabian dialects as well as in the modern languages of southern Ethiopia and in the Aramaic dialect of Ma'lūla.

8.43. In the Ethiopian sphere many cases of spirantization and palatalization of velar plosives can be observed, but none of them is certain for the classical period (Ullendorff, SLE, pp. 49—74). In addition, Ethiopic has evolved, under the impact of its Cushitic substratum, a series of labio-velars which exist alongside the ordinary velars. This labialization embraces, in addition to the three velar plosives, the velar fricative $\underset{.}{h}$—thus producing: k^w, g^w, q^w, $\underset{.}{h}^w$. At times the labialized consonants take the place of the simple ones in such correspondences as: Akk. $kal\bar{u}$ "all", Ug. kl, Heb. kol, Syr. kol, Ar. $kull$, Eth. $k^w\partial l$.

9. Velar Fricatives

8.44. Proto-Semitic has two velar fricatives, voiceless $\underset{.}{h}$ and voiced $\dot{g}$, i.e. I.P.A. [x] and [γ].

8.45. In a series of studies Růžička has maintained that $\dot{g}$ is not a Proto-Semitic consonant but an Arabic innovation. Originally, the argument in support of this thesis lay in the fact that $\dot{g}$ was to be found in Arabic only, and even there it was in some cases secondary, i.e. derived from the pharyngal ' (e.g. *musawwaǧ* "permitted", a variant of *musawwa'*). When an independent $\dot{g}$—or at least an independent graphic symbol—was identified in South Arabian and in Ugaritic, Růžička dismissed the South Arabian evidence as a mere extension of the Arabic phenomenon and claimed that the symbol taken for $\dot{g}$ in Ugaritic corresponded in some instances to '. From this he inferred that $\dot{g}$ did not exist in Ugaritic but that the symbol in question was simply one of a number of attempts at fashioning a suitable graphic sign for '. Růžička's contentions have been partially supported by Petráček (ArOr 21 [1953], pp. 240 to 262; 23 [1955], pp. 475—78) who has endeavoured to show, in a statistical investigation, that in Arabic $\dot{g}$ is of a complex phonemic nature, being partly a variant of ' and partly an independent phoneme. This condition can be explained in terms of the acquisition of independent phonemic status of what was originally a mere variant. Against this set of observations there still remains the fact that in classical Arabic, South Arabian, and Ugaritic $\dot{g}$ possesses a clearly circumscribed independence which is not invalidated by a number of peripheral developments. Moreover, it has recently been pointed out (Rössler, ZA 54 [1961], pp. 158—72) that Proto-Semitic $\dot{g}$—as distinct from Proto-Semitic '—does not always occasion the Old Akkadian change $a > e$: a fact which would point to its independent existence in the most ancient phase of East Semitic. It appears, therefore, that $\dot{g}$ is to be retained among the Proto-Semitic consonants.

8.46. The correspondences of the velar fricatives in the principal Semitic languages are as follows:

Proto-Semitic	Akkadian	Ugaritic	Hebrew	Syriac	Arabic	ESA	Ethiopic
ḫ	ḫ	ḫ	ḥ	ḥ	ḫ	ḫ	ḫ
ġ	'	ġ	'	'	ġ	ġ	'

Examples: ḫ: Akk. *aḫu* "brother", Ug. *åḫ*, Heb. *'āḫ*, Syr. *'aḥā*, Ar. *'aḫ*, ESA *'ḫ*, Eth. *'əḫʷ*;—ġ: Akk. *'rb* "to enter", Heb. Syr. Eth. *'rb*, Ar. ESA *ġrb*; Ug. *ġlm* "boy", Heb. *'elem*, Syr. *'əlaymā*, Ar. *ġulām*, ESA *ġlm*.

8.47. In Akkadian interchanges occur between *ḫ* and *k* (e.g. *ḫnš* instead of the usual *knš* "to submit"). Akkadian *ḫ* corresponds in some cases to Semitic *ḥ* (e.g. *ḫkm* "to understand", cf. Ar. *ḥkm*, whereas the normal Akkadian development [see § 8.54] is *ḥ > ʾ*) or to *ġ* (e.g. *ṣḫr* "to be small", cf. Ar. *ṣġr*).

8.48. In North-West Semitic of the second millennium B.C. the existence of *ḫ* and *ġ* is attested both in Ugaritic and in the Egyptian transcriptions of Semitic names. In these transcriptions "ḫ" is used for *ḫ*, and "g" (or "q") for *ġ*, while "h" is employed for *ḥ* and " ʿ " for ʿ (e.g. Egyptian *nḥr* = Heb. *naḥal*, Akk. *naḫlu*; Egyptian *mġrt* = Heb. *məʿārā*, Ar. *maġārat*; Egyptian *qdt* = Heb. *ʿAzzā*, Ar. *Ġazzat*). Some Ugaritic uses of the symbol "ġ" for *ḫ* as well as the correspondence between Ugaritic "ġ" and Akkadian "ḫ" in a syllabary from Ugarit may suggest voiceless articulations of Ugaritic *ġ* (Garbini, SNO, p. 52).

8.49. In North-West Semitic of the first millennium the process *ḫ > ḥ*, *ġ > ʿ* is complete. The only problem in this connexion is posed by the Greek and Latin transcriptions of Hebrew which show for *ḥ*: χ (*ch*), ε, zero; for ʿ: γ (*g*), ε, zero. It has been suggested that the transcriptions χ (*ch*), γ (*g*) stand for the original consonants *ḫ*, *ġ*, respectively, while the others stand for original *ḥ*, ʿ. This hypothesis can, of course, be tested by a comparative examination, and the result of such a test militates against the hypothesis (e.g. χ corresponds to *ḥ* in Aβιχαιλ, Heb. *ʾăbiḥayil*; γ corresponds to ʿ in Γοφερα, from the root *ʿfr*). The variations in the transcriptions seem instead to relate to different periods: χ (*ch*) and γ (*g*) predominate in the earlier period, while ε and zero belong to a later one. Another feature characteristic of late North-West Semitic, which appears in Eastern Syriac and in a sector of the Jewish-Ashkenazi tradition (though European languages are bound to have affected Ashkenazi pronunciation), is the rendering of *ḥ* as *ḫ*. The correspondences exclude the possibility of a survival of an original *ḫ*.

8.50. In Ethiopic the pronunciation of *ḫ* gradually coalesces with that of *ḥ*; this is reflected in graphic interchanges of increasing frequency and arbitrariness.

10. Pharyngal Fricatives; Laryngals

8.51. Proto-Semitic has two fricative pharyngals, voiceless $ḥ$ and voiced ' (I.P.A. [ħ] and [ʕ], respectively).

8.52. Proto-Semitic has two laryngals: one glottal plosive, ' (I.P.A. [ʔ]) and one voiceless laryngal fricative h (of which, however, there are some voiced manifestations in modern Arabic dialects).

8.53. The consonants of the pharyngal fricative and laryngal series have regular correspondences in the various Semitic languages, with the exception of Akkadian where they are reduced to ' (or to zero). There are, however, extensive phonetic reductions and losses which it is well to examine individually (for phenomena of syncope, cf. § 9.20).

8.54. In Akkadian (as has just been mentioned) these consonants have been reduced to '—under the influence of Sumerian which did not possess the consonants of this series. The reduction is not yet complete in Old Akkadian (cf. the use of the symbol É for the phonetic values $'à$ and $à'$, probably corresponding to the Proto-Semitic consonants h and $ḫ$); in Old Babylonian, too, there are indications that some laryngals at least were still pronounced (*'adānum* "limit" written with initial $ḫ$); in New Assyrian it is probable that h reappears, because *anniu* "this" is often spelt *ḫanniu* (pronounced [hanniu]?). It is only from the Middle Babylonian and Middle Assyrian periods onwards that ' has symbols of its own which even then are not regularly employed. Apart from the use of specific symbols, ' may be graphically expressed in various ways: by the symbol for the vowel which follows (e.g. *iš-a-am* for *iš'am*) or by the symbols for $ḫ$ (e.g. *e-ḫi-il-tum* for *e-'i-il-tum*). It should be observed that the graphic notation of ', partial and irregular in medial position, is usually absent at the beginning of words (cf. von Soden, GAG, p. 24 for some rare exceptions). The Assyriological custom of not transliterating even initial ' is followed in the present work; it should be clear, however, that the absence of a symbol does not necessarily coincide with phonetic reality. There is no reason to suppose that the situation in Akkadian ran counter to the general Semitic rule which requires that every

syllable should begin with a consonant (cf. § 10.2). An identification
of the consonants which had coalesced in ' is at times possible on
the basis of modifications to which neighbouring vowels have
been subjected: for ' derived from $ġ$, $ḫ$, ' occasions the change a into
e (e.g. *'aprum "dust" > eprum). This transition does not, however,
always take place in the case of $ġ$ (cf. § 8.45), while on the other
hand it sometimes occurs with $ḥ$ (e.g. ewūm "to become" compared
with Aram. həwā).

8.55. In Canaanite, a weakening of the pharyngals is suggested
for pre-Masoretic Hebrew by Greek and Latin transcriptions
(cf. § 8.49) and by interchanges with ' and h which are attested in
the Dead Sea documents. It is, therefore, not altogether impossible
that the Masoretes may have aimed at restoring the ancient pronunciation by means of their peculiar system of vocalizing the
pharyngals. A characteristic feature of Punic, as distinct from
Phoenician, is the gradual weakening and eventual reduction to '
(or zero) of $ḫ$, ', $ḥ$. This phenomenon becomes manifest to only
a limited degree in official documents where the traditional orthography prevails; but it is prevalent in popular inscriptions in which
constant interchanges and losses occur in the pharyngal and
laryngal series (e.g. 'd for 'ḥd "one").

8.56. Aramaic, prior to the division into West and East Aramaic,
retains by and large the independent articulation of the pharyngals
and laryngals (some weakening which may be observed in the
Aramaic of Assyria is probably due to Assyrian influence: e.g.
' > ' in 'rṣt' for 'rṣt' as well as many cases in which intervocalic ' is
dropped: mry for mr'y, etc.). Later, extensive areas of phonetic
uncertainty occur which are reflected in the orthography. In the
languages of the Western group the consonants in question are
frequently interchanged or dropped altogether; in those of the
Eastern group the reductions ' > ', $ḥ$ > h are very frequent and
may, in fact, extend further to ' > zero, h > ' > zero. Syriac, in
particular, shows many cases in which ' loses its consonantal value
and is then dropped in the current spelling convention (e.g. ḥad
"one", cf. Heb. 'eḥad, Ar. 'aḥad, etc.); h often loses its consonantal
character (e.g. the pronouns hū, hī "he, she" lose h in enclitic
position): for details cf. Brockelmann, SG, pp. 25—26.

8.57. In the Arabian area, Old South Arabian displays the transition ' > ' in the dialect of the Ḥaḍramawt (e.g. *'d* "up to" for *'d*). Classical Arabic exhibits a remarkable stability of the pharyngals and laryngals, though a few traces of the development ' > ', *ḥ* > *h* are attested in some ancient dialects. As for ', it is possessed of an exceptional constancy in the orthography of the classical language.

8.58. In Ethiopic we observe a gradual phonetic reduction of *ḥ* to *h* and of ' to '; this uncertainty (resulting eventually in almost complete arbitrariness) does not appear in the most ancient inscriptions of Aksum and may well be due to the influence of Amharic. The latter affects the orthography of classical Ethiopic, so that with the passage of time inconsistencies become ever more prevalent. But there are, of course, no grounds for denying the original phonemic independence of the consonants of this series.

11. Synopsis of the Consonantal System

8.59. To return to the table of the Proto-Semitic consonant system (cf. § 8.3), the evolution of this system in the principal languages of the group may be envisaged as follows:

Proto-Semitic	Akkadian	Ugaritic	Hebrew	Syriac	Arabic	ESA	Ethiopic
p	*p*	*p*	*p*	*p*	*f*	*f*	*f*
b	*b*	*b*	*b*	*b*	*b*	*b*	*b*
m	*m*	*m*	*m*	*m*	*m*	*m*	*m*
ṯ	*š*	*ṯ*	*š*	*t*	*ṯ*	*ṯ*	*s*
ḏ	*z*	*d (ḏ?)*	*z*	*d*	*ḏ*	*ḏ*	*z*
ṯ̣	*ṣ*	*ṯ̣*	*ṣ*	*ṭ*	*ẓ*	*ẓ*	*ṣ*
ḍ	*ṣ*	*ṣ*	*ṣ*	'	*ḍ*	*ḍ*	*ḍ*
t	*t*	*t*	*t*	*t*	*t*	*t*	*t*
d	*d*	*d*	*d*	*d*	*d*	*d*	*d*
ṭ	*ṭ*	*ṭ*	*ṭ*	*ṭ*	*ṭ*	*ṭ*	*ṭ*
n	*n*	*n*	*n*	*n*	*n*	*n*	*n*
l	*l*	*l*	*l*	*l*	*l*	*l*	*l*

Proto-Semitic	Akkadian	Ugaritic	Hebrew	Syriac	Arabic	ESA	Ethiopic
r	r	r	r	r	r	r	r
s	s	s	s	s	s	s^3	s
z	z	z	z	z	z	z	z
ṣ	ṣ	ṣ	ṣ	ṣ	ṣ	ṣ	ṣ
ś	š	š	ś	s	š	s^2	š
š	š	š	š	š	s	s^1	s
k	k	k	k	k	k	k	k
g	g	g	g	g	ǧ	g	g
q	q	q	q	q	q	q	q
ḫ	ḫ	ḫ	ḥ	ḥ	ḫ	ḫ	ḫ
ġ	ʾ	ġ	ʿ	ʿ	ġ	ġ	ʿ
ḥ	ʾ	ḥ	ḥ	ḥ	ḥ	ḥ	ḥ
ʿ	ʾ	ʿ	ʿ	ʿ	ʿ	ʿ	ʿ
h	ʾ	h	h	h	h	h	h
ʾ	ʾ	ʾ	ʾ	ʾ	ʾ	ʾ	ʾ

8.60. The extent to which the original consonantal system has actually survived in the various languages (irrespective of etymological relationships) is shown in the following table:

Proto-Semitic	Akkadian	Ugaritic	Hebrew	Syriac	Arabic	ESA	Ethiopic
p	p	p	p	p	f	f	f
b	b	b	b	b	b	b	b
m	m	m	m	m	m	m	m
ṯ		ṯ			ṯ	ṯ	
ḏ		(ḏ)			ḏ	ḏ	
ṭ̱		ṯ̣			ẓ	ẓ	
ḍ					ḍ	ḍ	ḍ
t	t	t	t	t	t	t	t
d	d	d	d	d	d	d	d
ṭ	ṭ	ṭ	ṭ	ṭ	ṭ	ṭ	ṭ
n	n	n	n	n	n	n	n
l	l	l	l	l	l	l	l
r	r	r	r	r	r	r	r
s	s	s	s	s	s	s	s
z	z	z	z	z	z	z	z
ṣ	ṣ	ṣ	ṣ	ṣ	ṣ	ṣ	ṣ
ś		ś			ś		

Proto-Semitic	Akkadian	Ugaritic	Hebrew	Syriac	Arabic	ESA	Ethiopic
š	š	š	š	š	š	š	š
ġ	ġ	ġ	ġ	ġ	ǧ	ġ	ġ
q	q	q	q	q	q	q	q
ḫ	ḫ	ḫ			ḫ	ḫ	ḫ
ġ̇	ġ̇				ġ̇	ġ̇	
ḥ	ḥ	ḥ	ḥ	ḥ	ḥ	ḥ	ḥ
ʿ	ʿ	ʿ	ʿ	ʿ	ʿ	ʿ	ʿ
h		h	h	h	h	h	h
ʾ	ʾ	ʾ	ʾ	ʾ	ʾ	ʾ	ʾ

12. Semivowels

8.61. Proto-Semitic has a bilabial semivowel w and a palatal semivowel y, i.e. I.P.A. [j].

8.62. Both semivowels have regular correspondences in the various Semitic languages. They are, however, subject to changes and reductions (for some phenomena of syncope cf. § 9.20).

8.63. Since w is rare, and probably secondary, in the Sumerian writing-system (and language), its graphic notation in Akkadian is somewhat uncertain and imperfect. Up to the Old Babylonian and Old Assyrian periods the syllables *wa, we, wi, wu* are written with the Sumerian symbol PI; later on, for w the symbols for *m* are predominantly used in Babylonia, and in Assyria those for *b* (e.g. Old Bab. Ass. *awātum* "word", Mid.-Bab. *amātu*, Mid.-Ass. *abatu*). At the beginning of words, w is generally preserved until the Old Babylonian and Old Assyrian periods; afterwards it is either dropped (or reduced to ') or written with symbols for *m* (e.g. *wuššurum* "to send" $>$ *uššuru* and *muššuru*; *warādum* "to descend" $>$ *arādu*). For w in medial position cf. § 9.20. As regards the other semivowel, y, Sumerian possessed only the phonetic sequence *i-a*, and the symbols for this are used not only for the graphic expression of the Akkadian syllable *ya*, but also for *yi, ye, yu*; the symbols A-A are employed for the sequences *ay, āya, ayya, ayyi, ayye, ayyu* (other sequences are not encountered owing to elisions and contractions). In initial position y almost invariably disappears (or is reduced to '), at times leaving behind the vowel which

accompanied it (e.g. *yu* > *u*), while at other times the homorganic
vowel *i* (e.g. *ya* > *i*) remains. Finally, Old Akkadian spellings of
the type *i-ik-mi*, *i-ig-mu-ur* (Gelb, OA, p. 158) seem to suggest
the possibility of a prefix *yi-* as an intermediate phase in the change
ya- > *i-*. For *y* in medial position cf. § 9.20.

8.64. In North-West Semitic there is a characteristic development
w > *y* in initial position (e.g. Akk. Ar. Eth. *wld* "to bear", Ug.
Heb. Syr. *yld*). This phenomenon can already be seen in Amorite,
in the Egyptian transcriptions of the second millennium, in Ugaritic and in the Tell Amarna glosses. Some exceptions in the Egyptian transcriptions might suggest that this process was then still
in the evolutionary stage. Initial *w* is kept in the conjunction *w*
"and" and in a few nouns (e.g. Heb. *wālād* "child"). Some survivals
of *w* in Nabataean (in cases where the other North-Western languages have *y*) may be explained as due to Arabic influence.

8.65. In ancient Arabian dialects an occasional change *w* > *y*
in initial position is suggested by such cases as *yāzi'ahum* "their
protector" for *wāzi'ahum* (Rabin, WA, pp. 65, 83). Reductions
of initial *w*, *y* to ' are also found (e.g. *'uǧūhuhum* "their faces"
for *wuǧūhuhum*, *'iqā'* "protection" for *wiqā'*). Another phenomenon
attested in these dialects is the pronunciation of *y* as *ǧ*; but the
stock example usually cited, *'iyyal* "deer" > *'iǧǧal* (Rabin, WA,
p. 199), may conceivably be the result of dissimilation of the
semivowel in relation to the homorganic vowel *i* which precedes it.

13. Vowels

8.66. Proto-Semitic has three short vowels: open back velar
a, i.e. I.P.A. [ɑ], close front palatal *i*, and close back velar *u* with
strongly rounded lips. Proto-Semitic also possesses the three
corresponding long vowels: *ā*, *ī*, *ū*. Traces of vocalic *l* and *r* have
also been claimed (von Soden, GAG, p. 11), but further study is
required.

8.67. There are no certain grounds for supposing that Proto-
Semitic had once possessed additional vowel phonemes. In particular, the addition to the vowel-system of *ē*, which has more than
once been postulated (cf. most recently Rabin, WA, pp. 110—11),
meets with difficulties in demonstrating the phonemic status of

this vowel. From the phonetic point of view it may be taken for granted that not only this vowel but numerous other varieties have existed in Semitic since its most ancient phase.

8.68. The Proto-Semitic vowel system has an exact reflection in that of Arabic whose full network of graphic symbols mirrors the phonemic position. The history of Arabic and its dialects shows clearly in what manner vowels of other timbres have evolved in the Semitic languages and have, in the course of time, acquired phonemic status. These vowels have arisen in two main ways: by change under the influence of neighbouring consonants and by contraction of diphthongs ($aw > \bar{o}$, $ay > \bar{e}$). The non-phonemic variations e for a, o for u, e for i are so common that Arabic vowels are rightly classified according to the place of articulation rather than on the grounds of timbre (Fleisch, TPA, p. 63).

8.69. The graphic notation of vowels in the various Semitic languages is bound up with the system of writing adopted by each one; and these systems vary between certain extremes of phonemic and phonetic representation. The examination which follows will be especially concerned with the vowel-systems of those languages for which we possess the best sources of information. For other languages, and especially those of the North-West Semitic group, the consonantal system of writing does not offer sufficiently solid grounds for adequate reconstruction, even though there exists a good deal of circumstantial evidence (general Semitic comparisons, foreign transcriptions, *matres lectionis*); the principal data available will, of course, be recorded.

a. Akkadian

8.70. Akkadian presents a vowel-system identical with that of Proto-Semitic, but with the addition of the vowel e, either short or long (e, $\bar{e}$), which appears to be derived from a or i (a, $\bar{a}$; i, $\bar{i}$). In the writing-system the series of symbols with e is very incomplete; in the southern dialect of Old Babylonian i occurs so frequently for e that this feature has been regarded as reflecting a dialectal peculiarity.

8.71. The graphic interchanges between u and i and between u and a in certain forms (e.g. *mu-ru-iṣ* for *mu-ru-uṣ* "pain", *i-na-ṣur* for *i-na-ṣar* "he watches") have been claimed as evidence for the existence of vowel qualities of the type [y], [ɔ] (cf. von Soden, JCS 2 [1948], pp. 291—303).

8.72. The construct state (cf. §§ 12.78—79) in *-i* of some monosyllabic substantives (in contrast to the usual absence of endings in that form) has suggested the existence in Akkadian (known also in other Semitic languages) of a vowel of the *ə* type (von Soden, GAG, pp. 10, 82).

b. North-West Semitic of the Second Millennium B.C.

8.73. Amorite, which has come down to us in cuneiform script, exhibits a vowel-system identical with that of Akkadian—with the sole exception that *e* does not appear to be an independent phoneme but rather an allophone of *i* (Gelb, RANL 13 [1958], pp. 146—47). Some interchanges of *i* and *u* (e.g. *binum* and *bunum* "son") may possibly suggest the existence of vowel qualities of the [y] type. Similar considerations might apply to other interchanges, e.g. *u* and *a* (*sumum* and *samum* "name") where one might suppose a vowel of the [ɔ] type.

8.74. The language of the Tell Amarna glosses (likewise in cuneiform writing) also displays a vowel-system like that of Akkadian. The vowel *e*, frequently resulting from an original *a* or *i*, now appears to be established as part of the phonemic system, even though it started as a mere allophone. The glosses show the, apparently non-conditioned, change *ā > ō* (e.g. *a-nu-ki*, cf. Heb. *'anōkī*, against Akk. *anāku*: the writing of *u* for *o* is due to the absence in cuneiform of a proper notation for the vowel *o*); cf. § 8.83. An instance of the change *ā > ō* is now attested in an Old Babylonian inscription from Mari: (*ḫamāṣam >*) *ḫamūṣam iḫmuṣ* "he plundered thoroughly".

8.75. In Ugaritic the writing-system is consonantal, but the consonant ' has three symbols according to the vowel which follows, i.e. *a/ā, i/ī, u/ū*. From this we may probably infer that the Ugaritic vowel-system corresponds substantially to that of Proto-Semitic. The problem of representing unvocalized ' is open to argument, for the data are far from being consistent. In the majority of such cases the symbol for ' with the vowel *i* is used;

but sometimes the symbol used is that of ' plus the vowel identical with that which precedes it; and on other occasions it is the symbol for ' with any vowel indiscriminately (or at least so it appears to us in the absence of a rational explanation).

8.76. It has been observed that in Ugaritic the symbol for ' with $u/\bar{u}$ corresponds also to '(*$aw >$)$\bar{o}$ and that for ' with $i/\bar{\imath}$ to '(*$ay >$) $\bar{e}$ (Gordon, UM, p. 17). It might be averred in this connexion that the diphthongs aw, ay can also evolve into $\bar{u}$, $\bar{\imath}$ (cf. Akk. *$baytu > b\bar{\imath}tu$ "house"; *$mawtu > m\bar{u}tu$ "death"); but this Akkadian development is not attested in North-West Semitic. Moreover, it is probable that there existed vowels of the e, o timbre, not as independent phonemes but as allophones of a, i, u. Some vowel interchanges similar to those in Amorite (cf. § 8.73) have called forth the idea of vowel qualities of the [y], [ɔ] type. It is possible (cf. § 8.74) that the symbol for ' with the vowel i may in some cases represent a $\check{s}\partial w\bar{a}$ (cf. Garbini, SNO, pp. 63—64).

c. Canaanite

8.77. In the Canaanite area the Phoenician vowel-system (which can be partially reconstructed by means of Akkadian, Greek, and Latin transcriptions of Phoenician words) presents the usual Semitic phonemic vowels (§ 8.66) in a number of varying pronunciations. Thus we find a pronounced as e (ζερα for *zar' "seed"), i as e (Οζερβαλος for *$\bar{A}zir$-$ba'al$), u as o (Baliahon for *$Ba'al$-$yah\bar{u}n$). The original long vowels appear to be more stable than the short ones, but in Phoenician we may observe the non-conditioned change $\bar{a} > \bar{o}$ (e.g. macom for *$maq\bar{a}m$ "place"), for which cf. §8.83.

8.78. The vowel notation of Biblical Hebrew is the work of the Masoretes and originated during the second half of the first millennium A.D.; it therefore postdates the consonantal text by a very considerable margin. The reconstruction of the original vocalization has been attempted by utilizing the transcriptions of Hebrew names in other languages (Sperber's studies) as well as by the application of modern linguistic techniques (Z. S. Harris in JAOS 61 [1941] pp. 143—67). The tentative results show considerable divergences from the Masoretic system. Within the system itself three different traditions can be distinguished: the Babylonian, the Palestinian, and the Tiberian. The first and the second of these

indicate the vowels by means of supralinear signs, while the third
uses (with one exception) sublinear symbols. A characteristic
feature of the Masoretic vowel notation is the fairly elaborate
representation of qualitative distinctions.

8.79. According to the Tiberian system, which has prevailed
in Hebrew manuscripts and later on in printed books, the Biblical
vowel system may be represented as follows:

$$\overline{}\qquad\overline{\overline{}}\qquad\underline{\overline{}}\qquad\overline{}\qquad\overline{}\qquad\underline{}\qquad\overline{\cdot\cdot}$$

$$i\qquad e\qquad ä\qquad a\qquad ɔ\qquad o\qquad u$$

8.80. Vowel quantity is not in general indicated by the symbol
as such, but depends on the position of the vowel within the word;
only of *a* can it be said that it is normally a short vowel. As for ɔ,
it has two different pronunciations: it is either long when it corresponds etymologically to *ā* or short when it corresponds to an
original *u*. On etymological grounds, naturally paramount in
a comparative grammar, as well as for other reasons set out above
(cf. §§ 6.12—15), the present treatise will employ the following
transliterations (taking the seven vowels in the same order as in
the preceding paragraph):

$$i/ī\qquad ẹ/ẹ̄\qquad e/ē\qquad a\qquad ā/o\qquad o/ō\qquad u/ū$$

8.81. Combinations of vowel symbols with *matres lectionis* serve
to indicate a series of predominantly long vowels: *w* is used as
mater lectionis for vowels of the timbre *u* or *o*; *y* for those of timbre
i or *e*; *h* at the end of a word for those of timbre *e*, *a* or *o*; ' in the
middle or at the end of a word for those of any timbre. The indication of vowel quantity by means of *matres lectionis* is very
imperfect—in contrast to the position in Arabic (§ 8.91)—for in
Hebrew we have long vowels without *matres lectionis* and short
ones with *matres lectionis*. The use of *matres lectionis* in the Dead
Sea documents is somewhat peculiar: ' is extensively used at the
end of words, and *y* appears frequently instead of *h* (at the end of
words) to indicate vowels of the *e* timbre.

8.82. To the symbols enumerated above we have to add $\overline{}$ (*šəwā*)
which originally marked the absence of a vowel but which has come
to indicate in certain positions (at the beginning of syllables) the
vowel of the type *ə* (*Murmelvokal*). In combination with other

symbols *šəwā* produces the compounds $\overline{\cdot\hspace{-0.3em}\cdot}$, $\overline{\cdot\hspace{-0.3em}\cdot\hspace{-0.3em}\cdot}$, $\overline{\cdot\hspace{-0.3em}\cdot}$, employed with the pharyngal and laryngal consonants and here transliterated *ă*, *ĕ*, *ŏ*, respectively.

8.83. Compared with the Proto-Semitic system Hebrew vocalization displays a noteworthy development. This is, however, closely linked to syllabic structure and stress patterns and will, therefore, be dealt with at the appropriate entries below. Only one of the vowel changes in Hebrew appears to be non-conditioned, i.e. *ā > ō* (e.g. Akk. *samāne* "eight", Heb. *šəmōnē*). This change, which can already be observed in the Tell Amarna glosses and in Phoenician (§§ 8.74, 8.77), has long been considered a characteristic of "Canaanite" (in the traditional sense of that term); but in fact, while it does not occur in Ugaritic, it reappears in the early centuries of the Christian era both in West Aramaic (cf. §§ 8.84, 8.88) and in pre-Islamic Arabic (Rabin, WA, pp. 28, 105—10).

d. Aramaic

8.84. While Biblical Aramaic uses the same system as Hebrew, some earlier data are furnished by a magical text in cuneiform from the third century B.C. (A. Dupont-Sommer, RA 39 [1942—44], pp. 35—62). The vocalization of this text has—as compared with the general development of North-West Semitic—a rather archaic appearance: for example, the original *i* remains in *la-bi-iš* as against Heb. *lābēš*. Some cases of the change *ā > ō* (not attested in Old Aramaic) occur in Palmyrene (cf. § 8.83); this process is, later on, characteristic of Western Syriac (cf. § 8.88).

8.85. Syriac has a vowel notation going back, like that of Hebrew, to the second half of the first millennium of the Christian era; again like the Hebrew system it is characterized by the predominance of qualitative over quantitative distinctions.

8.86. There are two different methods of vowel notation, the Eastern (used by the Nestorians) and the Western (used by the Monophysites or Jacobites); the latter is based on Greek vowel symbols:

Eastern: $\underset{\cdot}{\cdot}$ *a*, $\overset{\cdot}{\cdot}$ *ā*, $\underline{\cdot}$ *e*, $\overline{\cdot}$ *ē*, ◦ *i/ī*, ꞇ *u/ū*, ◦◦ *o/ō*

Western: ⸲ *a/ā*, ⸲ *o/ō*, ⸲ *e/ē*, ⸱ *i/ī*, ⸲ *u/ū*

8.87. This notation makes use, for the vowels *i*, *u*, *o*, of *matres lectionis* which are widely employed in Syriac: *w* for *u/ū*, *o/ō*; *y* for *i/ī*, and in medial position sometimes for *ē*; ' for *ā* (Western *ō*), and for *ē* (Western *ī*) in final (occasionally also medial) position.

8.88. In addition to the difference in the actual system of notation there is a phonetic distinction between the Eastern vocalization (which is used in the present treatise) and the Western one. East Syriac preserves a more ancient vocalism, whereas West Syriac presents the following developments: *ā* > *ō* (cf. Hebrew: § 8.83); *ō* > *ū*; *o* > *u*; *ē* > *ī* (in certain types of words). Examples: ESyr. *pārōqā* "saviour", WSyr. *pōrūqō*; ESyr. *rēšā* "head", WSyr. *rīšō*.

8.89. Syriac possesses no symbol to indicate the absence of a vowel or to mark a vowel of type *ə*, though the existence of such a *Murmelvokal* (a central vowel whose precise timbre is determined by the nature of surrounding consonants as well as by the effects of vowel harmony) must be assumed in certain positions.

8.90. Compared with the Proto-Semitic system Syriac vocalization presents important developments which are connected—as indeed is the case in Hebrew—with syllabic structure and the incidence of stress; they will be dealt with at the appropriate place below.

e. Arabic

8.91. Pre-classical Arabic does not furnish sufficient indications for a reconstruction of its vowel system, and in any event it is improbable that this system differed appreciably (at least from the phonemic point of view) from that of classical Arabic (for the vexed question of *ē* cf. § 8.67). The classical language presents a vowel system which corresponds phonemically to the Proto-Semitic one. As for its notation, *matres lectionis* were consistently used for the indication of long vowels: *w* for *ū*, *y* for *ī*, ' for *ā*. This is natural in the case of *w* and *y* in view of the Aramaic (or rather Nabataean) origin of the Arabic script; only the use of ' to mark *ā* may be regarded as a specifically Arabic development (and is not, in fact, customary in the more ancient texts). For short vowels (and for long ones in combination with *matres lectionis*) a system of symbols was introduced (in the late ninth century A.D.) which is derived from somewhat simplified forms of the *matres lectionis*:

$$\underset{\smile}{}\ a \qquad \underset{\overline{}}{}\ i \qquad \overset{\smallsmile}{}\ u$$

8.92. There is a special symbol (‿) to denote the absence of a vowel; a vowel of type ǝ does not exist in Arabic.

8.93. From the phonetic point of view, traditional grammar and the history of the dialects provide some idea of the extensive variations in the timbre of Arabic vowels. The principal tendencies noted by Arab grammarians are: a) *'imāla*, i.e. [a:] > [e:], a non-conditioned phenomenon of palatalization whose realization is at times prevented by the operation of conservative forces; b) *tafḫīm*, i.e. [a:] > [o:], a less frequently occurring phenomenon of velarization, sometimes conditioned by the neighbourhood of emphatic consonants; c) *'išmām*, i.e. [i:] > [u:], another phenomenon of velarization whose true nature is, however, somewhat less certain (cf. Rabin, WA, p. 159).

f. Ethiopic

8.94. Old Ethiopic was at first written without vowel signs, but in the fourth century A.D. it introduced a very special type of vowel notation which operates by means of partial alterations in the form of the consonantal symbol. The vocalism which is manifested by this notation consists of seven elements; and it may now be regarded as established that these elements reflect essentially qualitative distinctions.

8.95. The qualitative values of the Ethiopic vowel series are as follows (for the purposes of exemplification it is convenient to use the consonant symbol *l*):

ለ	ሉ	ሊ	ላ	ሌ	ል	ሎ
ä	*u*	*i*	*a*	*e*	(*ǝ*)	*o*

8.96. Etymologically, *u i a* correspond in general to Proto-Semitic *ū ī ā*, respectively; *e o* to the diphthongs *ay aw*, respectively; and *ä* to *a*. Two elements of the Proto-Semitic system appear at first sight to be unrepresented, i.e. short *i u*, but in Ethiopic they have coalesced in the vowel *ǝ* (e.g. Ar. *'uḏn* "ear", Eth. *'ǝzn*; Ar. *sinn* "tooth", Eth. *sǝn*) in conformity with some general relationship which, in many instances in Semitic, seems to exist between these two vowels in opposition to *a*. For reasons of etymological correspondence, paramount in a comparative grammar, the present treatise will use the following transliterations (in the same order in which the Ethiopic vowels appear in the preceding paragraph):

$$a \quad \bar{u} \quad i \quad \bar{a} \quad \bar{e} \quad (\partial) \quad \bar{o}$$

As regards the sixth vowel, the transliteration ə is not free from ambiguity, for though this vowel may correspond to the sound of *šəwā mobile* of other languages, it is a stable vowel which may even be long (Ullendorff, SLE, p. 160). The ambiguity of the Ethiopic sixth order as either ə or zero causes difficulty not only to Europeans, but even Ethiopian scholars sometimes disagree about it in the traditional pronunciation of Gəʻəz.

14. Diphthongs

8.97. The combination of semivowels and vowels produces a series of rising or falling diphthongs; these are subject to a number of conditioned changes which will be dealt with at the appropriate place. Some changes, however, are not necessarily conditioned: they affect the diphthongs *aw, ay* whose treatment is a differentiating feature between certain Semitic areas.

8.98. In Akkadian the Proto-Semitic diphthongs *aw, ay* generally appear as *ū, ī*: e.g. **mawtu* "death" > *mūtu*, **'aynu* "eye" > *īnu*. In Assyrian, and partly in New Babylonian, *ē* takes the place of *ī* (*ēnu*). The Akkadian phenomenon may possibly be explained as the result of assimilation (cf. § 9.8). An exception occurs in the case of *ay* before *y* (e.g. *ayyābu* "enemy") and in some instances of the vetitive particle *ay* "not".

8.99. In the North-West Semitic of the second millennium B.C. Amorite shows the preservation of *aw* as well as the developments *am* and *ā*; for *ay* we find *ā* and *ē/ī*. The Egyptian transcriptions of Semitic names attest sometimes to the loss and sometimes to the retention of the semivowel element: perhaps they reflect a stage in the course of actual evolution. The reduction is shown to be complete in the Tell Amarna glosses and in Ugaritic where we encounter the result of the changes *aw > ō, ay > ē* (cf. however § 8.76). Before *y* (as in Akkadian) *ay* does not seem to be reduced in Ugaritic (Gordon, UM, p. 27): it is conceivable that syllabic

extension (through anaptyxis) might have occurred as in Hebrew
(§ 8.100).

8.100. In the Canaanite sphere, Phoenician exhibits the reductions
aw > *ō*, *ay* > *ē*: e.g. *Ιωμιλκον* for *Yeḥaw-milk, *caneth* for *qanaytī
"I acquired". In Hebrew the same reductions are generally found:
e.g. *yawm > *yōm* "day". In some cases, however, the diphthongs
remain unreduced, especially in final position: e.g. *qaw* (< *qaww)
"cord", *ḥay* (< *ḥayy) "living". In doubly-closed syllables we
meet instances of syllabic extension through the insertion of a new
vowel: e.g. *mawt > *māwet* "death", *bayt > *bayit* "house".
These are probably cases of anaptyxis (cf. § 9.17).

8.101. "Defective" writing in Aramaic shows that the reduction
of the diphthongs had taken place even in the most ancient inscriptions; some exceptions in Egyptian Aramaic are doubtless
to be explained as instances of historical spelling. In Biblical
Aramaic *aw* is reduced unless it is followed by *w*; *ay* sometimes
remains uncontracted and may give rise to syllabic extension as
in Hebrew (§ 8.100). In Syriac the diphthongs are preserved—
except when their preservation would result in a doubly-closed
syllable: e.g. *'aynā* "eye", but st. constr. *'ēn*.

8.102. Whereas Old South Arabian shows graphic variations
(e.g. *ywm* and *ym* "day") which may suggest that the process of
reduction was at an active stage (cf. Höfner, *Altsüdarabische
Grammatik*, pp. 9—11, 22—23), classical Arabic preserves the
original diphthongs in their entirety; but they undergo extensive
contractions in the modern dialects.

8.103. In Ethiopic the diphthongs appear in reduced form (e.g.
*yawm > *yōm* "today", *layl > *lēlīt* "night"), but there are a
number of divergent formations (cf. Dillmann, EG, § 39, pp. 78—79).

8.104. A number of secondary diphthongizations are to be found
in the Semitic languages, and those in Ethiopic (for which cf.
Ullendorff, SLE, pp. 170—83) are particularly noteworthy. They
are, however, secondary phenomena in the various languages,
even if they occurred at an ancient period: cf. ESyr. *haykal* from
Akk. *ekallu* "palace" (a Sumerian word).

C. Conditioned Phonetic Changes

9.1. The manifold phenomena of conditioned phonetic evolution
have not yet been sufficiently investigated from the point of view
of comparative Semitic linguistics: a study of these phenomena and
processes in the various languages and groups, as well as the
determination of their frequency, will undoubtedly contribute
to a better comparative appraisal of the Semitic languages. In
the treatment which follows some of these instances will be
identified and illustrated; attention will be drawn to salient aspects
and characteristic features in individual languages and groups,
while for detailed discussion the reader is referred to the grammars
of the various languages concerned.

1. Assimilation

9.2. The Semitic languages present assimilatory processes of
various kinds: assimilation may take place between consonants,
or between vowels, or of consonant to vowel, or vowel to consonant,
or of diphthongs; it may be progressive or regressive or reciprocal;
it may be partial or total; and it may be contiguous or at distance.

9.3. a) Between consonants.—Progressive, partial and
contiguous: e.g. Ar. *'*iṣtabaǵa* "it was dyed" > *'iṣtabaǵa*; Akk.
(New Ass.) *aqtirib* "I approached" > *aqṭirib*, *amtaḫiṣ* "I fought"
> (later Bab.) *amdaḫiṣ* (voicing). Contiguous assimilation may
be the cause of the voicing of *t*, in some roots with second radical *b*,
which occurs in some West Semitic languages, both Northern and
Southern: e.g. Akk. *'bt*, WSem. *'bd* "to perish"; Akk. *kbt*, WSem.
kbd "to be heavy". It was probably contiguous assimilation that
gave rise to the "emphaticization" (in North-West Semitic) of
t in the root *qṭl* "to kill" as compared with Ar. Eth. *qtl* (though
dissimilation might conceivably have occurred in the South
Semitic languages).—Progressive, partial and at distance: possibly
Syr. *purqəsā* "tower", from Greek *πύργος*.—Regressive, partial
and contiguous: Eth. *'agā'əzt* lords" > *'agā'əst* (devoicing).—Regressive, partial and at distance: e.g. Ar. *buq'at* "plain", Heb.
biq'ā, but Syr. *pəqa'tā* (devoicing).—Progressive total: e.g. Ar.
'ittalaba "he sought" > *ittalaba*; Akk. *'aṭṭarad* "I sent" > *aṭṭarad*
(the assimilation of *t* in the Akkadian infixes *ta* and *tan* is always

total when following *d, ṭ, z, ṣ, s*: e.g. **uṣtabbit* "he imprisoned" >
uṣṣabbit).—Regressive total: e.g. Heb. **yinten* "he gives" > *yitten*;
the assimilation of vowelless *n* to the following consonant is
characteristic of North Semitic; it does not occur in South Semitic
with the exception of some instances in South Arabian (cf. §§ 16.116
to 117); the assimilation of vowelless *l* to the following consonant
(which is sporadically found in various languages) takes place most
prominently in the case of the Arabic article before all interdental,
dental, and palato-alveolar consonants, yet *l* continues to appear
in the graphic pattern: e.g. *'al-šams* "the sun", pronounced
[aʃʃams]. Reciprocal assimilation: e.g. Ar. **'idtakara* "he remembered" > *'iddakara*.

9.4. b) **Between vowels.**—Assimilation of vowels (or vowel
harmony) is always at distance, since the structure of the Semitic
syllable does not admit vowels in positions of direct contact (cf.
§ 10.2). Vowel harmony is particularly extensive in Akkadian
(von Soden, GAG, pp. 12—13).—Progressive partial: e.g. Akk.
ḫiblātu "damage" > *ḫiblētu*.—Regressive partial: e.g. Akk. *uḫappi*
"he struck" > *uḫeppi*.—Progressive total: e.g. Ar. **riǧlihu* "of
his foot" > *riǧlihi* (vowel harmony in the suffix-pronoun of the
third-person m. singular is standard in Arabic).—Regressive total:
e.g. Ug. *ulp* "prince", cf. Heb. *'allūp*; Ar. **sanina* (c.obl.) "years" >
sinīna. A typical case of regressive total assimilation occurs in
Assyrian vowel harmony whereby *a* is assimilated to the vowel
of a case-ending which follows it: e.g. nom. *qaqqudu* "head", gen.
qaqqidi, acc. *qaqqada*; cf. also Ar. *'imru'ᵘⁿ* "man", *'imri'ⁱⁿ*, *'imra'ᵃⁿ*.

9.5. c) **Consonant to vowel.**—In Hebrew and in Aramaic,
after the latter's division into Eastern and Western dialects, the
plosives *p, b, t, d, k, g* are articulated as fricatives in postvocalic
position (cf. § 8.10): e.g. Heb. *dābār* "word" is pronounced [dāḇār].
This phenomenon, consisting of the transition of plosives to fricatives, may be regarded as an instance of partial assimilation: i.e. the
plosive articulation of the consonant passes towards the continuant
pronunciation characteristic of vowel articulation. This spirantization may continue after the elision of the vowel which occasioned
it: e.g. Syr. **dahabā* "gold" > *dahbā*, pronounced [dahḇā]. Another
phenomenon of assimilation of consonant to vowel must be seen
in the palatalization of *k* in the neighbourhood of palatal vowels:

for example, in Arabic dialects, *dič* for *dīk* "cock" (cf. § 8.42).
This process is wide-spread also in some of the modern Ethiopian
languages. Some phenomena of spirantization in Akkadian require
further investigation.

9.6. d) V o w e l   t o   c o n s o n a n t.—The pharyngal and laryngal
consonants frequently occasion a change of other vowels to *a*
(cf. for details § 16.110): e.g. Ar. **yaftuḫu* "he opens" > *yaftaḫu*;
Heb. **yišloḥ* "he sends" > *yišlaḥ*. The meticulous phonetic notation which characterizes Hebrew Masoretic pointing marks the
appearance of *a*-timbre vowels after the consonants ʻ and *h* (and
more rarely *ḫ*) in conditions when they would otherwise be vowelless:
thus **yaʻmod* "he stands" > *yaʻămod*. Such vowels are also indicated between long vowels of other timbres and pharyngal or
laryngal consonants (e.g. **rūḥ* "spirit" > *rūăḥ*). This is the
so-called *pataḥ furtivum* which does not, incidentally, run counter
to the rules of Semitic syllabic structure (where two contiguous
vowels are impossible—except when a glottal stop intervenes
between them: cf. § 10.2), because it serves merely as a "catalyst"
in the articulatory process (a similar phenomenon may be observed
in Arabic, though its strictly phonemic vowel notation fails to
indicate it). Labial consonants are liable to cause other vowels to
change into *u*, generally in preceding rather than following position:
e.g. Sem. **libb* "heart" > Ar. *lubb*.

9.7. e) R i s i n g   D i p h t h o n g s   A s s i m i l a t e d   o r   R e d u c e d.—
Assimilated: e.g. Ar. **ʼaywām* "days" > *ʼayyām*. Reduced by
assimilation: e.g. Akk. **yakšud* "he conquered" > **yikšud* > *ikšud*
(total progressive assimilation). In Hebrew a reduction might
possibly be inferred from Greek transcriptions: e.g. *Ισαακ* for
Yiṣḥāq (and cf. later on Syr. *ʼIsḥāq*).

9.8. f) F a l l i n g   D i p h t h o n g s   A s s i m i l a t e d   o r   R e d u c e d.—
Assimilated: e.g. Ar. **kawy* "burning" > *kayy*. Reduced by
assimilation: e.g. Akk. **iwbil* "he carried" > *ūbil* (reciprocal
assimilation), **baytu* "house" > *bītu* (total regressive assimilation).
Cf. for this section the treatment of the diphthongs in §§ 8.97—104.

2. Dissimilation

9.9. The Semitic languages present phenomena of dissimilation
between consonants, between semivowels, between vowels, and

between semivowel and vowel; both progressive and regressive, contiguous as well as at distance.

9.10. a) **Between Consonants.**—Progressive and contiguous: e.g. Ar. *ḥarrūb* "carob-bean" and *ḥarnūb* (but dissimilation is not the only way in which this variant may be accounted for, and in any event this type of dissimilation is infrequent).—Progressive and at distance: e.g. Ar. *layl* "night", *lūn* "to spend the night" (Heb. *lūn*, *līn*, Ug. *lyn*).—Regressive and contiguous: e.g. Akk. *inaddin* "he gives" and *inandin* (or *inamdin*); dissimilation by means of *n* is extensive in Akkadian, and particularly in Babylonian, in respect of *d*, *b*, and despite phonetic difficulties also *z*: e.g. *inazziq* "he grieves" > *inanziq*.—Regressive and at distance: e.g. Sem. **šamš* "sun" > Ar. **sams* (?) > *šams*, cf. Akk. *šamšu*, Ug. *špš*.

9.11. b) **Between Semivowels.**—This occurs particularly in Arabic: e.g. **wawāqī* "ounces" > *'awāqī* (regressive and at distance).

9.12. c) **Between Vowels.**—E.g. Ar. **madīnīy* "Medinese" > *madānīy* > *madanīy* (qualitative and quantitative). In Hebrew and Syriac the succession of two vowels of *u* or *o* timbre occasions the dissimilation of one of them to *i* or *e*: e.g. Heb. **ḥūṣōn* "external" > *ḥiṣōn* (qualitative); Syr. *Šəlēmōn* for Heb. *Šəlōmō* "Solomon" (qualitative).

9.13. d) **Between Semivowel and Vowel.**—E.g. Ar. *wuǧūh* "faces" > *'uǧūh* (regressive and contiguous); Eth. **zərūw* "sown" > *zərəw* (regressive and contiguous), though in the Ethiopian example other factors may be at work as well.

3. Prosthesis

9.14. As will be explained when dealing with syllabic structure (cf. § 10.2), the Semitic languages do not permit the presence of more than one consonant at the beginning of a word. To obviate such initial consonant clusters a supplementary vowel (introduced by ') is generally prefixed to the first consonant to produce a new syllable. In some cases, though more rarely, the new vowel is instead placed after the first consonant (cf. §§ 9.16—17).

9.15. In Hebrew and in Syriac the prosthetic vowel is *e*: e.g. Heb. **zrōắ* "arm" > *'ezrōắ* (but also *zərōắ* [in this case the more usual form], i.e. the alternative procedure just mentioned); Syr. **tqaṭṭal* "he was killed" > *'etqaṭṭal*. In Hebrew we have *hi-* in the verbal theme Hithpael—possibly by analogy with the theme Hiphil: e.g. Syr. *'etqaṭṭal*, Heb. *hitqaṭṭẹl* (so also in the imperative of the Niphal). In Arabic the prosthetic vowel is *i*: e.g. **bn* "son" > *'ibn*; **nqatala* "he was killed" > *'inqatala*; more rarely it is *u*: e.g. **qtul* "kill!" > *'uqtul* (vowel harmony?). In Ethiopic the vowel is *ə*: e.g. **mna* "from" > *'əmna*, **gzī* "lord" > *'əgzī*. The process continues in some modern dialects and becomes operative also in foreign borrowings such as the modern Eastern Aramaic *'usṭol* "table" from the Russian *stol*. Further examples in Ullendorff, SLE, pp. 198—201.

4. Anaptyxis

9.16. A consonant cluster at the end of a word (which would be contrary to the principles of Semitic syllabic structure, cf. § 10.2) is frequently resolved by the insertion of a secondary vowel and the consequent creation of a new syllable. The same method of resolving consonant clusters is employed (as we have seen—cf. §§ 9.14—15) also at the beginning of a word.

9.17. In Akkadian the anaptyctic vowel is generally identical with that of the principal syllable: e.g. in the construct state, **uzn* "ear" > *uzun*, **kalb* "dog" > *kalab* (in Assyrian *a* occurs at times after *i* or *u*: e.g. *uzan*). Similarly at the beginning of words: **kšud* "reach!" > *kušud*, **ṣbat* "take!" > *ṣabat* (but some verbs use *i* instead of *a*: e.g. **lmad* "learn!" > *limad*). In late Akkadian the weakening of stress favours the rise of secondary vowels in the middle of words: e.g. New Bab. *šipirētu* "letters" alongside *šiprētu*. In Hebrew the anaptyctic vowel is *e* which assimilates to itself the vowels *a*, *i* (but not *u*) of the preceding syllable: this is the origin of the "segolate" nouns, e.g. **'abd* "slave" > *'ebed* (but before laryngals and pharyngals *a* remains and even harmonizes the anaptyctic vowel), **sifr* "book" > *sefer*, **'uzn* "ear" > *'ozen* (the original forms reappear upon attachment of suffixes: e.g. *'abdī* "my slave"). For the diphthongs *aw*, *ay* (when they are not contracted) we have the development *aw* > *awu* > *awe* > *āwe* (e.g. *mawt "death" > māwet) and ay > ayi (e.g. *bayt "house" > bayit); cf. also § 8.100. In Syriac, too, the anaptyctic vowel is e; the preceding vowel tends to be reduced or dropped as its position becomes pre-tonic: e.g. *'abd "slave" > *'abéd > 'ǝbéd.

9.18. In Arabic the case-endings prevent the formation of consonant clusters at the end of a word: 'abd^{un} and 'abd^{u} "slave", riǧl^{un} and riǧl^{u} "foot". A special situation may, however, arise as a consequence of the effects of sentence stress (cf. § 10.14). As for Ethiopic, the ambiguity of the sixth vowel (which represents both ǝ and zero) does not allow us to arrive at safe conclusions; it does appear, however, that consonantal clusters were avoided either by the addition of final ǝ (e.g. gabr "slave", pronounced [gäbrǝ]) or by the insertion of ǝ between the consonants ([gäbǝr]): cf. Ullendorff, SLE, pp. 201—207.

5. Syncope and Contraction

9.19. The syncope of vowels or consonants, when occasioned by the succession of two of them, is basically a phenomenon of dissimilation: e.g. Heb. qīqālōn "shame", cf. Syr. qulqālā. In the example just quoted there occurs compensatory lengthening of the vowel.

9.20. There is ample evidence, throughout the whole of the Semitic area, of the syncope of ', w, y and, more rarely, h in intervocalic or paravocalic position. The syncope brings about vowel contraction or compensatory lengthening. The concomitant action of assimilation, dissimilation, analogy, as well as interchanges between the "weak" consonants, makes it difficult to establish generally valid rules of contraction or lengthening. In many cases, moreover, the explanation of forms as resulting from syncope or contraction is purely conventional. What may, in fact, have happened is much rather the secondary constitution of "weak" consonants or the lengthening of originally short vowels through the adaptation, by analogy, of biliteral roots to the predominant triliteral system (cf. §§ 11.5—9, 16.108—27). For detailed information the grammars of the various languages have to be consulted; but it may be said here that as a general rule vowel lengthening is unaccompanied by changes in the quality of the vowel—unless it is occasioned by assimilation to a semivowel. Of contraction it is generally true that (a) the combination of two like vowels results in the same vowel; (b) where one vowel is long and the other short it is the timbre of the long vowel that tends to prevail (but in some such cases contraction does not, in fact, take place: cf. e.g. the participles Akk. *šā'imu* "determining", Ar. *qā'im* "standing", in verbs with medial *w/y*); (c) the quality of a stressed vowel tends to prevail over that of an unstressed one; (d) two vowels markedly distant in their basis of articulation may produce a vowel with an intermediate point of articulation; (e) the vowel resulting from contraction is generally a long one; (f) Old Akkadian and Arabic agree that contraction does not generally take place when the second of the two vowels is *a*, either short or long; in later Akkadian contraction usually takes place, with *a* prevailing. The following may serve as examples of the principal changes: (a) postvocalic ': e.g. Sem. **ra'š* "head" > Akk. *rēšu*, Heb. *rōš*, Syr. *rēšā*, against Ar. *ra's*, Eth. *rə's*; (b) intervocalic ': e.g. Sem. **bada'a* "he began" > Heb. *bādā*, Syr. *bədā* (the Heb. and Syr. verbs differ in meaning from Arabic), against Ar. *bada'a*; Sem. **ṭami'a* "he thirsted" > Heb. *ṣāmē*, against Ar. *ẓami'a*; (c) intervocalic *w*: e.g. Sem. **gawir* "guest" > Heb. *gēr* (but Ar. *ǧār*); Sem. **dalawa* "he drew" > Heb. *dālā*, Syr. *dəlā*, Ar. *dalā*, against Eth. *dalawa*; (d) intervocalic *y*: e.g. Sem. **bakaya* "he wept" > Heb. *bākā*, Syr. *bəkā*, Ar. *bakā*, against Eth. *bakaya*; (e) *h*: e.g. Sem. **qatalahu* "he killed him" > Heb. *qəṭālō*, Eth. *qatalō*, against Syr. *qaṭleh*, Ar. *qatalahu*. For a detailed treatment of syncope and contraction in Arabic cf. Fleisch, TPA, pp. 98—138.

6. Haplology

9.21. The omission of one of two contiguous syllables with identical consonants (and sometimes vowels) is a phenomenon of dissimilatory origin which occurs in various Semitic languages. Certain combinations arise from Arabic morphology and may be eliminated by haplology: e.g. *tataqātalūna* "you fight" > *taqātalūna*; *yaqtulūnanā* "they kill us" > *yaqtulūnā* (cf. Fleisch, TPA, pp. 149—53). A few cases of haplology may also be observed in other languages: e.g. Syr. **'aryayā* "lion" > *'aryā*.

7. Metathesis

9.22. Examples of metathesis are to be found in all the Semitic languages: e.g. Akk. *dipšu* "honey" > *dišpu*; Heb. *śimlā* "coat" and *śalmā*; Syr. *taʿrā* "gate" > *tarʿā*; Ar. *'atraba* and *'artaba* "he was poor"; Eth. *nsk* and *nks* "to bite". Some metatheses can only be detected by comparison with other languages: e.g. Akk. *simmiltu* "ladder", Heb. *sullām*. Very wide-spread in the Semitic languages is the metathesis of *t* (as part of the verbal theme, cf. §§ 16.17—23) with the first radical of the verb when this is a dental or palato-alveolar fricative: e.g. Heb. **hitšammẹr* "he was on his guard" > *hištammẹr*; Syr. **'etsǝmek* "he leaned" > *'estǝmek*; Ug. **ttšḥwy* "she is prostrate" > *tštḥwy*. Consequently, when the verbal theme with prefix *š* is combined with that with prefix *t*, the two consonants change places with each other (cf. § 16.21): Akk. *šutaqbur*, Ar. *'istaqbara*, Eth. *'astaqbara* (for the paradigm *qbr* cf. § 12.3). In Akkadian the non-prefixed forms of the verbal themes with *t* and *tn* and the adjectives of the pattern *qitbār*, in which the element *t* would normally be infixed, show a metathesis in the opposite direction, i.e. the *t* becoming a prefix, when the first radical is *z*, *s*, *ṣ*, and sometimes *š* and also *d*: e.g. **ṣitbutu* "grasp" > *tiṣbutu*; **ṣitmur* "he desires" > *tiṣmur*; **ditūku* "combat" > *tidūku*.

8. Sandhi

9.23. A particular aspect of sentence-phonetics is that constituted by the extension of certain phenomena beyond the limits of the word itself, i.e. by their effect on the boundaries of neighbouring words (syntactic phonetics or *sandhi*). Thus, in the case of assimilation, the fricative pronunciation in post-vocalic position of the consonants *p*, *b*, *t*, *d*, *k*, *g* (§ 9.5) becomes operative also at the beginning of a word when the preceding one ends in a vowel. Phenomena of syncope and assimilation are widely attested in Arabic—affecting contiguous words—by the tradition of Koranic reading: thus in *sūra* 24,44 *ḥalaqa kullᵃ dābbatⁱⁿ* "he created all the animals" > [ḥalakkulla dābbatin].

D. Syllable and Stress

1. Syllabic Constitution

10.1. There are two types of syllables in Semitic: a) consonant followed by vowel (open syllable); b) consonant followed by vowel

followed by consonant (closed syllable). Quantitatively, a syllable
may be: a) short, when it ends in a short vowel; b) long, when it
ends in a long vowel or in a consonant. For example: *qa*, open short
syllable; *qā*, open long syllable; *qab*, closed (and therefore long)
syllable. The term "ultra-long" is used of syllables (cf. § 10.3)
which are closed in addition to having a long vowel (e.g. *qāb*).
For syllables in final position, ending in two consonants, see next §.

10.2. It follows from § 10.1 that in Semitic every syllable normally
begins with one consonant and one only. Two vowels cannot be in
contact. Two consonants may generally be contiguous only in the
middle of a word (final consonant of a closed syllable and initial
consonant of the following syllable). A sequence of two consonants
at the end of a word may result from the shedding of final
vowels. There prevails in the Semitic languages a widespread
tendency to eliminate exceptions to these rules, either by means
of prosthetic vowels (graphically supported by ') or anaptyctic
ones (cf. §§ 9.14—17) or else through word juncture. As examples
of prostehtic vowels cf. Ar. **nkasara* > *'inkasara* "it was broken";
and in transcriptions of foreign words Syr. *'espērā* from σφαῖρα,
Eth. *'atrōnes* from ϑϱόνος. For anaptyctic vowels cf. **'uzn* "ear" >
Akk. *uzun*, Heb. *'ozen*. Liaison of words occurs in Ar. **ṯumma
nkasara* [ṯummankasara] "then it was broken". Among modern
Semitic languages, the Ethiopian tongues make fairly extensive
use of prosthetic and anaptyctic vowels (Ullendorff, SLE, pp. 199
to 200). In North-West Semitic, conclusions about syllabic constitution depend to a large extent on one's judgment as to the nature
of the *šəwā* (§ 8.82). The pronunciation of *šəwā* as ə in certain
conditions has been considered by some scholars as a secondary
phenomenon of an anaptyctic character (Gesenius-Bergsträsser,
Hebräische Grammatik, pp. 134—35); and in this connexion one
may compare fluctuating pronunciations of the type of Syr.
deḥeltā for *deḥlətā* "fear". If one maintains the primarily vocalic
character of *šəwā*, one has yet to recognize that Masoretic pointing
acknowledges the succession of two consonants in initial position
(it does not register the second consonant as a fricative—as it
should have done in post-vocalic position) in *štayim* "two" (to
which *štā* corresponds in Syriac). It is possible, however, that the
infringement of the general rule is due to the workings of analogy.

10.3. According to Brockelmann (GVG, I, p. 63), Semitic originally postulated short vowels in closed syllables. This rule is mainly based on the position in Arabic, and its general application over the Semitic field may be subject to some doubt. Nevertheless, it is a fact that long vowels show a tendency to become short when their syllable closes. This phenomenon is connected with the incidence of stress and will, therefore, be dealt with in that connexion (§§ 10.5—11). In Arabic the shortening of long vowels in closed syllables is a rule (e.g. *qūm > qum* "rise!"); the only exceptions occur in certain syllables of secondary origin, e.g. where the final vowel is dropped in pause (*nāzilūna > nāzilūn* "descendants"). The shortening of long vowels in closed syllables is characteristic also of Eastern Syriac (e.g. *'ālmīn* "eternity" > *'almīn*).

10.4. Fairly common is the tendency to lengthen short vowels in open syllables. This trend is likewise connected with the operation of stress and will, therefore, be dealt with in that connexion (§§ 10.5—11). But some cases occur also irrespective of stress: e.g. Akk. *mil'u* "fullness" > *milu* > *mīlu* (compensatory lengthening to restore the syllable rhythm of the word). Sometimes consonant-doubling (gemination) takes the place of vowel-lengthening and so restores the closed syllable with short vowel: e.g. Akk. *ḫiṭṭu* for *ḫīṭu* "sin" (this occurs predominantly, though not exclusively, in the later period of the language: cf. Old Bab. *kuṣṣum* alongside *kūṣum* "cold"); Heb. *gāmāl* "camel", plur. *gəmallīm*. There are also some cases of consonant-doubling without any parallel vowel-lengthening, especially in Aramaic: e.g. Syr. *qalīl* "little" > *qallīl*, *'atānā* "she-ass" > *'attānā*.

2. Stress and Associated Changes

10.5. We lack sufficient data to determine the position of stress in Proto-Semitic or to distinguish clearly between expiratory stress and pitch accent. To restrict ourselves to the more readily identifiable expiratory stress, we may say, in the first place, that in Proto-Semitic it is unlikely to have had distinctive or phonemic status; and, secondly, that the almost complete agreement between Arabic and Akkadian might facilitate a hypothetical reconstruction of Proto-Semitic stress modelled on these two languages.

The risks inherent in this procedure need hardly be underlined when we recall that the situation in Arabic, and particularly in Akkadian, is subject to much uncertainty (cf. §§ 10.6—7).

10.6. In Akkadian, so far as our limited evidence permits a reconstruction, the position of the stress may be expressed as follows: a) if the final syllable is the result of contraction it generally bears the stress; b) otherwise stress does not fall on the ultima, even if it is long, but recedes as far as possible until it meets a long syllable (if there is no long syllable stress comes to rest on the first syllable of the word). Only in rare instances (cf. von Soden, GAG, p. 38) does stress fall on a short syllable in the middle of a word. Examples: a) accent on ultima: *šanû* (< **šaniyu*) "second"; b) accent on long syllable: *bēlútu* "lordship" (long vowel), *napištu* "life" (closed syllable); on antepenult (short): *kúbburu* "stout". If stress falls on a short syllable it may cause it to be lengthened, either by the lengthening of the vowel, e.g. *imqútū* > *imqûtū* "they fell", or by the doubling of the following consonant, so as to form a closed syllable, e.g. *iškúnū* > *iškúnnū* "they put". Strong expiratory stress may occasion reduction in neighbouring vowels, e.g. **wášibat* > *wášbat* "she dwells": cf. §§ 10.3—4. Secondary stress patterns arise in compound words of some length, e.g. with pronominal suffixes: so *ušèribú-šu* "they let him enter". In any case, stress is non-phonemic in Akkadian.

10.7. For classical Arabic the rule given in the preceding paragraph is of universal application, i.e. stress does not fall on a final syllable (even if it be the result of contraction) but goes back as far as possible till it meets a long syllable or, failing that, the initial syllable. Examples: *qatáltum* "you killed"; *qátalū* "they killed"; *mámlakat* "kingdom". We do not, however, know any express Arab tradition of acceptable antiquity which might elucidate for us the origin of the stress rules now observed in reading classical Arabic. According to some recent studies (Birkeland) it would appear that these rules might derive from the stress patterns of certain Arabic dialects. In these dialects considerable developments have taken place which—with regard to this particular feature—have brought about some affinity to the situation which prevails in other Semitic languages (cf. §§ 10.8—10), in notable contrast to the pattern in classical Arabic. As stress in Arabic is bound, it can obviously not be phonemic.

10.8. In Hebrew (at least as far as can be judged from the Masoretic tradition) stress falls on the last syllable—save for some cases of penultimate patterns. In contrast to Akkadian and Arabic, stress in Hebrew may have distinctive or phonemic value: e.g. *šábū* "they returned", but *šābú* "they took prisoner". Stress patterns and syllabic constitution are bound up with complex rules of vowel evolution which (leaving out of account the difficult question of their origin) may be summarized as follows:

a) final short vowels are dropped (**qábara* > **qábar*);

b) stress shifts to the last syllable which the development under (a) has left closed and therefore long (**qábar* > **qabár*);

c) short accented vowels undergo lengthening or change of timbre, or both, either under the influence of the word-accent or by contextual stress patterns (pause) (cf. § 10.13): $a > ā$, $i > ẹ/ḕ$, $u > o$ (**dábaru* > *dābár*; **qábiru* > *qōbḕr*; **yáqburu* > *yiqbór*); before two successive consonants, however, $i > a$ instead of $i > ẹ/ḕ$ (**zāqínta* > *zāqánta*);

d) in contrast to the general Semitic tendency, and probably by a relatively late process of restoration, open pre-tonic syllables undergo lengthening and sometimes change of vowel quality: $a > ā$, $i > ḕ$ (or else *ə* according to the development referred to under g); u remains, but the following consonant is doubled (cf. § 10.4): e.g. **dábaru* > *dābár*, **'inabu* > *'ẹnáb* (but **himáru* > **həmŕ* > *hămŕ*), **luqáh* > *luqqáh*;

e) short vowels in closed unstressed syllables may undergo change of quality: $a > i$, $i > e$, $u > o$ (**madbár* > *midbár* [dissimilation?]; *'imrātŕ* and *'emrātŕ*; **'udnī* > *'ozní*);

f) in final open stressed syllables *ī* becomes *ē* (Ar. *ṯamānī*, Heb. *šəmōnḕ*);

g) short vowels in open unstressed syllables are reduced to *ə* in accordance with the general Semitic tendency and in contrast to the instances listed under (d) where pre-tonic syllables frequently undergo lengthening; it is likely that these two opposed tendencies were operative at different periods: e.g. **dabarím* > *dəbārím*; **qābarú* > *qābərú*.

As for the pre-Masoretic stress-accent, this must have diverged notably from its later Masoretic version (as has been shown by Brønno from Greek transcriptions): cases such as φέϑεϑα for *pittáḥtā*, ἄννωϑεν for *hannōtén*, ζωημέϱου for *zammərú*, δάβϱη for *dibrḗ*, etc., testify to stress conditions contrasting with our notions derived from the Masoretic recension of the Hebrew text.

10.9. Compared with the ample documentation of Masoretic Hebrew, the evidence concerning North-West Semitic of the second millennium B.C. and the rest of Canaanite is exceedingly scanty:

a) there are indications of a reduction of short vowels in unstressed open syllables (cf. § 10.8 g) in Amorite (e.g. *A-ma-na-nu-um* and *Am-na-nu-um*, *ya-ta-ra-tum* and *ya-at-ra-tum*), in the Tell Amarna glosses (e.g. *miḫṣū* for *maḫiṣu*, *ṣiḫrū* for *ṣaḫirū*), and possibly in Ugaritic (Garbini, SNO, pp. 75—77);

b) in Phoenician we have some lengthenings of short stressed vowels, accompanied by changes of vowel quality ($a > ō$, $i > ē$, $u > ō$), which reveal remarkable similarities to the Hebrew changes (cf. § 10.8 c).

10.10. In the Aramaic area, while Biblical Aramaic reflects the situation in Masoretic Hebrew, Syriac stress always falls on the final syllable. As in Hebrew (indeed, the Masoretes worked under the impact of Aramaic) there are complex rules of vowel development, connected with the incidence of stress and with syllabic constitution, which may be summarized as follows:

a) final vowels, whether long or short, are dropped (**qábara > *qábar*; **qábarū > *qábar* [the final *ū* is written but not pronounced]);

b) stress passes to the final syllable which is now closed and hence long (**qábar > *qabár*);

c) short vowels in open unstressed syllables are reduced to ə or dropped (**qabár > qəbár*);

d) in closed syllables short *a* and *i* may become *e* (**qabrát > qebrát*; **sifrá́ > sefrá́*);

e) a short stressed *u* becomes *ō*, whether by the action of the word-accent (as for the change $u > o$, cf. also the opposition between West and East Syriac, § 8.88) or by analogy with pronominal forms and verbal suffixes (**qabártumu > *qabártum > *qabartúm > *qabartṓn > qəbartṓn*);

f) *ī* becomes *ē* in final open and stressed syllables (Ar. *ṭamānī*, Syr. *təmānḗ*).

After the close of the classical period (about A.D. 700) final open syllables tend to lose their stress: e.g. *néhwē* "he is" in Maronite usage; the Nestorians stress the penult even in cases when the final syllable is closed: e.g. *kétbat* "she wrote".

10.11. In Ethiopic it is usually assumed that stress falls on the final syllable of a noun but the penult of a verb. Recent research by Ullendorff (SLE, pp. 189—97) shows, however, that the whole question remains complicated and more than a little uncertain. The very existence of expiratory stress in Gəʿəz is doubtful, and in the traditional pronunciation it is difficult to distinguish between stress and pitch. In any event, the accent in Ethiopic (whatever its precise nature may have been) is non-phonemic.

3. Sentence Stress

10.12. In addition to word-accent, the Semitic languages have a sentence stress determined (especially in pause) by the traditional recitation of the text. This stress occasions a number of changes in some languages.

10.13. In Hebrew the principal alterations are as follows:

a) stress is thrown back on to the penult (e.g. *'ānōkî* > *'ānóki*);

b) a short accented vowel is lengthened (e.g. *máyim* > *mǻyim*) sometimes causing change of quality (e.g. *'éreṣ* > *'ǻreṣ*).

10.14. In Arabic the principal changes are as follows (cf. Fleisch, TPA, pp. 172—90):

a) final short vowels are dropped (e.g. *qatala* > *qatal*); this may in some cases affect the constitution of a final consonant group (cf. § 9.18) with consequent anaptyxis (e.g. *al-bakr^u* "young [camel]", in pause *al-bakur*).

b) the indefinite case-endings *-un*, *-in* are dropped, and *-an* becomes *-ā* (e.g. *malik^{un}* > *malik*, *malik^{in}* > *malik*, *malik ^{an}* > *malikā*);

c) the feminine noun ending *-at* becomes *-ah* (e.g. *malikat^{un}* > *malikat* > *malikah*); for a possible Hebrew and Syriac parallel cf. §. 12.33.

10.15. For the other languages we possess no adequate indications about sentence stress, or, at any rate, no changes occur of the type we have witnessed in Hebrew and Arabic. There are, however, one or two hints: thus in Akkadian the word on which sentence stress falls, in interrogative sentences, shows a shift of the stress on to the penult or ultima with consequent secondary vowel lengthening: e.g. *ippušú* or *ippúšū* "will they do?" instead of *íppušū*.

III. Morphology

A. Preliminaries

1. Morphemes

11.1. The Semitic languages present a system of consonantal roots (mostly triconsonantal), each of which is associated with a basic meaning range common to all members of that root: e.g. *ktb* "to write", *qbr* "to bury", *qrb* "to approach", etc. These roots (root morphemes) constitute a fundamental category of lexical morphemes (cf. Petráček, ArOr 28 [1960], pp. 564—68). The linguistic reality of consonantal roots is shown not only by their lexical implications but also by the laws governing the compatibility or otherwise of radicals (which do not concern the vowels: cf. § 11.10) and in the transcription of foreign words. Only the pronouns and some particles lie outside this system of roots.

11.2. The task of lexical individualization (lexical morphemes) and grammatical categorization (grammatical morphemes) is assumed by vowels and by affixes (prefixes, infixes, suffixes): e.g. in Arabic, from the root *ktb* "to write": *kitāb* "book", *kātib* "writer", *maktabat* "library", *kataba* "he wrote", *yaktubu* "he writes", etc. The linguistic reality of vocalization and affixes, in their morphemic function, is clearly attested by their specific semantic implications.

11.3. Grammatical morphemes may be external, internal, or syntactical. External morphemes are elements attached to a root (affixes, cf. the preceding paragraph). Internal morphemes are constituted by the nature or disposition of certain phonetic elements (consonants, vowels, stress), and in the Semitic languages they appear especially in the "inner" (or "broken") plurals and in the passive conjugation of the verb: e.g. Ar. *kitāb* "book", pl. *kutub* "books"; *qatala* "he killed", *qutila* "he was killed". Petráček's important studies (ArOr 28 [1960], pp. 547—606; 29 [1961], pp. 513—545 and to be continued) show that inner inflection is particularly developed in South Semitic, though it is not without precedent in Hamito-Semitic generally. The importance of vowel-alternation (apophony) in Semitic morphology has been stressed by Kuryłowicz. Syntactical morphemes are constituted by the order of words or by independent elements; the latter are of relatively low frequency in the Semitic languages (for example in the Arabic formation of the future tense by means of the particle *sawfa*).

11.4. The above account is concerned with consonantal radicals only, and it has long been usual to conceive of Semitic roots as purely consonantal; such a reconstruction is unreservedly maintained by some scholars (so Fleisch, TPA, pp. 247—51) but is disputed by others. Von Soden, in particular, (GAG, pp. 51—52, 96—97) holds that vowel elements should be regarded as forming part of the root (see also E. Ullendorff in Or 28 [1958], pp. 69—70). Such elements, which can be identified in the imperative of verbs and in the prefix conjugation, are short in triconsonantal roots (e.g. *pqid* "to guard, to deposit") but predominantly long in biconsonantal ones (e.g. *dūk* "to kill", *bnī* "to build"). It should be observed that these latter roots exhibit stable vowels in other parts of the Hamito-Semitic area as well (§ 11.6 c), so that the incorporation of original semivowel radicals (*dwk, bny*) may be ascribed to artificial reconstruction. A similar stability is seen in the vowel elements of nominal roots (e.g. Sem. *kalb* "dog") which have to be differentiated from the verbal ones which, in their turn, are to be divided into those indicating states or conditions and those connoting actions (cf. § 16.2). The distinction between the three semantic spheres of noun, adjective and stative verb, and active verb is reflected in a differentiation in the structure of the root.

2. The Proto-Semitic Root

11.5. In the historically attested Semitic languages triconsonantal roots form the great majority; roots with two or with four radicals are much less numerous, while those with one or with five are rare (in roots with more than three consonants there is a possibility of secondary formations by metaplasm, dissimilation, etc.). Examination of the dictionary reveals the following phenomenon: there are many groups of roots having two radicals in common which express identical or similar meanings. Thus for example in Hebrew: *prd* "to separate", *prm* "to tear", *prs* "to split", *prṣ* "to break down", *prq* "to pull apart", *prr* "to dissolve", *prš* "to distinguish" etc. All these verbs have in common the radicals *pr* and the basic notion "to divide". This phenomenon, which is widespread in the Semitic lexicon, raises the question whether many triconsonantal roots are not, in fact, derived from biconsonantal ones; and whether a system of biconsonantal roots may, perhaps, have preceded the triconsonantal theme in Semitic.

11.6. For a solution of this problem the following data must be borne in mind:

a) The Semitic languages have many biconsonantal nouns (in addition to some monoconsonantal ones) which, from the objects they denote, must be adjudged fairly ancient: e.g. *dam* "blood", *yad* "hand", *yam* "sea", etc. The assignation of these nouns to triconsonantal roots must be ruled out as contrived and far-fetched.

b) The so-called "weak" verbs exhibit many biradical forms: e.g. Heb. *qām* "he rose" (root *qwm*), *'ē-šeb* "I dwell" (root *yšb*), Ar. *ram-at* "she threw" (root *rmy*), etc. It is our grammatical systematization which looks upon these forms as having "dropped" a radical, while one might maintain with as much reason that the "weak" radical—in those forms which contain it—was, in fact, added to the root for the sake of adaptation to the triconsonantal system. This consideration seems particularly cogent where the roots in question coincide semantically with others on a biconsonantal basis.

c) Comparison with other languages of the Hamito-Semitic group strengthens the biconsonantal hypothesis: e.g. Sem. *qtl* "to kill", Cushitic *qal*; Sem. *p'l* (*f'l*) "to make", Cushitic *fal*; (it should be noted—as indeed appears from these examples—that Cushitic possesses biconsonantal roots with stable vowel).

11.7. The data just set forth show that biconsonantal roots in the Semitic languages are not a hypothesis relating to a pre-historic period but constitute an historical reality attested by a group of nouns and by a series of verbal forms; this is further supported by the semantic concurrence of many roots in two of their radicals. There is, however, no sufficient reason for maintaining, as some have done, that the entire Semitic stock of roots was originally biconsonantal. It is a more likely supposition that originally there existed roots with either two or three consonants (as well as a smaller number with one only or with more than three) and that at a certain stage in the development of the Semitic languages the triconsonantal system prevailed—extending by analogy and thus bringing into line biconsonantal roots through the adoption of a third radical. Cf. also Fleisch, TPA, pp. 247—61.

11.8. As regards this third radical, or "determinant", the following questions arise: which consonants can be so used and with what specific semantic value? A lexical probe leads to the following tentative conclusions:

a) all consonants may be used as "determinants";

b) apart from some grammatical formatives which retain some trace of their original function (e.g. *š*- causative), it may be said that the present state of the dictionary does not appear to permit the identification of specific semantic values attached to these "determinants".

11.9. In the examination of biconsonantal roots it is to be borne in mind that the radicals may have undergone certain phonetic changes: thus alongside the series *pr* "to divide" (§ 11.5) Hebrew also possesses the groups *pl* and *br*, i.e. by interchange between consonants with the same (or a similar) point of articulation (*plḥ* "to furrow", *brr* "to separate", *šbr* "to break", etc.).

11.10. Leaving aside biconsonantal roots and their development, the Semitic languages reveal certain structural incompatibilities which reduce the number of possible combinations in triconsonantal roots. In no Semitic language can two identical consonants—or two consonants with a similar point of articulation—appear next to each other in first and second position; and it is rare for such consonants to be found as first and third radicals (e.g. Akk. *ḥašāḥu* "to desire"). In positions two and three, identical consonants are frequently found but not different consonants with a similar basis of articulation. There exist other incompatibilities in individual languages or groups: thus in Akkadian *g* and *z* are never found in third position, nor can all three radicals be voiced, and of two emphatic consonants one is reduced to non-emphatic status (e.g.

Akk. *qatnu* "thin", Sem. root *qtn*); in West Semitic, both Northern and Southern, there are many incompatibilities between dental and velar plosives: in Hebrew *gṭ, ṭg, kṭ, ṭk, qṭ, ṭq* are normally incompatible—but not *tq, qṭ*; in Arabic (taking into account the transition *g > ǧ*) *ṭǧ, ǧṭ, ṭǧ, ǧṭ, ṭq, ṭq, ṭk, ṭk, kṭ* are generally incompatible. The foregoing considerations apply particularly to verbal morphemes. In nominal morphemes the position varies to some extent: e.g. Sem. *šamš* "sun", *nūn* "fish", *layl* "night", *šuršš* "root", etc.

3. Morphological Development

11.11. Morphology manifests the action of two fundamental forces in the development of forms:

a) phonetic laws (e.g. assimilation, dissimilation, etc.) which have already been considered in the section on phonology (cf. §§ 9.1—22);

b) analogy, both morphological and lexical, sometimes in opposition to phonetic laws; an example of morphological analogy (cf. the evidence adduced in §§ 16.44—45) is offered by the Proto-Semitic endings of the first and second persons singular in the verbal suffix-conjugation (**-ku, *-ta, *-ti*) and their development in Arabic (*-tu, -ta, -ti*) or Ethiopic (*-ku, -ka, -ki*), with analogical extension of the elements *t* and *k*, respectively; as an example of lexical analogy one might mention Heb. *ḥămiššā* "five" instead of **ḥamšā*, by analogy with *šiššā* "six" (cf. § 14.2).

Further aspects of morphological development are shown in such contrasting forms as (in the case of verbs *primae* ') Akk. *i''abit* "was destroyed" alongside *innabit* "he fled"—despite identical phonetic origin. In later phases of the language the possibility of the normative influence of grammarians on morphological as well as phonological development cannot be discounted.

B. The Noun

1. Themes or Patterns

12.1. In the Semitic dictionary the system of roots is combined with that of themes or patterns. These are morphological types which are frequently associated with specific meanings or uses. For example: Ar. *'abyaḍ* "white", *'aḥmar* "red", *'azraq* "blue" are formed from the roots *byḍ*, *ḥmr*, *zrq*, respectively, and the pattern *'aqbar* (cf. § 12.3) to render the names of colours.

12.2. The system of nominal themes weakens in the course of morphological development, particularly in those languages in which stress and syllabic constitution affect the vocalic structure. Hebrew is a typical example of such a language: e.g. *dābār* "word", construct state *dəbar*, construct before "light" suffixes *dəbār*, construct plural *dibr(-ē*, plural ending): four "themes" which are conditioned allomorphs or combinatory morphological variants.

2. Nominal Patterns

12.3. Nominal patterns may be "simple" (when the root is modified by vowels only) or "extended", i.e. when affixes are added. From a semantic point of view (partly also owing to the insufficiently developed state of these studies) we are only occasionally able to assign specific values and uses to individual patterns. In the following, some of the principal nominal themes will be presented together with their main spheres of employment—where these can be reasonably well established. For these purposes the paradigm used for the identification of patterns will be *qbr* ("to bury"): this is, of course, merely an arbitrary choice and may therefore serve even when the resultant forms are not in fact attested. The root *qbr* is found throughout the Semitic area and is one of very few verbal roots which combine this advantage with a suitable phonetic constitution. It is greatly preferable to the usual paradigm *qtl* "to kill" which is not so far attested in Ugaritic, while in Hebrew and Syriac it is subject to the assimilation $t > ṭ$ (cf. § 9.3); but, above all, *qtl* contains the obnoxious *t* which may so easily be confused with its other functions (infixes etc.) in the morphological scheme. For these reasons *qbr* will be employed for paradigmatic purposes throughout this book. The fact that in Akkadian the verbal inflexion of *qbr* shows the vowel *i* as against *u* in the other languages carries little or no weight, as we are merely concerned with conventional patterns. For further details the grammars of the various languages concerned have to be consulted; for phonological developments which have a bearing on certain nominal patterns see the section on phonology.

12.4. Noun-patterns can be studied to best advantage in Akkadian and Arabic, while some of the other languages (apart from those whose vocalization is not attested) exhibit a lesser number of independent themes but a great variety of formal developments resulting from the incidence of stress and syllabic constitution. From an examination of Akkadian and Arabic patterns certain preliminary conclusions may be drawn: a) not all patterns are necessarily differentiated in origin: some of them can be explained as secondary developments brought about by phonetic processes and analogy— not infrequently corroborated by their meaning (on the other hand, the same forces have also caused a measure of uniformity and levelling as well as reductions in the number of patterns); b) nominal themes with rising rhythm (with final long syllable) appear to be predominating (cf. the wider diffusion of *qabār* as compared with *qabar*); c) the distinctions between noun and adjective, concrete and abstract, are not always apparent from a purely thematic point of view: while in some cases differentiation and opposition may be recognized (particularly in Akkadian), by and large these patterns occur indiscriminately for the various categories just mentioned (cf. Fleisch, TPA, pp. 349—76).

a. Simple Patterns

12.5. a) Monosyllables with short vowel: *qabr, qibr, qubr*. Owing to the requirements of Semitic syllabic constitution these patterns are liable to anaptyxis: e.g. Ar. *'abd*, Akk. *abdu*, but Heb. *'ebed* (the "segolate" nouns: cf. § 9.17).

12.6. b) Disyllables with short vowels: *qabar, qabir, qabur, qibar, qibir, qubar, qubur*. These themes may be variants of the preceding ones occasioned by the influence of stress or by anaptyxis or by the extension of pausal forms: an example of the elision of a vowel under the impact of stress is Akk. **rapašu > rapšu* "wide", fem. *rapaštu* (in Akkadian the first three patterns are generally employed as adjectives).

12.7. c) Disyllables with long vowel or diphthong in the first syllable: *qābar, qābir, qābūr, qaybar, qaybār, qaybūr, qawbar, qawbār*. Of these patterns *qābir* usually has the function of an active participle and is widespread throughout the Semitic lan-

guages (cf. § 16.68): Akk. *māliku* "counsellor", Ar. *kātib* "writer",
Heb. *kōṭēb*, Syr. *kāteb*, Eth. *wārəs* "heir". The other patterns are
more common in Arabic than elsewhere; *qābūr* serves in Syriac
as *nomen agentis* (e.g. *pārōqā* "saviour"; for the alternation *u : o*
see § 8.88).

12.8. d) Disyllables with long vowel or diphthong in the second
syllable; here the long vowel may be replaced by the feminine
ending -*at* (whose addition places these patterns into the category
of extended themes): *qabār* and *qabarat*, *qabīr* and *qabirat*, *qabūr*,
qibār and *qibarat*, *qubār* and *qubarat*, *qubayr*, *qubūr*. Of these
patterns *qabīr* and *qabūr* are predominantly adjectival (e.g. Ar.
kabīr "great", Heb. *ṣāʿīr* "small", Eth. *marīr* "bitter"; Ar. *farūq*
"timid", Heb. *ʿāṣūm* "strong", Akk. *batūlu* "young"); *qabīr*, in
particular, is used in Syriac as a passive participle (*qabīr >
qəbīr, with reduction of the pretonic vowel—cf. § 10.10 c), and
qabūr in Hebrew (*qabūr > *qābūr*, with lengthening of the pre-
tonic vowel—cf. § 10.8 d) as well as similar uses of both forms to
be sporadically encountered in other languages (e.g. Ar. *qatīl*
"killed", *rasūl* "messenger"—cf. § 16.69). The pattern *qubayr* is
largely used as a diminutive: it occurs principally in Arabic (e.g.
ʿabd "servant", *ʿubayd* "little servant"—cf. Fleisch, TPA, pp. 380
to 389), though traces of it are found in other Semitic languages
(e.g. Syr. *ʿulaymā "lad" > *ʿəlaymā*; in Akkadian in nouns with
diminutive or pejorative connotation: e.g. *kusaypu > *kusīpu*
"morsel of bread"). The pattern *qibār* is employed in some languages for tools or instruments: e.g. Ar. *niṭāq*, Heb. *ʾēzōr*, Eth.
qənāt (all three meaning "belt").

b. Patterns Extended by Gemination or Reduplication of Radicals

12.9. a) Patterns with doubled second radical: *qabbar*, *qabbār* and
qabbarat, *qabbir*, *qabbīr*, *qabbūr*, *qibbar*, *qibbār*, *qibbir*, *qibbīr*,
qibbūr, *qubbar*, *qubbār*, *qubbur*, *qubbūr*. Of these patterns, *qabbār*
is widespread throughout the Semitic languages and characterizes
intensives and names of professions (e.g. Ar. *ʿallām* "man of great
learning", *ǧammāl* "cameleer"; Akk. *dayyānu* "judge"; Heb.
ṣayyād "huntsman"; Eth. *gabbār* "worker"). Other patterns with
long second vowel are chiefly employed to indicate adjectives
with intensive meaning (e.g. Ar. *farrūq* "very timid", *quddūs*

"very holy", *ṣiddīq* "very sincere", *kurrām* "very generous"). Of the patterns with short second vowel, *qabbar* and *qabbir* are used in Akkadian for adjectives with iterative or intensive significance (e.g. *kabbaru* "very thick"), and similarly *qubbur*, the adjective of the verb-stem with doubled second radical and intensive meaning (e.g. *dummuqu* "very good").

12.10. b) Patterns with reduplication of the second radical: *qababār*, *qubabīr* and others are attested in Akkadian (e.g. *zuqaqīpu* "scorpion") and the modern Ethiopian languages (Amh. *tāllāq* and *talāllāq* "great").

12.11. c) Patterns with doubled third radical: *qabarr*, *qaburr*, *qibarr*, *qibirr*, *qubarr*, *quburr* are fairly rare and occur chiefly in Akkadian and Arabic. In Akkadian they produce both nouns (e.g. *arammu* "dyke", *kirissu* "needle") and adjectives with intensive meaning (e.g. *namurru* "shining", *da'ummu* "pitch-dark"); in Arabic they are employed for adjectives (e.g. *niḥibb* "timid", *qumudd* "strong"). A development peculiar to Akkadian is the pattern *quburrā'* used for regular actions (e.g. *muḥurrā'u* "reception") and for certain situations or conditions (e.g. *uturrā'u* "superfluity"); it belongs, formally, to the class of patterns extended by affixes.

12.12. d) Patterns with repeated third radical: *qabrar*, *qabrār*, *qabrīr*, *qabrur*, *qabrūr*, *qibrar*, *qibrār*, *qibrir*, *qibrīr*, *qubrar*, *qubrār*, *qubrur*, *qubrūr*. These are infrequent types—attested chiefly as adjectives (e.g. Heb. **ra'nān > ra'ănān* "green", *'umlāl* "languishing"; Ar. *ri'dīd* "cowardly"), sometimes with diminutive or pejorative significance (e.g. Ar. *qu'dud* "ignoble" from the root *q'd* "to sit"). A few nouns of this type occur in Akkadian (e.g. *namrīru* "splendour", *kulbābu* "ant") and in Syriac (e.g. *zahrīrā* "ray", *partūtā* "piece"), again on occasion with diminutive or pejorative meaning.

12.13. e) Patterns with reduplicated second and third radicals: *qabarbar*, *qabarbār*, *qabarbīr*, *qabarbūr*, *qabirbir*. These are fairly infrequent and mainly attested in West Semitic as adjectives (e.g. Heb. **yaraqraq > yəraqraq* "greenish", Ar. *'arakrak* "thick", Eth. *ḥamalmīl* "greenish"), but there also exist a few nouns (e.g. Heb. *'ăsafsūf* "common people", Syr. *pərahruḥtā* "spark").

c. Patterns Extended by Prefixes

12.14. a) Patterns with vowel prefixes (introduced by ʼ): *ʼaqbar,*
ʼiqbar, ʼiqbir, ʼuqbur. The most frequent of these is *ʼaqbar* (cf.
§ 12.68 for Wehr's study, and see also Fleisch, TPA, pp. 408—17)
which serves in Arabic to characterize elatives and colours (e.g.
ʼaḥsan "most beautiful" from *ḥasan* "beautiful"; *ʼaḥmar* "red",
ʼabyaḍ "white", *ʼaswad* "black", etc.) and in Hebrew for certain
other types of adjectives (e.g. *ʼakzār* "cruel", *ʼakzāb* "mendacious").
In the other languages this pattern is rare (some animal names
occur in Ugaritic: e.g. *ảnḥr* "dolphin"). As for the other types,
they are fairly rare in Arabic and are probably variants of *ʼaqbar*;
in Akkadian *ʼiqbir* is found as a variant of *qibr*.

12.15. b) Patterns with prefix *y-*: *yaqbar, yaqbār, yaqbīr, yaqbūr,*
etc. These are rare and confined to West Semitic where *yaqbūr* in
particular is used for names of animals (e.g. Ar. Heb. *yaḥmūr*,
a kind of antelope) and, infrequently, of plants (e.g. Ar. *yabrūḥ*,
Syr. *yabrūḥā* "mandrake") as well as for adjectives (e.g. Ar.
yaḥmūm "black").

12.16. c) Patterns with prefix *m-*: *maqbar, maqbār, maqbir,*
maqbīr, maqbur, maqbūr, miqbar, miqbār, miqbir, miqbīr, muqbar,
muqbār (for prefix *n-* occasioned by dissimilation of *m-* before
a labial see § 12.19; for prefix *m-* and suffix *-n* [*maqbarān*] cf.
§12.21). Four principal meaning-variants are connected with the
prefix *m-*: local, temporal, instrumental, abstract. In the expression of these meanings the various patterns appear to be used
indiscriminately, yet in individual languages a measure of differentiation can be observed: In Akkadian *maqbar(t)* and *maqbār* are
employed for nouns of place and time (e.g. *maškanu* "place"),
maqbart also for nouns of instrument, and *muqbar(t)* and *muqbār*
for nouns of time (e.g. *muṣlālu* "midday"). Arabic indicates nouns
of place by *maqbar* and *maqbir* (e.g. *mawḍiʻ* "place" from the root
wḍʻ "to put") and nouns of instrument by *miqbar* and *miqbār*
(e.g. *miftāḥ* "key" from the root *ftḥ* "to open"). Hebrew uses for
abstracts *maqbar* and *miqbar* (e.g. *mamlākā* "kingdom" from the
root *mlk* "to reign", *mišpāṭ* "judgement" from the root *špṭ* "to
judge"), while *maqbir* and *miqbir* often designate instruments
(e.g. *maptēăḥ* "key"). In Ethiopic *məqbār* (< **miqbār*) predomi-

nates for nouns of place (e.g. *məšrāq* "east"), while *maqbar(t)* and *maqbər(t)* refer mainly to instruments (e.g. *malbas* "dress"). The theme *maqbūr* expresses the passive participle of the simple verb-stem in Arabic; for the participles of the derived stems—which are formed with the prefix *m-* in most of the Semitic languages—cf. §§ 16.96—101. Outside the Semitic area, patterns with prefix *m-* are attested in Egyptian (e.g. *m.śdm.t* "cosmetics" from the root *śdm*). For a detailed study of patterns with *m-* prefix cf. Fleisch, TPA, pp. 422—34.

12.17. d) Patterns with prefix *t-*: *taqbar, taqbār* and *taqbarat, taqbir, taqbīr* and *taqbirat, taqbur, taqbūr* and *taqburat, tiqbār*. These themes produce, for the most part, verbal nouns (e.g. Ar. *tardād* "repeating", Akk. *tallaktu* "going"), generally of the verbal stem with doubled second radical (e.g. Ar. *tibyān* "explaining", Eth. *tafṣām* "completing"). In particular, *taqbīr* is used in various languages as the verbal noun of the verbal stem with doubled second radical (e.g. Akk. *tamšīlu* "image", Syr. *ta'dīrā* "help", Ar. *tafrīq* "distribution"); *taqbur, taqbūr* and *taqburat* occur as verbal nouns of the simple stem (e.g. Akk. *tapšuḫtu* "repose", Heb. *tagmūl* "favour, recompense", Syr. *taktūšā* "battle", Ar. *tahlukat* "perdition"); *taqbār* and *taqbur(a)t* appear in Akkadian as verbal nouns of the simple stem with infixed *t* (e.g. *tamḫāru* "encounter", *taqrubtu* "approach").

12.18. e) Patterns with prefix *š-*: *šaqbār, šaqbur* and *šaqburat, šuqbur* and *šuqburat*, etc. These themes are used in Akkadian for verbal nouns of the stem with prefix *š-* and causative value (e.g. *šaḫluqtu* "ruin" from the root *ḫlq* "to perish") and also, though less frequently, as adjectives with intensive meaning (e.g. *šanūdu* "very famous", *šurbū* "huge"). To this group also belong the nominal forms of the verbal stem with *š* and *t*, for which cf. § 16.21. Outside Akkadian there are only a few traces in North-West Semitic: e.g. Heb. *šalhebet*, Jewish-Aram. *šalhōbītā* "flame", and perhaps Ug. *š'tqt* "she who causes to pass".

12.19. Patterns with prefix *n-*: *naqbār, naqbur*, etc. These themes are attested in Akkadian, generally as variants (by dissimilation) of the theme with prefix *m-* (e.g. **mapḫaru* "sum" > *napḫaru*, by dissimilation of the labials *m* and *p*), and in this sense do not

constitute an independent category (cf. § 12.16). They also appear,
however, as nouns and adjectives of the verbal stem with prefix *n-*:
e.g. *namungatu* "paralysis"; *nalbubu* "enraged". Outside Akkadian
a possible example is Ug. *nbldt* "flames".

d. Patterns Extended by Infixes

12.20. Patterns with infixed *t*: apart from the nominal forms of
the verbal stems with *t* (for which cf. § 16.17—23) we find in Akkadian *qitbār* for adjectives with intensive value (e.g. *gitmālu* "very
complete", *itbāru* "very friendly").

e. Patterns Extended by Suffixes

12.21. a) Patterns with suffix *-ān*: *qabarān, qabrān, qibrān,
qubrān, maqbarān*. These themes (in which the suffix *-ān* is attached
to other patterns already discussed) occur especially in abstracts
(e.g. Ar. *ṭayarān* "flight", Heb. **pitrān > pitrōn* "solution",
Syr. *puqdānā* "order", ESA *'ḫwn* "brotherhood", Eth. *rəš'ān*
"old age"); also in adjectives (e.g. Ar. *sakrān* "intoxicated", Heb.
*qadmān > qadmōn "eastern", Syr. *'ar'ān* "terrestrial"); and, finally,
in diminutives (e.g. Ar. *'aqrabān* "little scorpion", Heb. **'išān >
'išōn* "[little-man =] pupil [of the eye]", Akk. *mīrānu* "little
animal"). Hebrew has a number of nouns in which the usual
change *ā > ō* does not take place; the question arises, therefore,
whether they belong to the category at present under consideration:
e.g. *šulḥān* "table", *qorbān* "sacrifice", etc. A particular Akkadian
type of the patterns with suffix *-ān* is that which describes a
special person in a special condition (e.g. *nādinu* "vendor", *nādinānu*
the seller in a particular case of the particular object referred to).
The pattern *maqbarān* appears in a few cases in West Semitic
(e.g. Heb. *maššā'ōn* "deceit", from a root *nš'*, Palm. *maddə'ān*
"knowledge", Syr. *ma'bərānā* "passage"). In some cases (e.g. Ar.
ṭaysal as well as *ṭays* "great number", *hidmil* alongside *hidm*
"patched garment"; possibly Heb. *karmel*, cf. *kerem*) we may have
to identify independent patterns with suffix *-l*, even though of
rare occurrence.

12.22. b) Patterns with suffix *-m*: they are infrequent and occur
predominantly in Arabic adjectives (e.g. *ṭuṣḥum* "wide", *šadqam*

"wide-mouthed"). In Hebrew one may mention *śāfām* "moustache" (from *śāfā*), and in Ethiopic *qastam* "bow" (from *qast*); it is, however, conceivable that in some cases the *-m* might be a relic of mimation (cf. §§ 12.73, 76).

12.23. c) Patterns with suffixes *-īy*, *-āy*, *-āwī*. When attached to other themes these suffixes produce adjectives with the meaning "belonging to" (e.g. Ar. *'arḍīy* "terrestrial", Akk. *maḥrū* (< **maḥrīyu*) "first", Bibl.-Aram. *kaśdāy* "Chaldaean", Heb. *yəhūdī* "Jewish", etc.). The suffix *-āwī* is characteristic of Ethiopic (e.g. *nəgūšāwī* "royal"). The ending *-īy* is called *nisba* in Arabic, and this name has been extended to cover the same type of formation even outside the Semitic languages (the ending is attested, for example, in Egyptian: *ḥmw.ty* "artist" from *ḥmw.t* "art").

12.24. d) Patterns with suffixes *-ūt*, *-īt*: when attached to other patterns (resulting in *qabrūt*, *qabrīt*, etc.) these suffixes produce themes connoting abstracts. Patterns with *-ūt* occur in Akkadian (e.g. *šarrūtu* "kingship"), Hebrew (e.g. *malkūt* "kingship"), Syriac (e.g. *dakyūtā* "purity"), Ethiopic (e.g. *ḥirūt* "goodness"). In Ethiopic these forms are, however, infrequent, and the same applies to Arabic. Themes in *-īt* are found in North-West Semitic (e.g. Heb. *rēšīt* "beginning", Pun. *swyt* "curtain", Syr. *'ərawwītā* "fever", Bibl.-Aram. [as well as Heb.] *'aḥărīt* "end"), perhaps originally as feminine morphemes (cf. § 12.35). In Akkadian they appear only as feminines of the pattern *-īy*, while in Ethiopic they produce abstract nouns (e.g. *daḥārīt* "end", *qadāmīt* "beginning", etc.). In Ethiopic we also encounter the ending *-āt* (e.g. *na'asāt* "youth", *qədsāt* "holiness"). Outside Semitic, nominal formation with the suffix *-t* is attested in Egyptian (e.g. *m.śdm.t* "cosmetics", from the root *śdm*).

f. Patterns from Roots with One, Two, Four, and Five Radicals

12.25. a) Monoconsonantal patterns; these are fairly rare: e.g. Akk. *pū* "mouth", Ug. *p*, Heb. *pē*, Phoen. *p*, Ar. *fū* (cf. Eth. *'af*); Ug. *š* "sheep", Heb. *śē* (cf. Akk. *šu'u*, Ar. *šā'*). Further examples are found in the various languages, e.g. Ug. *g* "voice".

12.26. b) Biconsonantal patterns with short vowel: *qab*, *qib*, *qub* (e.g. Akk. *aḫu* "brother", Ug. *aḫ*, Heb. *'aḥ*, Syr. *'aḥā*, Ar. *'aḥ*,

Eth. *'əẖ*[W]; Akk. *šumu* "name", Ug. *šm*, Heb. *šēm*, Aram. *šum*, Ar. *'ism*, Eth. *səm*).

12.27. c) Biconsonantal patterns with long vowel or diphthong: *qāb, qayb, qawb, qīb, qūb* (e.g. for *qāb*: Akk. *ṭābu* "good", Heb. *ṭōb*, Syr. *ṭābā*, Ar. *ṭāb*; for *qawb*: Ar. *ṯawr* "bull", Syr. *tawrā*, Akk. *šūru*, Heb. *šōr*).

12.28. d) Biconsonantal patterns with doubled second radical: *qabb, qibb, qubb* (e.g. for *qabb*: Akk. *kappu* "palm [of hand]", Heb. *kap* [*kappī* "my palm"], Syr. *kappā*, Ar. *kaff*).

12.29. e) Biconsonantal patterns with reduplication of both radicals: *qabqab, qabqāb, qabqūb, qibqib, qubqub, qubqūb*, etc. (e.g. for *qabqab*: Sem. **kabkab* "star" > Akk. *kakkabu*, Heb. *kōkāb*, Syr. *kawkəbā*, Ar. *kawkab*, Eth. *kōkab*; for examples in individual languages: Akk. *kimkimmu* "wrist"; Ug. *'p'p* "eye"; Heb. *galgal* "wheel"; Syr. *gargərā* "threshing flail"; Ar. *dakdak* "plain"; Eth. *ḥazḥaz* "swamp").

12.30. f) Four-consonant patterns. In addition to those already discussed (constituted by the attachment of affixes or the reduplication of radicals), forms are attested over the entire Semitic area on the pattern $C_1aC_2C_3aC_4u$: e.g. Heb. *'aqrāb*, Syr. *'əqarbā*, Eth. *'aqrab* "scorpion". Examples of other four-radical patterns are Akk. *ḥumṣīru* "mouse", Heb. *'akkabīš* "spider", Syr. *'uqbərā* "mouse", Ar. *qunfuḏ* "hedgehog", Eth. *ḥanbāl* "saddle". Names of animals figure prominently in these patterns; the same is true of words of foreign origin.

12.31. g) Five-consonant patterns. These are infrequent (e.g. Akk. *išḫilṣu* "potsherd", Heb. *ṣəfardēǎ'* "frog") and often of foreign origin. Others of this type are formed, by attachment of affixes or reduplication of radicals, from roots with a smaller number of radicals.

3. Gender

12.32. The Semitic languages distinguish two genders: masculine and feminine. The masculine possesses no special endings (zero morpheme), whereas the feminine is associated with a special morpheme which probably goes back to a more complex and ancient system of classes (cf. §§ 12.34—35), i.e. the ending *-(a)t* which extends over the whole of the Semitic area (and beyond: cf. Egyptian *s³* "son", *s³.t* "daughter"). For example: Akk. *šarrat-u* "queen" (from *šarr-u* "king"); Ug. *ilt* "goddess" (from *il* "god"); Heb. *taḥtīt* "lower" (fem.) (from *taḥtī* "lower"); Syr. *bīštā* "bad" (fem.) (from *bīšā* "bad", in the emphatic state: cf. § 12.74); Ar. *malikat* "queen" (from *malik* "king"); Eth. *bə'əsīt* "woman" (from *bə'əsī* "man"). The fem. gender is not always marked—in relation to the corresponding masculine—by the feminine morpheme, but is sometimes expressed by means of lexical opposition (e.g. Ar. *ḥimār* "he-ass", *'atān* "she-ass"). Grammatical gender does not necessarily and invariably correspond either to sex or to the formal constitution of the noun (cf. §§ 12.34—35).

12.33. In Hebrew and Syriac the Proto-Semitic feminine ending (retained consistently in the construct state: e.g. *mamlākā* "kingdom", constr. *mamleket*) develops in the majority of cases (in the status absolutus) into *-ā*: e.g. Heb. *ṭōbā* (fem. of *ṭōb*) "good"; Syr. *bīšā* (fem. of *bīš*) "bad". According to Brockelmann (GVG, I, p. 409), this development may be understood from the Arabic pausal form *-ah* which has extended beyond its original function (*-at* > *-ah* > *-a* > *-ā*), but this explanation appears somewhat doubtful. A process similar to that in Hebrew and Syriac seems to take place in Neo-Punic—to judge by Latin transcriptions such as *Anna* for *ḥnt*, *alma* for *'lmt*, while neither Phoenician nor Moabite manifests this phenomenon. In Arabic also exist the feminine endings *-ā'* (type *qabrā'*, fem. of *'aqbar*, for colour-nouns: e.g. *ṣafrā'*, fem. of *'aṣfar* "yellow") and *-ā* (type *qubrā*, fem. of *'aqbar*, elative: e.g. *ṣuġrā*, fem. of *'aṣġar* "smallest"). It should be noted, however, that these morphemes are attached to nominal patterns different from those of the corresponding masculine—thus constituting an instance of inner morphemes (cf. § 11.3). Finally, there are the very rare endings, in Hebrew and Syriac, *-ay* (for which may be adduced such words as Heb. *śāray* "lady" and Syr. *ṭu'yay* "error") and *-ē* (from *-ay*?—cf. the feminine numeral Heb. *'eśrē* "ten", Syr. *'əsrē*, in the compounds from 11 to 19). The Ethiopic ending *-ē* (e.g. *sarwē* "army", *'arwē* "beast", *gīzē* "time") is not associated with the feminine.

12.34. The Semitic languages show instances of the fairly general phenomenon of masculine nouns with feminine gender morphemes and feminine nouns without them. Examples of masculine nouns with (apparently) feminine ending: Ar. *ḫalīfat* "caliph", Heb. *qōhelet* n.pr.m. Examples of feminine nouns without feminine ending: Ar. *nafs*, Heb. *nepeš*, Syr. *napšā*, Eth. *nafs* "soul" (also masc.); Ar. *'arḍ*, Heb. *'ereṣ*, Syr. *'ar'ā* "earth". It is interesting to note that in these latter cases Akkadian attaches the feminine ending (*napištu, erṣetu*). Some nominal patterns in Akkadian present variant forms with or without the feminine ending but without a corresponding difference in meaning (*qibr*: *qibirt*; *maqbar*: *maqbart*; *taqbir*: *taqbirt*, etc.); and similarly in Hebrew: *naqām* and *nəqāmā* "vengeance", *mā'ōn* and *mə'ōnā* "dwelling". The names of paired parts of the body are generally feminine, yet without feminine ending (e.g. Akk. *uznu* "ear", Ar. *'uḏn*, Heb. *'ozen*, Syr. *'ednā*, Eth. *'əzən*). Finally, it is noteworthy that the cardinal numerals from 3 to 10 use the forms without gender-ending as feminine and those with the usual feminine morpheme as masculine (cf. § 14.2).

12.35. The feminine morpheme is employed not only to indicate the corresponding natural gender but also *nomina unitatis*, diminutives and pejoratives, abstract and collective nouns. This multiplicity of function points to the probable origin of the feminine ending in a more complex system of classes within which the category of number has to be included as well (by way of the collective). Examples of *nomina unitatis*: Syr. *zəbattā* "time" = French "fois" (cf. *zabnā* "time" = "temps"), Heb. *'ŏniyyā* "ship" (cf. *'ŏnī* "fleet"), Ar. *waraqat* "leaf" (cf. *waraq* "foliage"). Examples of diminutives or pejoratives: Heb. *məlūnā* "hut" (cf. *mālōn* "inn"), Syr. *yammətā* "lake" (cf. *yammā* "sea"). Examples of abstracts: Ar. *waqāḥat* "insolence" (cf. *waqāḥ* "insolent"), Heb. *rā'ā* "wickedness" (cf. *ra'* "wicked"), Eth. *šannāyt* "goodness" (but also the masc. *šannāy*). Examples of collectives: Ar. *ṣūfiyyat* "the mystics" (cf. *ṣūfiy* "mystic"), Heb. *'ōrəḥā* "caravan" (cf. *'ōrĕaḥ* "guest", "traveller").

4. Number

12.36. The Semitic languages possess three numbers: singular, plural, and dual. The dual is formed by the attachment to the singular of special endings; the plural may be formed by the addition of endings, and in that case it is referred to as "external" or "sound" plural; or it may be expressed by a change of pattern (i.e. the use

of a pattern different from that employed for the singular), and in
that case it is called an "internal" or "broken" plural. An example
of the "external" plural is Ar. *qaṣṣāb* "butcher", pl. *qaṣṣābūna*;
of the "internal" plural, Ar. *malik* "king", pl. *mulūk*. For the
characteristics of inner inflexion, cf. § 11.3. In some languages we
find hybrid plurals, i.e. pluralizations of forms already plural; this
occurs both in the form of internal plurals of internal plurals (e.g.
Ar. *balad* "locality", pl. *bilād*, further pl. *buldān*) or in that of
external plurals of internal ones (e.g. *ṭarīq* "way", internal pl.
ṭuruq plus external fem. *ṭuruqāt*).

a. External Masculine Plural

12.37. A comparative examination of the Semitic languages
suggests the following Proto-Semitic morphemes for the external
masculine plural: nominative -*ū* (cf. also Egyptian -*w*: e.g. *nṭr*
"god", pl. *nṭr.w*), genitive/accusative -*ī*. These endings seem to
be the result of the lengthening of the corresponding singular
morphemes of the nominative (-*u*) and genitive (-*i*), while the independent ending of the accusative singular (-*a*) merges with that
of the genitive in the plural.

12.38. In Akkadian the endings of the masculine plural are nom.
-*ū*, gen./acc. -*ī* (Assyrian -*ē*, later extended in part to Late Babylonian) from the earliest occurrence until the Neo-Babylonian and
Neo-Assyrian period, where -*ī* (-*ē*) prevails and is extended to the
nominative: e.g. sing. *šarru* "king", pl. nom. *šarrū*, gen./acc.
šarrī/ē; Neo-Bab. and Neo-Ass. pl. nom./gen./acc. *šarrī/ē*. The
fairly frequent appearance of plural endings of feminine form
(cf. § 12.56 and von Soden, GAG, pp. 77—78) for masculine nouns
(e.g. *ikkāru* "peasant", pl. *ikkārātu*; *nāru* "river", pl. *nārātu*)
recalls the similar phenomenon in Ethiopic (cf. § 12.41); for some
cases in other languages cf. § 12.66. Akkadian adjectives exhibit
the special endings nom. -*ūtu*, gen./acc. -*ūti*: e.g. *rabū* "great",
pl. nom. *rabūtu*, gen./acc. *rabūti*.

12.39. In North-West Semitic the original endings -*ū*, -*ī* are
preserved in Ugaritic: e.g. nom. *rpum*, gen./acc. *rpim* "demigods,
shades of the dead" (for the final -*m* or -*n*, with or without an
accompanying vowel, cf. below §§ 12.70—77); and later in Ya'udic:

e.g. *mlkw* "kings", gen./acc. *mlky*. Elsewhere *-ī* predominates and
is extended to the nominative: e.g. Heb. *sūs* "horse", pl. *sūsīm*;
Syr. *bīš* "bad" (status absolutus), pl. *bīšīn*.

12.40. In classical Arabic the Proto-Semitic endings remain:
nom. *-ū*, gen./acc. *-ī*: e.g. *qaṣṣāb* "butcher", pl. nom. *qaṣṣābūna*,
gen./acc. *qaṣṣābīna*. For the pre-classical phase of Arabic, the
indications furnished by South Arabian and Liḥyānite (drawn
from forms in the construct state, since in the absolute state the
purely consonantal spelling does not allow any valid conclusions)
suggest the same state of affairs: e.g. Liḥyānite pl. nom. constr.
bnw "sons", gen./acc. *bny*.

12.41. In Ethiopic the plural endings are *-ān* for the masculine
and *-āt* for the feminine (cf. below § 12.52): e.g. *ṣādəq* "just",
pl. masc. *ṣādəqān*, fem. *ṣādəqāt*. However, the feminine ending has
greatly expanded at the expense of the masc. morpheme: e.g. *māy*
"water", pl. *māyāt* (cf. also §§ 12.38, 12.56). The ending *-ān*
remains in use for adjectives, participles, and a smaller number
of substantives: e.g. *ḥadīs* "new", pl. *ḥadīsān*; *masīḥ* "Messiah",
pl. *masīḥān*.

12.42. The masculine external plural *-ān* current in Ethiopic
(cf. the preceding paragraph) appears also in other parts of the
Semitic area. In Akkadian we find nom. *-ānū*, gen./acc. *-ānī*
(combination of *-ān* with *-ū*, *-ī*) in the Old and Middle periods,
-ānī for all cases in Late Akkadian: e.g. *šarru* "king", pl. nom.
šarrānū, gen./acc. *šarrānī* (Late period *šarrānī* for all cases). In
Syriac we find *-ānīn* (combination of *-ān* with *-īn*): e.g. *rabbā*
"master", pl. *rabbānīn*. According to Goetze (Language 22 [1946],
pp. 121—30) the ending *-ān* designates "individual" plurals as
distinct from "general" ones (e.g. Akk. *ilū* "the gods", *ilānū*
"some gods" or "the gods taken individually"). Gelb (Morphology
of Akkadian, pp. 14—15) regards it as an ending without specific
significance which is used to reinforce short nouns. The ending
-ān appears also with internal plurals (cf. § 12.50).

b. Internal Masculine Plural

12.43. Internal plurals are formed, as has been explained, by the
use of patterns different from those of the singular. The patterns

so used may be regarded as original collectives; their employment as plurals cannot be established—except when they are construed as plurals in terms of grammatical concord. Cf. Fleisch, TPA, pp. 470—505 for a detailed discussion.

12.44. The internal plurals may be regarded as Proto-Semitic, in the sense that their patterns are Proto-Semitic. However, their use as plurals is regularly found only in the South Semitic area (Arabic and Ethiopic). In North-West Semitic there are some late and rather doubtful traces: e.g. Heb. *rekeb* from the singular *rōkēb* "horseman" (Ar. *rakb* from sing. *rākib*), Syr. *quryā* from the singular *qərītā* "village" (Ar. *qurā* from sing. *qaryat*), Syr. *ḥemrā* from the singular *ḥəmārā* "ass". The existence of internal plurals in Ugaritic has not been demonstrated. For Akkadian, attention might be invited to Old Assyrian *ṣuḥrum*, a collective corresponding to the singular Ass. *ṣaḥrum*, Bab. *ṣeḥrum* "small". It must therefore be supposed that internal plurals are a particular development of South Semitic, although Petráček's studies (cf. § 11.3) have shown the existence of precedents in Hamito-Semitic. The following paragraphs will indicate the principal patterns used for internal plurals—together with the singular themes to which they correspond.

12.45. a) Disyllabic patterns with short vowel: *qabar, qibar, qubar, qubur*. Of these themes, *qibar* corresponds in Arabic to the singular *qibrat* (e.g. *qiṭaʿ*, pl. of *qiṭʿat* "piece") and *qubar* to the singular *qubrat* (e.g. *ʿulab*, pl. of *ʿulbat* "box"). In South Arabian the situation must be similar, though the vocalization is, of course, unknown to us (e.g. *s̊ḥf*, pl. of *s̊ḥft* "trench" [?]; *fnw*, pl. of *fnwt* "plain"). *qubur* corresponds in Arabic to various singular patterns, but chiefly to those with the second vowel long (e.g. *kutub*, pl. of *kitāb* "book"). In Ethiopic, the merging in *ə* of the Proto-Semitic short vowels *i* and *u* (cf. § 8.96) produces the pattern *qəbar*, corresponding to singular *qəbr* (e.g. *ʾəzan*, pl. of *ʾəzn* "ear").

12.46. b) Monosyllabic patterns with short vowel: Arabic *qubr*, plural of *ʾaqbar* (nouns of colour, cf. § 12.14): e.g. *ḥumr*, pl. of *ʾaḥmar* "red".

12.47. c) Disyllabic patterns with long vowel in the second syllable, or with short second vowel and feminine suffix: *qabīr*, *qibār, qubūr; qabarat, qibarat, qubarat.* Of these themes, *qibār* and *qubūr* correspond in Arabic mainly to the monosyllabic singulars *qabr, qibr, qubr*: e.g. *biḥār,* pl. of *baḥr* "sea"; *ǧunūd,* pl. of *ǧund* "army". The situation in South Arabian may have been similar, though we remain ignorant of the vocalization: e.g. *ḫrwf* and *ḫryf,* plurals of *ḫrf* "year". The themes *qabarat* and *qubarat* correspond in Arabic to the participial pattern *qābir* in the singular: e.g. *kafarat,* pl. of *kāfir* "unbeliever". In Ethiopic the situation is similar: the internal plural pattern *qabart* corresponds to the singular participial theme *qabārī* (e.g. *ṣaḥaft,* pl. of *ṣaḥāfī* "writer") as well as to the pattern *qabīr* (e.g. *ṭababt,* pl. of *ṭabīb* "wise").

12.48. d) Patterns marked by doubling: Arabic presents *qubbar* and *qubbār,* both corresponding to the singular participial theme *qābir* (e.g. *ruǧǧaʿ,* pl. of *rāǧiʿ* "returning"; *kuttāb,* pl. of *kātib* "scribe").

12.49. e) Patterns extended by prefixes: *ʾaqbār, ʾaqbirat, ʾaqbirāʾ, ʾaqbur, ʾaqburat.* In Arabic all these themes, except the last two, are frequent: *ʾaqbār* corresponds mainly to the singular pattern *qabar* (e.g. *ʾamrāḍ,* pl. of *maraḍ* "illness"); *ʾaqbirat* correlates to singular themes with long vowel following the second radical (e.g. *ʾaġribat,* pl. of *ǧurāb* "crow"); *ʾaqbirāʾ* corresponds principally to the singular pattern *qabīr* (e.g. *ʾaqribāʾ,* pl. of *qarīb* "kinsman"); *ʾaqbur* corresponds frequently to the singular theme *qabr* (e.g. *ʾanfus,* pl. of *nafs* "soul"). Noteworthy is also the use of the themes *ʾaqbār, ʾaqbirat, ʾaqbur* (as well as *qibrat*) for the so-called *plural of paucity,* i.e. a plural for quantities not exceeding ten. In South Arabian the series of patterns extended by prefixes is fairly widespread: the consonantal schemes *ʾqbr, ʾqbrt, ʾqbrw* admit of the existence of all the patterns mentioned above, although their vocalization cannot be established (cf. for example *ʾbyt,* pl. of *byt* "house"; *ʾḫrft,* one of the plural patterns of *ḫrf* "year"; *ʾkbrw,* pl. of *kbr* "great"). In Ethiopic we have *ʾaqbār, ʾaqbər* (= *ʾaqbur*), *ʾaqbūr, ʾaqbərt* (= *ʾaqburat* or *ʾaqbirat*): of these patterns, *ʾaqbār* often corresponds to singular themes *qabr, qəbr, qabar* (e.g. *ʾaʿmād,* pl. of *ʿamd* "pillar"; *ʾalbās,* pl. of *ləbs* "dress"; *ʾadwāl,* pl. of *dawal* "district"); *ʾaqbər* corresponds mainly to the singular *qabr* (e.g. *ʾawgər,* pl. of *wagr* "hill"); *ʾaqbūr* frequently corresponds to singulars with two short vowels or with a single vowel (e.g. *ʾahgūr,* pl. of *hagar* "city"; *ʾaḥqūl,* pl. of *ḥaql* "field"); *ʾaqbərt* correlates mainly to a singular theme *qabr* (e.g. *'agbərt*, pl. of *gabr* "servant").

12.50. f) Patterns extended by suffixes: *qibrān, qubrān, qubarā'*. These are frequent in Arabic (e.g. *ǧīrān*, pl. of *ǧār* "neighbour"). *qubarā'* corresponds most often to a singular theme *qabīr*, but at times also to *qābir* (e.g. *'umarā'*, pl. of *'amīr* "Emir"; *šu'arā'*, pl. of *šā'ir* "poet").

12.51. g) Four-consonant themes: These are formed on the patterns $C_1aC_2\bar{a}C_3iC_4$ and $C_1aC_2\bar{a}C_3iC_4$. They correspond to four-consonant singular patterns (e.g. Ar. *'aqārib*, pl. of *'aqrab* "scorpion"; Eth. *sanāsəl*, pl. of *sansal* "chain"; Ar. *'anāqīd*, pl. of *'unqūd* "bunch") including those formed from triconsonantal roots by the attachment of an affix (e.g. Ar. *manāzil*, pl. of *manzil* "dwelling", root *nzl*; Eth. *malā'əkt*, pl. of *mal'ak* "messenger", root *l'k* plus suffix *-t*); they also correlate to triconsonantal singular patterns with long vowel (the plural theme being characterized by the insertion of ' or *w* or *y*): e.g. Ar. *fawāris*, pl. of *fāris* "horseman"; Ar. *'arā'is*, pl. of *'arūs* "bride"; Eth. *kəsāwəd*, pl. of *kəsād* "neck".

c. Feminine Plural

12.52. The feminine plural is of the external type. It appears to be formed on the same principle as the external masculine plural, i.e. by the lengthening of the vowel—contrasting with the short vowel of the singular:-(a)t, fem. pl. *-āt*; e.g. Ar. *malikat* "queen" (fem. of *malik* "king"), pl. *malikāt*.

12.53. In the languages which retain case-endings, these are attached to the feminine suffix; the same applies to the morphemes *-m* or *-n* (cf. §§ 12, 70—78). Thus we find in Akkadian *šarrum* "king" (nom. sg.), fem. sg. (nom.) *šarratum*, fem. pl. nom. *šarrātum*, gen./acc. *šarrātim*; and in Arabic *malik^{un}* "king" (nom. sg.), fem. sg. (nom.) *malikat^{un}*, fem. pl. nom. *malikāt^{un}*, gen./acc. *malikāt^{in}* (cf. on declension §§ 12.64—69 below).

12.54. In the North-West Semitic area, Hebrew (owing to the well-known transition $\bar{a} > \bar{o}$ [cf. § 8.83]) presents the feminine plural suffix *-ōt*: e.g. *bərākā* "blessing", pl. *bərākōt*. Syriac has *-āt* in the construct and emphatic states, but in the absolute state *-ān*, probably by analogy with the masculine plural *-īn*: e.g. *bīšā* "bad" (fem. sg. abs.), pl. cstr. *bīšāt*, emph. *bīšātā*, abs. *bīšān* (this 'innovation' in the Aramaic area is attested, as early as the eighth century B.C., in the Arpad inscriptions where *-n* occurs alongside the more common *-t*; later on it appears as the established form in Biblical Aramaic).

12.55. At times the feminine ending of the plural is superimposed upon that of the singular—instead of being substituted for it. This phenomenon is not uncommon in Ethiopic (e.g. *barakat* "blessing", pl. *barakatāt*); here it may, however, be accounted for by the fact that the plural ending *-āt* is no longer limited to the feminine and has, in fact, been extended to masculine nouns as well (cf. § 12.41); it is rare in other languages (e.g. Akk. *išātu* "fire", pl. *išātātu*; Heb. *qešet* "bow", pl. *qəšātōt*).

12.56. In several of the Semitic languages we encounter instances of nouns of feminine form in the singular and of masc. form in the plural: e.g. Heb. *šānā* "year", pl. *šānīm* (but in the construct state a feminine morpheme reappears: *šənōt*); Syr. *gannətā* "garden", pl. *gannē*; Ar. *ḥarrat* "stony ground", pl. *ḥirrūna* (also *ḥarrāt*). These formations, which do not normally occur in Akkadian and Ethiopic (cf. however Akk. *kabūtu* "dung", pl. *kabū*), are rare in Arabic, though fairly frequent in North-West Semitic. The converse of this phenomenon, i.e. the appearance of feminine endings in the plural of nouns of masculine singular, is rather more widespread: it occurs particularly in nouns which are of feminine gender but lack the feminine morpheme in the singular (e.g. Akk. *ḥarrānu* "road", pl. *ḥarrānātu*; Heb. *'ātōn* "she-ass", pl. *'ătōnōt*; Syr. *ḥaqlā* "field", pl. *ḥaqlātā*); similarly in some nouns of trade or occupation (e.g. Akk. *ikkāru* "peasant", pl. *ikkārātu*; Syr. *'āsyā* "doctor", pl. *'āsawwātā*) and a number of other substantives. This phenomenon, developed to varying extents in individual languages (esp. in Akkadian), has assumed somewhat larger propórtions in Ethiopic where the original feminine ending *-āt* has been extended to masculine nouns over a fairly wide range (§ 12.41).

d. Plurals of Biconsonantal Nouns

12.57. In West Semitic many biconsonantal nouns form their plurals by adding a third consonant to the singular pattern;

this consonant is mostly *h*: e.g. Heb. *'āmā* "maid-servant", pl.
'ămāhōt; Syr. *šəmā* "name", pl. *šəmāhē*; Ar. *šafat* "lip", pl. *šifāh*
and *šafawāt*, *sanat* "year", pl. *sanawāt*. In Akkadian some biconsonantal nouns double the second consonant in the plural: e.g. *abu*
"father", pl. *abbū*, *iṣu* "tree", pl. *iṣṣū*.

12.58. In West Semitic there are also traces of a plural formation
by reduplicating the singular of biconsonantal nouns (and then
adding the external plural ending): e.g. Syr. *rab* "great", pl. **rab-
rəbē* > *rawrəbē*; ESA *'l* "god", pl. *'l'lt*. Similar cases occur in
Hebrew with nouns which were perhaps originally monoconsonantal, such as *mayim* "water", cstr. *mē* or *mēmē*. It is possible (Brockelmann, GVG, I, p. 439) that this type of plural arose from a distributive context: cf. Syr. *ḥadhədānē* and Amharic *'andānd* "some"
(from *ḥad* and *'and*, respectively, "one"), and Tigre *kəlkəl'ōt*
"every two".

e. Dual

12.59. The dual is used for the linguistic expression of natural
pairs, but it also serves, in some of the Semitic languages, to indicate duality outside these narrow limits. Its extensive use in Old
Akkadian, Ugaritic, and Arabic suggests that the restricted employment in other languages is secondary (cf. below). A comparative
examination proposes the following Proto-Semitic endings: nom.
-ā, gen./acc. *-ay*, followed by nunation or mimation.

12.60. The Akkadian dual has *-ān* for the nominative and
(**-ayn* >) *-ēn/-īn* for the genitive-accusative. Nunation is dropped
in the more recent period. The distinction between the cases is
gradually lost, and in Middle Akkadian *-ēn/-īn* predominate over
-ān. An interesting feature in Akkadian is the use of the dual as
a plural of paucity: e.g. *ubānāšu* "his fingers", *šinnāšu* "his teeth".

12.61. In North-West Semitic, the unvocalized Ugaritic texts
reveal no formal distinction between dual and plural: Gordon
(UM, pp. 43, 223) reconstructs the dual endings as nom. *-āmi*,
gen./acc. *-ēmi* (the latter by contraction of original *-ay* followed by
mimation). Hebrew exhibits a restricted use of the dual (at any
rate during the historically attested period) with the ending *-ayim*
predominating and extending to all the cases. The position is
very similar in Aramaic, but here we have nunation instead of

mimation: -*ayn*; and in Syriac the dual appears to occur in only two words (*tərēn* [*tartēn*] "two" and *matēn* "two hundred").

12.62. Arabic presents the Proto-Semitic endings followed by -*ni*: nom. -*āni*, gen./acc. -*ayni*. It has been suggested that -*ni* is a secondary derivative of -*na* (the suffix having been added to the plural ending); and the hypothesis has been advanced (though with doubtful justification) that the change took place by way of vowel dissimilation (Brockelmann, GVG, I, p. 456). In Arabic dialects, the ending of the oblique cases predominates over that of the nominative—just as it does in the other Semitic languages. South Arabian has the dual morphemes -*ān* and -*ayn*, but their employment appears to be quite indiscriminate in relation to the various cases.

12.63. Ethiopic preserves only a few traces of the dual, represented by the ending (**ay* >) *ē*: *kəl'ē* "two" (cf. § 14.2), *'ədē* "hands" (before suffixes), *ḥaq^wē* "loins".

5. Declension

12.64. The Semitic languages originally possessed three basic cases: nominative (subject), genitive (complement governed by a noun), accusative (complement governed by a verb). For the plural and dual endings of these cases see the preceding paragraphs; if we append to them the endings of the singular the following picture emerges:

	Singular	Plural	Dual
Nominative	-*u*	-*ū*	-*ā*
Genitive	-*i*	-*ī*	-*ay*
Accusative	-*a*		

According to Brockelmann (GVG, I, p. 459) the singular endings are quantitatively ambivalent (-*ŭ*, -*ĭ*, -*ă*); but since their opposition to the plural morphemes depends on a quantitative distinction they must be regarded as short.

12.65. To the three basic cases in Proto-Semitic we might have to add a locative in -*u* which is attested in Akkadian and traces of which may perhaps be detected in other languages as well—esp.

in adverbs such as Ar. *taḥtu* "below" and *qablu* "before", Eth. *lāʿlū* "above" and *kantū* "gratuitously". Some of these examples may be open to doubt. They also raise the problem of the quantity of the locative ending *-u* (on this cf. the following paragraph).

12.66. Akkadian retains the basic case-endings in their entirety: nom. *ṭābu* "good", gen. *ṭābi*, acc. *ṭāba*. Only in the course of time do these distinctions become progressively blurred: in Neo-Babylonian and Neo-Assyrian the three case-morphemes are used indiscriminately or even omitted altogether. The Akkadian locative in *-u* (cf. § 12.65) is often used with prepositions (e.g. *ina libbu* "in the midst of, within") or appears joined to prepositions (e.g. *balu[m]* "without", *ištu[m]* "from"; for the ending *-m* cf. § 12.71). According to Gelb (OA, pp. 144—45) the vowel of the locative ending was originally long; according to von Soden (GAG, pp. 87—88) its length is a late and secondary development. The material at our disposal seems to favour this latter view. Finally, Akkadian has a fifth case, the dative-adverbial in *-iš* (cf. the element *š* which characterizes the dative of the pronouns: § 13.3). As a dative this occurs in only the most ancient phase of the language (e.g. *muātiš* "to die", *amāriš* "to see"); for *-iš* in comparisons note *iliš* "like a god". As an adverbial, however, it remains throughout the entire period of Akkadian (e.g. *mādiš* "much", *damqiš* "well", etc.). In conjunction with the ending *-am* (more rarely *-um*), used adverbially, *-iš* assumes either terminative or distributive function (e.g. *annišam* "hither", *ūmišam* "daily").

12.67. In the North-West Semitic area, Amorite and the Tell Amarna glosses retain the Proto-Semitic case-endings—and so does Ugaritic, as may be seen in nouns whose final consonant is ' (vocalized with *a, i, u*). In the later languages the endings disappear and with them the formal distinction between the cases, leaving only a few faint traces: in Hebrew the ending *-ā* denoting motion towards a place (e.g. *Bābél* "Babylon", *Bābélā* "towards Babylon") is regarded by some scholars as such a survival; in Aramaic, Brockelmann (GVG, I, p. 465) considers adverbs such as *taḥtā* "below", *bārā* "outside", etc., also as survivals, but this remains highly conjectural.

12.68. Classical Arabic (as indeed the pre-classical language—so far as we can judge) retains the Proto-Semitic declension system in its entirety: nom. *malik^u* "king", gen. *malik^i*, acc. *malik^a*. There exists, however, a series of nouns whose declension is limited to two endings only: *-u* for the nominative and *-a* for the genitive/ accusative (cf. Fleisch, TPA, pp. 269—80). Wehr's studies on the nominal pattern *'aqbar^u* conjecture that this diptote declension originated within that theme. It would then have spread to other adjectival themes (*qabrān^u*) and internal plurals (*'aqbirā'*, *qubarā'*, $C_1aC_2\bar{a}C_3iC_4u$, $C_1aC_2\bar{a}C_3\bar{i}C_4u$, and others) as also to a series of proper nouns with the feminine ending (e.g. *Makkat^u* "Mecca"), to some verbal forms (e.g. *Yazīd^u*, "Yezid") and to some names of foreign origin (e.g. *'Ibrāhīm^u* "Abraham"). For a possible occurrence of diptotes in Ugaritic see Gordon, UM, p. 45. It is noteworthy that diptotes do not take nunation. In modern Arabic dialects case-endings have disappeared altogether—just as they have done in the other Semitic languages.

12.69. Ethiopic retains only one oblique case ending (indicating also motion towards a place): e.g. nom. *gabr* "servant", acc. and constr. *gabra*. The ending *-a* appears both in the singular and in the plural of nouns terminating in a consonant: e.g. nom. *'agbərt* "servants", acc. and constr. *'agbərta*. The ending *-a* of the construct state has possibly arisen from an analogical extension of the accusative morpheme. The final *-ū* of certain numerals may be a survival of the nominative ending: e.g. *'aḥadū* "one" (thus Dillmann, EG, § 142, p. 318, though other explanations have been proposed for this element—cf. Brockelmann, GVG, II, p. 274). Proper names are either indeclinable or form an accusative by the attachment of stressed *-hā* (e.g. *Yəsḥaqhā* "Isaac" [acc.]).

6. Definiteness and Indefiniteness

12.70. It is not possible to reconstruct Proto-Semitic forms for the expression of definiteness or indefiniteness. It will, therefore, be well to examine first the various languages separately and then to consider what common features emerge from this investigation.

12.71. In Akkadian all nouns, whether definite or indefinite, have the ending *-m* (mimation) in the masculine singular and in the feminine singular and plural, the ending *-n* (nunation) in the dual, and neither mimation nor nunation in the masculine plural:

	Singular		Plural		Dual	
	(Masc.)	(Fem.)	(Masc.)	(Fem.)	(Masc.)	(Fem.)
Nom.	*šarrum*	*šarratum*	*šarrū*	*šarrātum*	*šarrān*	*šarratān*
Gen.	*šarrim*	*šarratim*	*šarrī*	*šarrātim*	*šarrēn*	*šarratēn*
Acc.	*šarram*	*šarratam*				

It can thus be seen that mimation and nunation co-exist in Akkadian, but they do not possess the function of distinguishing definiteness and indefiniteness—as is the case in some other languages. In any event, mimation and nunation fall into disuse from the end of the Old Babylonian and Old Assyrian periods. It should be observed that in Old Babylonian nunation occurs instead of mimation in some personal pronouns (*yattun*, *yuttun*, *kattun*, *kuttun*, *šuttun*: cf. § 13.18) and demonstratives (*annūtun*, *annātun*: cf. § 13.29); in the case of the latter there may possibly be some connexion with the indication of nearness, but the relationship of this phenomenon with the problem under examination remains somewhat uncertain. Noteworthy is also the absence of mimation in some proper names in Old Akkadian as well as in some common nouns used as proper names: e.g. *abu* "father" and *aḫu* "brother" when denoting gods (von Soden, GAG, p. 80; Gelb, OA, p. 145).

12.72. In the North-West Semitic area mimation is found in the majority of Amorite proper names (of the type *Ṣaduqum*, *Yaplaḫum* etc.) as well as in some Egyptian transcriptions. In the Tell Amarna glosses we encounter only a few traces of this phenomenon. Ugaritic shows neither mimation nor nunation in the singular or in the feminine plural, but it presents endings with *-m* in the dual and in the masculine plural. Gordon's hypothetical vocalization produces (UM, pp. 43—44, 223) the following picture:

	Plural		Dual	
	(Masc.)	(Fem.)	(Masc.)	(Fem.)
Nom.	*ṭābūma*	*ṭābātu*	*ṭābāmi*	*ṭāb(a)tāmi*
Gen./Acc.	*ṭābīma*	*ṭābāti*	*ṭābēmi*	*ṭāb(a)tēmi*

In North-West Semitic, as indeed in North-East Semitic, no properly established relationship can be ascertained between mimation and nunation, on one hand, and aspects of determination, on the other.

12.73. Hebrew possesses neither mimation nor nunation in the singular. Traces of mimation have been seen in forms such as *dārōm* "south", *ḥarṭōm* "soothsayer", etc., and particularly in such proper names as *Milkōm* and the series of adverbs (ending in *-ām*) which includes *'omnām* "truly", *ḥinnām* "gratuitously", etc. (cf. Torczyner's studies). Yet, the interpretation of these data remains uncertain. Some formations in *-n* are also found, such as *Gid'ōn*, but they may well be secondary—or, at any rate, can be explained as nominal patterns with suffixes. Mimation is a prominent feature in the masculine plural and in the dual (*-īm*, *-ayim*) which tallies with the state of affairs in Ugaritic (cf. preceding paragraph). This mimation is not, however, related to a differentiation between the definite and the indefinite; instead, definiteness is expressed, in all three numbers, by a prefixed article *ha-* followed by doubling (or reinforcement) of the initial consonant of the noun (e.g. *melek* "king", *ham-melek* "the king"; *məlākīm* "kings", *ham-məlākīm* "the kings"). The position in Phoenician resembles that in Hebrew—at least as far as can be judged from the purely consonantal script; the transition, in late Punic, of the article *h-* to *'-* is due to a general phonetic change in that area (cf. § 8.55). Moabite differs from the other Canaanite languages and agrees with Aramaic in the appearance of nunation (*-n*) in the plural.

12.74. Syriac (and Aramaic in general) agrees with Hebrew in possessing neither mimation nor nunation in the singular. Nominal forms such as *'īmāmā* "day", *pummā* "mouth" may, however, be regarded as preserving traces of mimation. In the plural (there is no dual) nunation occurs in the ending *-īn*, but—as in Hebrew—it is not connected with the differentiation between definite and indefinite. Definiteness is formally expressed, from the most ancient Aramaic inscriptions onwards, by a suffixed article *-ā* (emphatic state of the noun) which in the Eastern Aramaic dialects (and in Syriac in particular) loses this specific function and becomes the normal ending of all nouns. Remnants of a nominal ending *-a*, though not entirely agreeing in the specifically determinative function, have been detected in Old Akkadian, Old Assyrian, and Amorite (cf. Garbini, SNO, pp. 118—21).

12.75. In the Arabic area, Epigraphic South Arabian presents a fairly complex situation (Beeston). The absolute state occurs either with or without mimation, and the ending -*m* does not by itself necessarily correspond to the indefinite article ('*s¹m* "a man" or "the man"). The factors governing the use of mimated or un-mimated forms remain obscure, especially as the syntactical function of mimation appears to be negligible. Mimation occurs in the singular, the internal plural, and the external feminine plural. In the dual and the external masculine plural we encounter unmimated forms only. On the other hand, the ending -*n* is attached to the singular, internal plural, and external feminine plural (it is not attested in external masc. plurals). It has the function either of a demonstrative or of a definite article, e.g. *ṣlmn* "this statue" or "the statue". In pre-classical North Arabic -*m* occurs occasionally in Ṭamūdic to indicate indefiniteness, while definiteness is expressed by the prefixed article *h*-. In the earliest Liḥyānite inscriptions we still encounter -*n* to mark definiteness, whereas more recent epigraphic documents have brought to light two instances of (')*l*-. Finally, classical Arabic has -*n* for the expression of indefiniteness and the prefixed element '*al*- as a definite article.

12.76. Ethiopic possesses neither mimation nor nunation, for the element -*ān* of the masculine external plural can scarcely be regarded as a form of nunation. Traces of mimation have been seen by some scholars in nominal forms such as *qastam* "bow" (alongside *qast*), but this opinion does not seem to be well substantiated. Ethiopic has no prefix-article, but a suffix-substitute has been evolved from the pronominal suffixes (cf. Praetorius, *Grammatica Aethiopica*, p. 33, § 38; Dillmann, EG, p. 426, § 172 [b]): *bə'əsīhū* "the man", *dabrū* "the mountain", etc. From these elements of frozen suffixes, no longer dependent on any antecedents, Amharic has developed a type of suffix-article. Ethiopic possesses very elaborate syntactical means for the periphrasis of the definite article (Dillmann, EG, pp. 423—30, §§ 172—73).

12.77. The evidence adduced in the foregoing confirms the view that it is impossible to identify any Proto-Semitic means of ex-

7*

pressing definiteness or indefiniteness. In this respect singular, dual, and plural seem to behave differently, so that observations valid for the singular cannot always be applied to the other numbers in which mimation or nunation are sometimes preserved after having been dropped in the singular. On this basis it may be suggested, by way of hypothesis, that originally there existed a mimation of nouns independent of any semantic function as regards definiteness or indefiniteness; and that this usage is reflected in the most ancient Semitic linguistic material. It may further be assumed that mimation developed into nunation in some languages, such as Arabic and Aramaic, following upon the change $m > n$ which occurs also in other connexions in these languages. It may then be shown how, in the course of the historical development of the Semitic languages, new and special means of indicating definiteness make their appearance in a number of different guises: the prefixes h- in Hebrew (and also in some pre-Islamic Arabic dialects) and 'al- in Arabic (a connexion between these may be seen both in the alternation h:' and in the doubling of the following consonant in Hebrew and Arabic—in the latter as a substitute for the total assimilation of l to certain consonants); the suffixes $-\bar{a}$ in Aramaic, $-n$ in South Arabian, and $-\bar{u}$ in Ethiopic. Where definiteness is expressed by a prefix it may bring about a modification in the use of mimation or nunation, i.e. it may become a means of indicating indefiniteness by virtue of the contrast to the definiteness connoted by the article. This happens in the singular in classical Arabic (where the article excludes nunation: e.g. $qaṣṣāb^{un}$ "a butcher", but 'al-$qaṣṣāb^u$ "the butcher"), while in Hebrew, where mimation appears in the plural only, it is semantically irrelevant and is retained together with the article (e.g. $məlākīm$ "kings", ham-$məlākīm$ "the kings"). Where definiteness is expressed by a suffix, this replaces mimation or nunation which now become an indication of indefiniteness: e.g. in Aramaic where the endings of the status emphaticus have extended their use at the expense of the forms with nunation (Syr. $biš\bar{e}$ prevailing over $bišin$).

12.78. The Semitic "construct state" is closely connected with the function of definiteness or indefiniteness; this is the special form taken by a noun when it is defined by a following genitive (or pronominal suffix). In these conditions the *nomen regens* merges with the *nomen rectum* in a single complex whose principal stress falls on the *rectum*, i.e. the "genitival" element. The two nouns cannot ordinarily be separated, though there are certain exceptions to this rule, e.g. in South Arabian: *nfs[1] wqbr HNTS[1]R* "*HNTS[1]R*'s monument and tomb" (classical Arabic would have changed the construction to "*Hntsr*'s monument and his tomb"). A noun in the construct state has neither mimation (nunation) nor the article (e.g. Ar. *qaṣṣāb[un]* "a butcher", *'al-qaṣṣāb[u]* "the butcher", *qaṣṣāb[u]* ... "the butcher of ...") except in certain instances of what is termed "improper annexation" (Akk. *damqam īnim* literally "good of eye", Ar. *'ar-raǧul[u] l-ḥasan[u] l-waǧh[i]* literally "the man handsome of face"; cf. von Soden, JNES 19 [1960], pp. 163—71). The case-endings are retained in their entirety in Arabic. In Akkadian their retention is less complete: they appear in some nouns ending in a vowel and before suffixes (e.g. *mārū-šu* "his son", gen. *mārī-šu*, acc. *mārā-šu*), but in general the autonomous genitive-ending contrasts with a case-element common to nominative and accusative. In Ethiopic the ending -*a*, characteristic of the accusative, serves also for the construct state (cf. § 12.69: extension by analogy?). The unity of the noun with the following "genitive" (with the principal stress on the latter) and the consequent reduction in the case-endings may occasion changes in the form of the noun in the construct state. For details the grammars of the various languages have to be consulted, but it may be said that these changes are often either of an anaptyctic type (e.g. Akk. *uznu* "ear", cstr. *uzun*; Heb. *'ebed* "servant", cstr. **'abd*: cf. § 9.17) or involve modifications in vowel quantity owing to the displacement of the stress (e.g. Akk. *máru* "son", but before a suffix *márú-šu* "his son"; Heb. *dābár* "word", but cstr. *dəbar* owing to the shift of the principal stress to the following *nomen rectum*). In many cases the original Semitic form can still be recognized in the construct state: so in the example just cited, Heb. **'abd* (nominal pattern *qabr*: cf. § 12.5) and in the Hebrew and Syriac feminine-ending (e.g. Heb. *yōnā* "dove", cstr. *yōnat*: cf. § 12.33).

12.79. In Akkadian and Aramaic three "states" of the noun may be distinguished. In addition to the construct state there is that

called *rectus* or "emphatic", in which Akkadian exhibits mimation
and Syriac the ending *-ā* (e.g. Akk. *aḫum* "brother", Syr. *'aḫā*).
These endings do not, however, retain any significance in terms of
defining the noun. Thirdly, the "absolute" state is devoid of any
endings; it is comparatively rare and occurs mainly in distributive
expressions (e.g. Akk. *ina kār kār-ma* "in every colony", Syr.
rappīn rappīn "in flocks"), adverbial contexts (e.g. Akk. *ana dār*
"for ever", Syr. *ba-'gal* "in haste"), in some numerals (e.g. Akk.
ištēn "one", Syr. *ḥad*), and as predicates (cf. von Soden, GAG,
p. 79; Brockelmann, SG, pp. 104—105).

C. The Pronoun

1. Independent Personal Pronouns

13.1. The independent personal pronouns of the principal Semitic
languages are as follows:

		Akkadian	Ugaritic	Hebrew	Syriac	Arabic	Ethiopic
Sg.	1	*anāku*	*ȧn(k)*	*'ănī, 'ānōkī*	*'enā*	*'anā*	*'ana*
	2 m.	*attā*	*ȧt*	*'attā*	*'att*	*'anta*	*'anta*
	f.	*attī*	*ȧt*	*'att*	*'att*	*'anti*	*'antī*
	3 m.	*šū*	*hw*	*hū*	*hū*	*huwa*	*wǝ'ǝtū*
	f.	*šī*	*hy*	*hī*	*hī*	*hiya*	*yǝ'ǝtī*
Pl.	1	*nīnu*		*('ă)naḥnū*	*('ena)ḥnan*	*naḥnu*	*nǝḥna*
	2 m.	*attunu*		*'attem*	*'attōn*	*'antum(ū)*	*'antǝmmu*
	f.	*attina*		*'atten(ā)*	*'attēn*	*'antunna*	*'antǝn*
	3 m.	*šunu*	*hm*	*hem(mā)*	*hennōn*	*hum(ū)*	*'ǝmūntū*
	f.	*šina*		*hen(nā)*	*hennēn*	*hunna*	*'ǝmāntū*
Du.	2					*'antumā*	
	3		[*hm*]			*humā*	

13.2. A few general remarks on this table:
a) The first and second persons singular and plural belong to the
same system (*'an-* plus suffixes), while the third person is formed
from elements related to the demonstratives (cf. § 12.32).

13.3. b) The Akkadian series is used for the nominative only,
while the other cases employ considerably different elements related
to the forms of the suffix pronouns (cf. § 13.14):

		Genitive/Accusative	*Dative*
Sg.	1	*yāti*	*yāši(m)*
	2 m.	*kāti/a*	*kāšim*
	f.	*kāti*	*kāši(m)*
	3 m.	*šuāti/u, šāti/u*	*šuāšim, šāšu/i(m)*
	f.	*šu/iāti, šāti*	*šu/iāšim, šāši(m)*
Pl.	1	*niāti*	*niāšim*
	2 m.	*kunūti*	*kunūši(m)*
	f.	*[kināti]*	*[kināši(m)]*
	3 m.	*šunūti*	*šunūši(m)*
	f.	*šināti*	*[šināši(m)]*

13.4. c) Old Assyrian uses the genitive/accusative forms for the dative as well, and for the second person singular, masculine or feminine, it possesses a form of its own, *ku(w)āti*; in later dialects new forms may be observed: for the genitive/accusative, 2 m. pl. *kātun(u)*, 3 m. *šuātunu, šātun(u)*, 3 f. *šātina, šuātina*; and for the dative, 2 m. pl. *kāšun(u)*, 3 m. *šāšun(u)*, 3 f. *šāšina*. In the later dialects there also occur extensive fluctuations between the genitive/accusative and dative forms. For a connexion between the *š* element characteristic of the dative forms and the ending -*iš* of the dative-adverbial case of the noun, cf. § 12.66.

13.5. d) Ugaritic, too, shows variant forms for the genitive/accusative, but they are confined to the third person: the characteristic element in these forms is a suffixed -*t* (*hwt, hyt, hmt*).

13.6. e) The suffixed element -*t* in the third person also occurs in Phoenician (*hmt*), as a variant form in South Arabian demonstratives (cf. § 13.9), and in Ethiopic (*wəʾtū, yəʾtī, ʾəmūntū, ʾəmāntū*), but it is not connected in these languages with any distinction between the cases.

13.7. To pass now to a consideration of individual forms, we may posit a Proto-Semitic *ʾanā(ku)* for the first person singular; the additional element -*k* appears in North-East and North-West Semitic (cf. also *a-nu-ki* in the Tell Amarna glosses, *ʾnk[y]* in both Phoenician and Old Aramaic, *ʾnk* in Moabite; but contrast *ana* which is attested as a secondary form in Old Babylonian). In North-West Semitic there is a distinction in the vowel (-*kī*),

perhaps by analogy with the suffix-pronoun of the same person (*-nī*).
In Egyptian, too, the element *-k* is attested (*ink*). As regards the
quantity of the final vowel in *'anā* as well as in other pronouns,
one should bear in mind the existence of considerable fluctuations
and the difficulty of determining Proto-Semitic vowel-quantity
with any degree of certainty (cf. Brockelmann, GVG, I, pp. 296—
313; Gray, SCL, pp. 61—65).

13.8. For the second person singular we may postulate the
Proto-Semitic forms *'anta*, *'anti* (Kienast's recent reconstruction
offering as Proto-Semitic forms *kā*, *tī* raises several difficulties);
noteworthy are: a) the frequent assimilation of *n* (the form *atta*
of the Tell Amarna glosses confirms the extension of this assimilation to a great part of the North Semitic area; *'nt*, *'nty* in Egyptian
Aramaic and *'ant*, *'antī* in Biblical Aramaic are probably historical
spellings); b) the dropping of unstressed final vowels in the North-
West Semitic area, in accordance with the phonetic laws of that
region (cf. § 10.8)—with the exception of the second person masculine in Hebrew where the final vowel remains (important survivals
are also the Hebrew spelling "'attī" and the Syriac form with *-y*
in the feminine).

13.9. As to the third person singular: a) Akkadian uses for this
pronoun a consonantal element different from that encountered
elsewhere (*š* instead of *h*), and this element is to be found (cf. in
Egyptian: masc. *św*, fem. *śy*) in the South Arabian dialects as
well—with the exception of Sabaean. The South Arabian third-
person pronoun has the forms given in the following table (semantically, South Arabian keeps the original demonstrative values):

	Sabaean	*Minaean*	*Qatabānian*
Sg. 3 m.	*h', hw', hwt*		s^1w, s^1wt
f.	*h', hy', hyt*		s^1yt
Pl. 3 m.	*hmw, hmt*	s^1mt	s^1m, s^1mt
Du.			s^1myt

b) It appears that the series with *h* and that with *š* are both of
Proto-Semitic origin. A reconstruction (supported by the Modern
South Arabian dialect of Mehrī which has a masculine *he* and
a feminine *se*) suggests Proto-Semitic *huwa* for the masculine and
šiya for the feminine; this would explain the position in the various

languages as due to analogy working in opposite directions. But this reconstruction remains highly conjectural, and it is equally possible to envisage the formation of the third person pronouns from either series. c) Some (cf. Gray, SCL, p. 62) prefer Proto-Semitic *hū'a* (*hū'ā* is now found in the Dead Sea Manuscripts), *hī'a*, *šū'a*, *šī'a* to *huwa*, *hiya*, *šuwa*, *šiya*; but it is easier to explain the loss of intervocalic *w* and *y* than their secondary insertion (though even this is possible by assimilation to the preceding vowel). d) The Ethiopic forms *wə'ətū*, *yə'ətī* are conceivably due to the omission of the initial *h*- followed by the process *'uw* > *wu* > *wə* and *'iy* > *yi* > *yə*—and subsequent attachment of final *-tū*, *-tī*.

13.10. For the first person plural we may propose the Proto-Semitic form *naḥnu* (or even *niḥnu*, on the basis of Akkadian, taking the *a* as due to the influence of the following pharyngal). It is improbable that Proto-Semitic had an initial vowel of *a* timbre (*'a-naḥnu* or *'a-niḥnu*); where such a vowel appears, it may owe its origin to analogy with the singular form (*'anā*). As for the variants in the final vowel, this may again be due to analogy with the vowel of the suffix pronoun of the same person—as may be seen (except in Arabic) from the tables (cf. §§ 13.1, 13.14; in Akkadian, alongside the form *nīnu*, there later appears *nīni*).

13.11. For the second person plural we may posit the Proto-Semitic forms *'antumu*, *'antina*: a) the distinctive vowel (*u*, *i*) and consonant (*m*, *n*) of these forms are subject to the effects of analogy (the consonant, in some cases, undergoes gemination); in Akkadian *n* prevails over *m*, in Arabic *u* over *i*, etc.; b) the dropping of final unstressed vowels in the North-West Semitic area corresponds to the phonetic laws of that region (cf. § 10.8), despite some instances in which the retention of the vowel is attested by Masoretic Hebrew for the second as well as the third person plural (*'attẹnā*, *hemmā*, *hennā*). The Dead Sea documents bear witness to a situation when this phenomenon was even more widespread (spellings *'tmh*, *'tnh*).

13.12. As to the third person plural it will be observed that a) for the consonantal element the same holds true as in the case of the third person singular (cf. § 13.9); b) taking into account the arguments adduced with regard to the singular, we may postulate, by way of reconstruction of the Proto-Semitic forms, a series *humu*, *hina* and a parallel one *šumu*, *šina*; c) in very much the same way

as has been shown for the second person plural (cf. preceding
paragraph), analogy affects both the first vowel (u, i) and the following consonant (m, n): again n prevails over m in Akkadian, u over i
in Arabic, etc. (for instances of gemination of the consonant
cf. § 13.11); d) final unstressed vowels are dropped in the North-
West Semitic area, in accordance with the phonetic laws of that
region, save for a few remnants in some Old Aramaic documents
(*hmw*); e) the Ethiopic forms *'əmūntū*, *'əmāntū* may possibly be
explained as due to the disappearance of initial *h-* (cf. the enclitic
forms *'ennōn*, *'ennēn* in Syriac and the Ethiopic singular forms,
§ 13.9 d); the element *-tū* has been added (as in the masculine
singular). Ethiopic makes use also of the variant forms *wə'ətōmū*
(masculine) and *wə'ətōn* (feminine), formed by the attachment of
the suffix pronouns (cf. § 13.14) to the masculine singular base,
thus recalling, in part, the Akkadian developments *šuātunu*,
šātina alongside *šunu*, *šina* (cf. § 13.4).

13.13. For the dual one may assume as Proto-Semitic the Arabic
forms *'antumā*, *humā*. The data available are, of course, extremely
limited.

2. Personal Pronoun Suffixes

13.14. The suffixed personal pronouns in the principal Semitic
languages are as follows:

		Akkadian	*Ugaritic*	*Hebrew*	*Syriac*	*Arabic*	*Ethiopic*
Sg. 1 (noun)		-*ya*, -*i*	(-*y*)	-*ī*		-*ya*, -*ī*	-*ya*
(verb)		-*ni*	-*n*	-*nī*	-*n*	-*nī*	-*nī*
2 m.		-*ka*	-*k*	-*kā*	-*k*	-*ka*	-*ka*
f.		-*ki*	-*k*	-*k*	-*k*	-*ki*	-*kī*
3 m.		-*š(u)*	-*h*	-*hū*, -*ō*	-(*h*)*i*, -*h*	-*hu*	-*hū*, -*ō*
f.		-*š(a)*	-*h*	-(*h*)*ā*, -*āh*	-*h*	-*hā*	-(*h*)*ā*
Pl. 1		-*ni*	-*n*	-*nū*	-*n*	-*nā*	-*na*
2 m.		-*kunu*	-*km*	-*kem*	-*kōn*	-*kum(u)*	-*kəmmū*
f.		-*kina*	-*kn*	-*ken*	-*kēn*	-*kunna*	-*kən*
3 m.		-*šunu*	-*hm*	-(*he*)*m*	-*hōn*	-*hum(u)*	-(*h*)*ōmū*
f.		-*šina*	-*hn*	-(*he*)*n*	-*hēn*	-*hunna*	-(*h*)*ōn*
Du. 1			-*ny*				
2			-*km*			-*kumā*	
3			-*hm*			-*humā*	

13.15. The attachment·of the suffixes may be effected by means of connecting (or glide-) vowels or by way of contraction (for details see the grammars of the various languages). In some languages the consonant n is inserted before the suffixes (cf. Garbini, SNO, p. 98); for the reappearance of Proto-Semitic endings before the suffixes cf. §§ 16.139—42.

13.16. Some general remarks on the above table:

a) The Akkadian series is used for the genitive, while for the accusative and dative the following forms appear (they are, for the most part, very different and correspond closely to those of the independent personal pronoun for the accusative/genitive and dative; cf. § 13.3):

		Accusative	*Dative*
Sg.	1	*-ni*	*-a(m)*, *-ni(m)*
	2 m.	*-ka*	*-ku(m)*
	f.	*-ki*	*-ki(m)*
	3 m.	*-š(u)*	*-šu(m)*
	f.	*-š(i)*	*-ši(m)*
Pl.	1	*-niāti*	*-niāši(m)*
	2 m.	*-kunūti*	*-kunūši(m)*
	f.	*-kināti*	*-kināši(m)*
	3 m.	*-šunūti*	*-šunūši(m)*
	f.	*-šināti*	*-šināši(m)*

13.17. b) Old Assyrian uses for the accusative the forms of the genitive (§ 13.14) and for the dative those of the accusative; in later dialects, the forms of the accusative and dative are no longer kept apart and are used fairly indiscriminately.

13.18. c) Furthermore, Akkadian employs an independent possessive pronoun which is based on the endings of the suffixes; it is infrequent in Old Akkadian and, for want of Semitic parallels, must be considered a secondary development; its principal forms are as follows (Assyrian in brackets):

	Masc. sing.	*Fem. sing.*	*Masc. plur.*	*Fem. plur.*
Sg. 1	*yā'um, yūm*	*yat(t)um/n*	*yā'ūtum, yūtum*	*yāt(t)um/n*
2	*kūm (ku'ā'um)*	*kattum/n*	*kuttun (kuwā'ūtum)*	*kāttun*
3	*šū(m)*	*šattum, šuttun*		
Pl. 1	*ni'ā'um,nūm*	*ni'ātum, nuttum*	*(ni'ā'ūtum), nuttum*	*(ni'ātum)*
2	*kunūm*	*(kunūtum)*		*(kunū'ātum)*
3	*šunūm*	*(šunūtum)*		

13.19. d) At a later period of Akkadian a new type of possessive occurs which is formed by adding the genitive suffixes to *attū* (*attū-ka*, *attū-kunu*, etc.); for the variant forms with final *-n* instead of *-m* (*yattun, yuttun, kattun, kuttun, šuttun*) see § 12.71.

13.20. e) An independent possessive pronoun occurs in some languages which is the result of a combination of the suffix-pronouns with elements of the relative pronoun (cf. §§ 13.34—39), at times connected by the particle *l* "to": thus in post-Biblical Hebrew *še-l* (e.g. *šellī* "mine", literally "which [belongs] to me") and in Syriac *dī-l* (e.g. *dīlan* "ours"). In Ethiopic the independent possessive is formed by adding the suffix-pronoun to *zi'a-* for the masculine singular, *'əntī'a-* for the feminine singular, *'əllī'a-* for the plural (e.g. *zi'aya* "mine" [masc.], *'əntī'aya* "mine" [fem.], *'əllī'aya* "ours").

13.21. f) Ethiopic has also produced independent pronoun forms by adding suffixes to *lalī-*, for the subject, and to *kiyā-*, for the object (*lalīya, lalīka, lalīkī*, etc.; *kiyāya, kiyāka, kiyākī*, etc.). Hebrew has created an independent pronoun for the direct object by using the element *'ōt-* (*'ōtī, 'ōtəkā*, etc.); Arabic employs *'iyyā-* for the same purpose (*'iyyāya, 'iyyāka*, etc.).

13.22. Turning to a consideration of individual forms, we may propose, for the first person singular, a Proto-Semitic form *-ya* or *-ī*. If the original form was *-ya*, then the *-ī* which appears in certain languages is due to the loss of the final short vowel and the subsequent transformation of the semivowel into the homorganic vowel; or, if the original form was *-ī*, the change *-ī > ya* in certain languages is due to analogy with the suffix of the second person singular masculine *-ka*. The predominance of *-ī* in Old Akkadian and in Amorite favours the latter hypothesis. The suffix attached to verbs is preceded by the consonantal element *n*, possibly by

analogy with the suffix of the first person plural. In Syriac the
final -*ī* of the suffix is written but is not pronounced, and the same
is true of the final vowel of the second person singular feminine and
the third person singular masculine (cf. the optional omission of
the final vowel in the suffixes of the Akkadian third person singular).

13.23. For the second person singular we may suggest the Proto-
Semitic forms -*ka*, -*ki*. Reference has already been made (§ 13.7)
to the uncertainty about the quantity of the vowel element of these
suffixes (as well as of the others—except, probably, those of the
third person singular where the vowel appears long). As to the
feminine form, the loss of the final vowel is already encountered in
the form -*k* of Amorite and the Tell Amarna glosses, whereas
Hebrew, on the other hand, has in some cases -*kī* (yet Greek
transcriptions point to instances of -*k* for the masculine: e.g. ωδεχ
for 'ōdəkā, ηναχ for 'ēnēkā).

13.24. For the third person singular one should note: a) Akkadian
forms the suffixes of this person with the consonantal element
š instead of *h*—just as it does with the independent pronoun. The
same occurs (again in consonance with the independent pronoun
forms) in the South Arabian dialects—with the exception of
Sabaean:

		Sabaean	Minaean	Qatabānian
Sg. 3	m.	-*h(w)*	-*s¹(w)*	-*s¹(w)*, -*s¹ww*
	f.	-*h*	-*s¹*	-*s¹*, -*s¹yw*
Pl. 3	m.	-*hm(w)*	-*s¹m*	-*s¹m*
	f.	-*hn*		[-*s¹n*]
Du. 3		-*hmy*	-*s¹mn*	-*s¹my*

b) The same considerations apply to the Proto-Semitic suffix-
pronoun as were formulated with regard to the independent
pronoun (cf. § 13.9): two series can be established, -*hū*, -*hā* (corroborated also by the Amorite documentation) and -*šū*, -*šā* (the
vowel is not invariably long)—unless it be conjectured that -*hū*
was originally the masculine and -*šā* the feminine form and that

the workings of analogy subsequently acted in opposite directions.
c) In Old Aramaic a variant form -*hī* is attested for the masculine.

13.25. For the first person plural we may posit the Proto-Semitic
form -*na* (corroborated by both the Amorite and the Old Aramaic
documentation). The variations in the vowel in North-East and
North-West Semitic (to the Hebrew -*nū* corresponds -*nu* in the
Tell Amarna glosses) must be considered the result of analogy with
the final vowels of the independent pronouns (cf. § 13.1).

13.26. For the second person plural we may suggest Proto-
Semitic -*kumu*, -*kina* (the observations on the independent pronoun
[§ 13.11] are relevant also in this context): a) the vowels (*u*, *i*) and
the consonantal elements (*m*, *n*) are subject to analogy working in
various ways: in Akkadian *n* prevails over *m*, in Arabic *u* over *i*,
etc.; b) final unstressed vowels are dropped in the North-West
Semitic area (cf. § 10.8), yet some cases of retention are attested in
the Dead Sea Manuscripts, for both the second and the third person
plural (*kmh*, *hmh*, *hnh*).

13.27. For the third person plural note the following: a) as regards
the consonantal element, the same observations hold good which
have already been made for the singular suffix and for the independent pronoun (cf. §§ 13.9, 13.24); b) on this basis we may propose
for the Proto-Semitic pronoun the forms -*humu*, -*hina* as well as
-*šumu*, -*šina*, while again referring to the possibility of a Proto-
Semitic masculine form -*humu* and a feminine -*šina*; c) in consonance with the second person plural (cf. § 13.26) and the independent
pronoun (cf. § 13.12), both the first vowel (*u*, *i*) and the following
consonant (*m*, *n*) are subject to the workings of analogy: once more
n prevails over *m* in Akkadian, and *u* over *i* in Arabic, etc.; d) final
unstressed vowels are dropped in the North-West Semitic area
(cf. § 10.8), but at times they are retained, e.g. in the Hebrew of the
Dead Sea documents (cf. § 13.26); e) the Ethiopic forms -(*h*)*ōmu*,
-(*h*)*ōn* (like the -*ō* of the third person singular masculine) might
be explained by way of contraction of the initial *u* of the suffix
with the final *a* of the noun or verb.

13.28. The agreement of Arabic and Ugaritic suggests that the
forms of the dual are Proto-Semitic. The first person dual—found

in Ugaritic alone among the Semitic languages—occurs also in
Egyptian and may thus be regarded as Proto-Semitic.

3. Demonstrative Pronouns

13.29. The principal forms of the "near" demonstrative pronoun
("this") are as follows:

		Akka-dian	Hebrew	Phoen.	Bibl. Aram.	Syriac	Arabic	ESA	Ethiopic
Sg.	m.	$ann\bar{u}$	$z\bar{e}$	$z(')$	$d\partial n\bar{a}$	$h\bar{a}n(\bar{a})$	$(h\bar{a})\underline{d}\bar{a}$	$\underline{d}n$	$z\partial(nt\bar{u})$
	f.	$ann\bar{\imath}tu$	$z\bar{o}t$		$d\bar{a}$	$h\bar{a}d(\bar{e})$	$(h\bar{a})\underline{d}ihi,$ $\underline{d}\bar{\imath}, t\bar{\imath}$	$\underline{d}t$	$z\bar{a}(tt\bar{\imath})$
Pl.	m.	$ann\bar{u}tu$	$'\underline{e}ll\bar{e}$	$'l$	$'\underline{e}l(l\bar{e}), 'ill\bar{e}n$	$h\bar{a}ll\bar{e}n$	$(h\bar{a})'ul\bar{a}('i)$	$'ln/t$	$'\partial ll\bar{u}(nt\bar{u}),$ $'\partial ll\bar{o}nt\bar{u}$ $'\partial ll\bar{a}(nt\bar{u})$
	f.	$ann\bar{a}tu$							
Du.	m.						$(h\bar{a})\underline{d}\bar{a}ni$		
	f.						$(h\bar{a})t\bar{a}ni$		

13.30. Observations on the above table: a) the Akkadian forms
are the result of contraction of more ancient ones: $annium >$
$ann\bar{u}(m)$, $anni\bar{u}tum > ann\bar{u}tu(m)$, $anni\bar{a}tum > ann\bar{a}tu(m)$; b) Old
Babylonian presents, apart from $ann\bar{u}m$, the expanded and declin-
able form $anni/umm\bar{u}m$, while in Neo-Babylonian a new demon-
strative appears: $ag\bar{a}$, fem. $ag\bar{a}tu/i$, m. pl. $agann\bar{u}tu$, f. pl. $agann\bar{e}tu$
and $ag\bar{a}ti$; c) for some Akkadian variant forms with final -n instead
of -m ($ann\bar{u}tun$, $anni\bar{a}tun$, $annimm\bar{u}tun$) cf. § 12.71; d) Ugaritic is
not listed because the forms of its demonstrative pronoun are rare
and doubtful (hn and hnd are probably a type of demonstrative);
the additional languages adduced in the comparative table, Phoenician, Biblical Aramaic, and South Arabian, are mentioned on
account of their special interest; e) Hebrew presents the variant
forms $z\bar{o}$ for the feminine and $'\underline{e}l$ for the plural which correspond to
the Phoenician forms; the indeclinable $z\bar{u}$ is used as a relative (cf.
§ 13.36), and the expanded forms masc. sing. $hall\bar{a}z\bar{e}$, fem. sing.
$hall\underline{e}z\bar{u}$, sing. masc. and fem. $hall\bar{a}z$ are related to the Arabic "far"
demonstratives (cf. § 13.37); f) the plural form indicated for South
Arabian is the Sabaean one, while Minaean has $'hlt$ and Qatabānian
$\underline{d}tn/w$.

13.31. The principal forms of the "far" demonstrative pronoun ("that") are as follows:

	Akkadian	Bibl. Aramaic	Syriac	Arabic	Ethiopic
Sg. m.	ullū	dēk, dikkēn	hāw	dā(li)ka	zəkū
f.	ullītu	dāk, dikkēn	hāy	tī/āka, tilka	'əntəkū, 'əntākti
Pl. m.	ullūtu	'illēk	hānōn	'ulā'ika	'əlləkū
f.	ullātu		hānēn		

13.32. Observations on the above table: a) instead of *ullū*, etc., Assyrian has *ammiu*, fem. *ammītu*, masc. plur. *amm(i)ūtu*, fem. plur. *amm(i)ātu*; b) Ugaritic does not offer any special forms for the "far" demonstrative; c) it is very common in the Semitic languages to use the personal pronoun as a demonstrative—or rather to employ the same pronominal element ("anaphoric" pronoun) for both functions: this occurs in Akkadian, Hebrew, Syriac, and South Arabian.

13.33. It is clear from a comparison of the forms set out in the preceding §§ that they cannot easily be reduced to Proto-Semitic forms. Instead, it will be possible to identify certain formative elements which make their appearance in various languages, either in isolation or combined with each other. The most frequent of those elements is the consonant *ḏ* for the singular (taking into account the phonetic changes which this consonant undergoes in the various languages: § 8.14) to which *'l* corresponds in the plural. The antiquity of the element *ḏ* is demonstrated by its occurrence in Amorite (written "zū") and in Old Aramaic (z'). A component of the "near" demonstrative is *hā* which appears in conjunction with *ḏ* in the Arabic series *hāḏā*, etc., as well as in the Syriac *hāḏ(ē)*, *hāllēn*. In other languages the "near" demonstrative is formed by adding to *ḏ* the consonantal element *n*: thus in the Phoenician dialect of Byblos *zn*, Old Aramaic *znh* (as well as z'), Biblical Aramaic *dənā*, South Arabian *ḏn*, Ethiopic *zəntū*, *zātti* (with regressive assimilation), *'əllōntū* and *'əllāntū* (with the additional element -tū). *n* combines also with *hā* in the Akkadian *anniu*, etc., and in the Syriac *hān(ā)*. According to Greenberg (JAOS 80 [1960], pp. 317 to 321) the element *n* is characteristic of the masculine singular and of the plural, but not of the feminine whose characteristic component is t: the series $n/t/n$ appears to be typical of the deictic element in the Hamito-Semitic area. The "far" demonstrative includes, in the majority of the Semitic languages, the suffixed consonantal element $-k$ (often preceded in Arabic by l); the forms which result from these combinations are generally $ḏk$ in the singular and $'lk$ in the plural.

4. Relative Pronouns

13.34. The relative pronouns are connected in the majority of the Semitic languages with the demonstrative ones, and more particularly with the consonantal element $ḏ$. However, in the North-East and North-West Semitic areas there are certain different forms of the relative which are made up of the element $š$.

13.35. In Akkadian we have the following series for the most ancient period:

Singular	m.:	nom. *šu*, gen. *ši*, acc. *ša*
	f.:	nom. acc. *šāt*, gen. *šāti*
Plural	m.:	*šūt*
	f.:	*šāt*
Dual		*ša*

This series, which can be recognized as being formally connected with the personal/demonstrative pronoun of the third person, is reduced to the single form *ša* from the Old Babylonian period onwards (only in rare cases have *šūt* and *šāt* survived).

13.36. In North-West Semitic, Amorite has *šū* (fem. *šī*), while Ugaritic has two forms: *d* personal and *dt* impersonal. In Hebrew the forms connected with the demonstrative element $ḏ$ (*zū, zē*) are rare; the usual forms are *še-*, *šə-* and *'ăšer* (cf. *ašar* in the Tell Amarna glosses and *'šr* in Moabite, while the occurrence of *ḏṯr* in Ugaritic is disputed); later on *'ăšer* makes room for the shorter form. In Phoenician the use of *z* (Byblos dialect) is also rare, the usual form being *š* or, more frequently, *'š*. In the Aramaic area (in accordance with the phonetic development of the conso-

nant *ḏ*) the most ancient inscriptions show a relative pronoun *zī*
which later becomes *ḏī* and, in Syriac, *ḏə-*.

13.37. Old South Arabian has a masculine sing. *ḏ* (used also for
the plural), a feminine *ḏt*, and a plur. *'lw* (Qatabānian variants:
masc. *ḏw*, *ḏm*, fem. *ḏtm*). Classical Arabic has two series (cf. below,
§ 13.39):

Singular	m.	*ḏū*	*'allaḏī*
	f.	*ḏātu*	*'allatī*
Plural	m.	*ḏawū*, *'ulū*	*'allaḏīna*, *'allā'i*
	f.	*ḏawātu*, *'ulātu*	*'allātī*, *'allā'i*
Dual	m.	*ḏawā*	*'allaḏāni*
	f.	*ḏawātā*	*'allatāni*

In the second series the element *ḏ* is preceded by the article
'al- and the infix *-la-*.

13.38. The Ethiopic relative is in the masculine singular *za*,
feminine singular *'ənta*, common plural *'əlla*.

13.39. The forms of the relative pronouns are used in some
Semitic languages for the expression of the so-called "determinative"
pronouns, conveying the meaning "that of ...", "he of ...", or
simply "of ...": e.g. Akk. *ša ḫuṭari* "he of the stick", i.e. the man
with the stick; *šarru ša māti* "the king of the region"; Ar. *ḏū l-māli*
"he of the money", i.e. the rich man, etc. The Arabic "determinative" *ḏū* is fully declinable (nom. *ḏū*, gen. *ḏī*, acc. *ḏā*) and in this
respect differs from the indeclinable demonstrative *ḏā*.

5. Interrogative and Indefinite Pronouns

13.40. The interrogative pronouns appear to go back to the
Proto-Semitic elements *man* in relation to persons (the form *my*,
peculiar to a large part of North-West Semitic, seems to be secondary from a comparative point of view) and *mā* for things. The
interrogative adjectives have the element *'ay* in common. The forms
assumed in the various languages are as follows:

	"Who ?"	"What ?"	"Which ?"
Akkadian	mannu	mīnu	ayyu
Ugaritic	my	mh	mn(m)
Hebrew	mī	mā	'ē̜-zē̄
Phoenician	my	m	
Biblical Aramaic	man	mā	
Syriac	man	mā(n), mānā	'aynā
Arabic	man	mā	'ayy^{un}
South Arabian	mn		'y
Ethiopic	mannū	mənt	'ay

13.41. Observations on the above table: a) Amorite has *manna* "who ?" and *mā* "what ?"; b) Ugaritic also possesses the element *'ay* but it is generally employed as an indefinite pronoun ("any")—in addition to the element *mn(m)* (cf. the following paragraph); c) Hebrew preserves the element *'ay* in its original form in the interrogative adverb *'ayyē̜* "where ?", while it has numerous interrogative adverbs composed of *'ē-* (*'ēzē* "which ?" and "where ?", *'ēkā* "how ?" etc.); d) the Syriac interrogative adjective *'aynā* has a feminine *'aydā* and a plural *'aylēn* in which the interrogative element is reinforced by a demonstrative one; e) in Arabic *man* is not declinable; *'ayy* has a feminine *'ayyat*, though the masculine form frequently takes its place.

13.42. The interrogative forms are also used in the Semitic languages as indefinite pronouns. The element *mā* may be placed in apposition to nouns (so in Arabic, e.g. *yaum^{an} mā* "on whatever day") or be used as a reinforcing suffix to pronominal forms (so in Akkadian, where the indefinite pronoun is **man-ma > mamma* for persons, **min-ma > mimma* for things, and *ayyumma* as an adjective; the component *ayyum* is declinable: *ayyum-ma, ayyam-ma* etc.). Finally, Akkadian *man-man > mamman* produces an indefinite form by reduplication of the interrogative.

D. The Numeral

1. Cardinals

14.1. The cardinal numerals in the principal Semitic languages are as follows:

	Akkadian	Ugaritic	Hebrew	Syriac	Arabic	Ethiopic
1 m.	ištēn	aḥd	'eḥād	ḥad	'aḥad	'aḥadū
f.	ištiat, ištēt	aḥt	'aḥat	ḥədā	'iḥdā	'aḥattī
2 m.	šina	ṯnm	š(ə)nayim	tərēn	'iṯnāni	kəl'ē(tū)
f.	šitta		š(ə)tayim	tartēn	'iṯnatāni, ṯintāni	kəl'ētī
3 m.	šalāšat		šəlōšā	təlātā	ṯalāṯat	šalastū
f.	šalaš	ṯlṯ	šālōš	təlāt	ṯalāṯ	šalās
4 m.	erbet		'arbā'ā	'arbə'ā	'arba'at	'arbā'tū
f.	erbe, arba'u	arb'(t)	'arba'	'arba'	'arba'	'arba'
5 m.	ḥamšat		ḥămiššā	ḥamšā	ḥamsat	ḥaməstū
f.	ḥamiš	ḫmš	ḥāmēš	hammeš	ḥams	ḥaməs
6 m.	šešet		šiššā	štā', 'eštā	sittat	sədəstū
f.	[šeššə]	ṯṯ	šēš	šet	sitt	səssū
7 m.	sebet		šib'ā	šab'ā	sab'at	sab'atū
f.	sebe	šb'(t)	šeba'	šəba'	sab'	sab'ū
8 m.	[samānīt]		šəmōnā	təmānyā	ṯamāniyat	samānītū
f.	samāne	ṯmn	šəmōnē	təmānē	ṯamānin	samānī
9 m.	tišīt		tiš'ā	teš'ā	tis'at	təs'atū
f.	tiše	tš'	tēša'	təša'	tis'	təs'ū
10 m.	ešeret		'ăšārā	'esrā	'ašarat	'ašartū
f.	ešer	'šr	'eśer	'əsar	'ašr	'ašrū

14.2. Observations on the above table: a) the forms given for Akkadian are those of the absolute state (cf. § 12.79); b) "one" fem. in Ethiopic might possibly be formed by analogy with the feminine personal pronoun *yə'ətī*; c) for the vocalizations of "two" in Hebrew and "six" in Syriac cf. § 10.2; d) regressive dissimilation occurs in Syriac "two" **tənēn > tərēn*; e) Ethiopic "two" is derived from a different root which also appears in Akkadian *kilallā/ūn*, Ugaritic *klåt*, Arabic *kilāni* "both" and Hebrew *kil'ayim*; f) Hebrew "five" is formed on the analogy of "six" (**ḥamšā > ḥămiššā* on the analogy of *šiššā*); g) Syriac "five" is formed on the analogy of "four" (**ḥəmeš > ḥammeš* on the analogy of *'arba'*); h) Akkadian "eight" has initial *s* (*samānū*) instead of *š* which might be expected in consonance with the other languages: analogy with the initial *s* of "seven" (*sebū*) might be the cause; i) the numerals "one" and "two" are adjectives, while the others are substantives; and by a singular peculiarity, which must be regarded as Proto-Semitic, they are used in the gender opposite to that of the noun which follows in the genitive plural (e.g. Ar. *'arba'at^u riǧāl^in* "four men"); this inversion of gender also operates when the numeral appears without an accompanying noun. In Ethiopic the numerals with the ending *t* are more frequently used, while in the Ugaritic cardinals from "two" to "ten" the forms without -*t* may be employed with either gender.

14.3. The numerals from "11" to "19" are normally formed by the juxtaposition of the unit-numbers (with inversion of gender from "13" onwards) and the numeral "10" which appears in some variant forms: Heb. *'āśār*, fem. *'eśrē*; Syr. fem. *'esrē*; Ar. *'ašara*, fem. *'ašrata*. In Arabic, moreover, all these numerals have the fixed ending -*a* also in the unit-numbers. Examples: Hebrew "13" masc. *šəlōšā 'āśar*, fem. *šəlōš 'eśrē*; Syriac "14" masc. *'arbəta'sar*, fem. *'arba'sərē*; Arabic "15" masc. *ḥamsat^a 'ašara*, fem. *ḥams^a 'ašrat^a*. For the other languages the following observations may be made: a) in Ugaritic (see the statement in the preceding paragraph) inversion of gender is not applicable; b) in Akkadian the numerals from "11" to "19" are not attested except the forms *sebēšer* "17" and *samānēšer* "18" (masc.) and *šinšeret* "12", *ḥamiššeret* "15", and *samānēšeret* "18" (fem.); c) in Ethiopic the component "ten" precedes that of the units and is joined to it by *wa-* "and", while the gender of both components is inverted (e.g. "13" masc. *'ašartū wa-šalastū*, fem. *'ašrū wa-šalās*).

14.4. It is generally held (Brockelmann, GVG, I, p. 490) that in Proto-Semitic "20" is expressed by the dual of "10" (**'ašrā >* *'išrā* by vowel dissimilation); that the numbers from "30" to "90" are plurals of those from "3" to "9"; that in Akkadian, South Arabian, and Ethiopic the ending of "20" is analogically extended to the others, whereas in the remaining languages this is not the case:

	Akkadian	Ugaritic	Hebrew	Syriac	Arabic	ESA	Ethiopic
20	*ešrā*	*'šrm*	*'eśrīm*	*'esrīn*	*'išrūna*	*s²ry*	*'əšrā*
30	*šalāšā*	*tltm*	*šəlōšīm*	*təlātīn*	*talātūna*	(*tlty*)	*šalāšā*
etc.							

Although this reconstruction enjoys a considerable degree of probability, it has nevertheless recently been disputed by von Soden (WZKM 57 [1961], pp. 24—28) who holds that the Akkadian, South Arabian, and Ethiopic forms are feminine plurals in the absolute state. As regards Akkadian, it has to be realized that,

owing to the adoption of the Sumerian sexagesimal system, its
numerals from "60" to "90" are not of the same type as those of
the other languages; "60" has the form *šūšu* or *šuššu* which may
be compared with that for "1/6" (cf. § 14.10).

14.5. The numerals "100" and "1000" are clearly derived from
a common origin (with the exception of "1000" in Akkadian
which is connected with a word meaning "people"):

	Akkadian	Ugaritic	Hebrew	Syriac	Arabic	ESA	Ethiopic
100	*me'at*	*mit*	*mē'ā*	*mā*	*mi'at*	*m't(m)*	*mə'ət*
1000	*lim*	*ảlp*	*'elep*	*'alpā*	*'alf*	*'lf(m)*	*'əlf*

(cf. § 14.6)

14.6. Observations on the above table: a) the usual form for
"1000" is related to the noun meaning "ox"; b) Ethiopic *'alf* is
used for "10,000" ("1000" being expressed as *'ašartū mə'ət* = "ten
hundred"); c) for higher figures cf. Ugaritic *rbt*, Heb. *ribbō*, Syr.
rebbō "10,000".

2. Ordinals and Fractions

14.7. The ordinals from "first" to "tenth" are as follows:

	Akkadian	Ugaritic	Hebrew	Syriac	Arabic	Ethiopic
1st	*maḫrū*		*rišōn*	*qadmāyā*	*'awwal*	*qadāmī*
2nd	*šanū*	*ṯn*	*šēnī*	*tenyānā*	*ṯānī*	*kālə'*
3rd	*šalšu*	*ṯlṯ*	*šəlīšī*	*təlītāyā*	*ṯālit*	*šāləs*
4th	*rebū*	*rb'*	*rəbī'ī*	*rəbī'āyā*	*rābi'*	*rābə'*
5th	*ḫamšu*	*ḫmš*	*ḫămīšī*	*ḫəmīšāyā*	*ḫāmis*	*ḫāməs*
6th	*šeššu*	*ṯdṯ*	*šiššī*	*šətītāyā*	*sādis*	*sādəs*
7th	*sebū*	*šb'*	*šəbī'ī*	*šəbī'āyā*	*sābi'*	*sābə'*
8th	*samnu*	*ṯmn*	*šəmīnī*	*təmīnāyā*	*ṯāmin*	*sāmən*
9th	*tišū*		*təši'ī*	*təši'āyā*	*tāsi'*	*tāsə'*
10th	*ešru*		*'ăšīrī*	*'əsīrāyā*	*'āšir*	*'āšər*

14.8. Observations on the above table: a) "1st" is formed on
a number of varying themes (in Akkadian another form is attested,
ištiyū, though this is rare); the Ethiopic and Syriac forms are connected with a Semitic root denoting "precedence". The other ordinals

are adjectives derived from the cardinals on the pattern *qabir* or *qabur* in Akkadian, *qabīr* in Hebrew and Syriac, *qābir* in Arabic and Ethiopic; b) in the Ugaritic documents hitherto discovered, the ordinals "7th" and "8th" are attested in the feminine only; c) in Hebrew, "6th" is formed from "6" (*šiššī*, instead of *šədīšī*) on the analogy of the cardinal *šēš*, *šiššā*; d) in Arabic, "6th" is *sādis* (instead of *sādit*) owing to progressive non-contiguous assimilation, or—possibly—by analogy with *ḫāmis* "5th"; e) in Ethiopic "2nd" is derived from different themes: in addition to *kālə'* we have *kā'əb* and *dāgəm*, but the normal pattern re-appears in the feminine *sānīt* with the meaning "the following day (or night)"; f) in Ethiopic there also exists a parallel series with the ending -*āwī* (*qadamāwī*, *dāgmāwī*, etc.); cf. § 12.23.

14.9. Above "tenth" there occur in Akkadian "11th" *ištenšerū*, "12th" *šinšerū*, "13th" *šalaššerū*, "14th" *erbēšerū*, "20th" *ešrū*, "30th" *šelāšū*. Otherwise the forms of the cardinal numbers are used. In Ugaritic no ordinals beyond "8th" have hitherto been found. In Hebrew and Syriac there are no special forms beyond "10th"; thereafter the cardinal forms are used. In Arabic we have "11th" *ḥādī 'ašar*ᵃ; and for the ordinals from "12th" to "19th" the ordinal is always followed by *'ašar*ᵃ; from "20th" onwards the cardinal forms are used. In Ethiopic 20th to 90th is expressed either by the cardinal or by the addition of the suffix -*āwī* (*'əšrāwī*, *šalāšāwī*, *'arbə'āwī*, etc.).

14.10. Fractions are generally formed on the pattern *qubr*: thus in Arabic *ṯulṯ* "a third", *rub'* "a quarter", etc., in Syriac *tultā*, *rub'ā*, etc., and occasionally in other languages also (Akk. *šudšu* > *šuššu* "a sixth", Heb. *ḥomeš* "a fifth"). Hebrew uses as fractions the feminine forms of the ordinals (*ḥămīšīt* "a fifth", etc.); a similar formation occurs in Akkadian (*rabītu* "a quarter", *sebītu* "a seventh"), while Ugaritic (whose vocalization is, of course, unknown) exhibits feminine endings and a prefix *m*- (*mṯlṯt*, *mrb't*, etc.). In other cases use is made of forms which cannot readily be reduced to common patterns. Ethiopic forms the fractions with the masculine and feminine ordinals followed by *'əd* "hand" (e.g. *rābə'ət 'əd* "a quarter").

14.11. The distributive numerals are usually expressed by a repetition of the cardinals, e.g. Heb. *šənayim šənayim* "two by two", Syr. *šəba' šəba'* "seven by seven" (for the use of the absolute state cf. § 12.79), Eth. *'aḥadū 'aḥadū* "one by one", etc. Akkadian has special forms: for "1" *ištēnā*, for "2" *šinnū*, for "3"—"10" the nominal pattern *quburā'* (*šulušā, rubu'ā*, etc.).

E. The Particles

15.1. Under the term "particles" are subsumed (for the sake of convenience rather than as a linguistically accurate classification) adverbs, prepositions, conjunctions, and interjections. An analysis of the particles often reveals a nominal or pronominal origin, but there remain many cases in which such relationships cannot be established.

1. Adverbs

15.2. In adverbs of nominal origin it is characteristic of Arabic (and to a lesser degree of other languages as well) to use the accusative ending: e.g. Ar. *'abad^{an}* "always", *ǧidd^{an}* "very", *yawm^{an}* "by day"; Akk. *ūmam* "by day"; Eth. *nagha* "in the morning"; etc. With this group are probably to be connected the Hebrew adverbs in *-ām* (*yōmām* "by day", *ḥinnām* "gratis", etc.). The accusative ending also appears without the nunation (or mimation): e.g. Ar. *ṣabāḥa masā'a* "morning and evening"; Akk. *maḥra* "before", *warka* "behind" (already used in Old Babylonian and Old Assyrian). Another characteristic formation, which is encountered in North-West Semitic, involves the feminine ending: Heb. *yəhūdīt* "in Hebrew", *rīšōnā* "at the beginning"; Syr. *ṭābā'īt* "well", etc. Akkadian uses the ending *-iš* for the formation of adverbs (cf. § 12.66) and more rarely *-atta* and *-um* to which correspond adverbial formations in *-u* in other languages (Ar. *qablu* "first", Eth. *tāḥtū* "underneath", etc.: cf. §§ 12.65—66). Finally, a simple adjective or substantive may be used as an adverb (e.g. Heb. *rab* "much", *yaḥad* "together"); and this adjective or substantive appears in the absolute state in those languages which have a distinctive form for it (cf. § 12.79) (e.g. Akk. *ūmakkal* "one day", Syr. *šappīr* "beautifully").

15.3. Apart from the adverbs of demonstrably nominal origin, there are others of some importance which have common roots in Semitic. These include the demonstrative adverb of place Heb. *šam(mā)*, Syr. *tammān*, Ar. *ṯamma* "there"; the interrogative adverb Akk. *ayyānu*, Heb. *'ē, 'ēkā, 'ayin*, Syr. *'aykā*, Ar. *'ayna*,

Eth. *'aytē* "where ?"; the temporal interrogative Akk. *matī*, Heb. *mātay*, Syr. *'emmat*, Ar. *matā* "when ?"; the adverb of existence (affirmative) Ug. *iṯ*, Heb. *yēš*, Syr. *'īt* "there is", and the negative form Ass. *laššu*, Ar. *laysa*, Syr. *layt* "there is not"; the negative adverb Akk. *lā*, Ug. *l*, Heb. *lō*, Syr. *lā* "not" as well as Akk. *ul*, Ug. *ul*, Heb. *'al*.

2. Prepositions

15.4. In some prepositions a nominal origin may be detected: e.g. Heb. *'aḥar* "after" (and as a noun "back"), *'ēṣel* "beside" (and as a noun "side"), *bēn* "between" (and as a noun "interval"), etc.

15.5. The more important prepositions are shown in the following comparative table:

	Akkadian	Ugaritic	Hebrew	Syriac	Arabic	Ethiopic
"in, by"		*b*	*bə*	*bə*	*bi*	*ba*
"to"		*l*	*lə*	*lə*	*li*	*la*
"to"		*l*	*'el*		*'ilā*	
"like"	*kī(ma)*	*k*	*kə(mō)*	*'ak*	*ka*	*kama*
"over"	*eli*	*'l*	*'al*	*'al*	*'alā*	*lā'la*
"from"			*min*	*men*	*min*	*'əmna*
"with"		*'m*	*'im*	*'am*	*ma'a*	
"up to"	*adi*	*'d*	*'ad*	*'adammā*		

15.6. Observations on the above table: blanks indicate either missing forms or forms of different origin (Akk. *ina* "in", *ana* "to", *ištu* "from", *itti* "with" [for this latter cf. also Heb. *'et*]; Ar. *ḥattā* "up to" (but South Arabian *'d[y]*); Eth. *məsla* "with", *'əska* "up to"; etc.).

3. Conjunctions

15.7. The principal conjunctions with common roots are as follows (among the independent forms note especially Akk. *šumma* "if"):

	Akkadian	Ugaritic	Hebrew	Syriac	Arabic	Ethiopic
"and"	*u*	*w*	*wə*	*wə*	*wa*	*wa*
"and, also"		*(ȧ)p*	*'ap*	*'āp*	*fa*	
"or"	*ū*	*u*	*'ō*	*'aw*	*'aw*	*'aw*
"if"		*hm*	*'im*	*'en*	*'in*	*'əmma*
"in order that"	*kīma*	*k*	*kī*		*kay*	*kama*

4. Interjections

15.8. For the interjections various vocalic elements are used:
Akk. *i, e;* Heb. *'ī, 'ō;* Syr. *'ō;* Ar. *'ī, 'ay;* Eth. *'ō.* Another common
interjection is Akk. *ennu/am,* Heb. *hinnē,* Ug. *hn* "behold". Sometimes the imperative is employed as an interjection, without
verbal meaning: e.g. Heb. *lēk* "away!".

F. The Verb

1. Verbal Themes or Stems

16.1. The Semitic verb has a set of themes or stems (cf. the following
paragraphs) in which formal changes correspond to certain semantic
variations and express different aspects of the action connoted by
the root. The semantic connexions may be somewhat fluctuating
and are not always readily identifiable, nor are all the stems attested
over the entire range of the Semitic languages. The linguistic
evidence brought to light during recent years (especially for
North-West Semitic of the second millennium B.C.) reveals a remarkable wealth of forms in the most ancient phase of the Semitic
languages. In the course of time (particularly in the North-Western
region) numerous reductions have occurred—accompanied, at the
same time, by innovations and analogical restorations. For the
paradigm *qbr* cf. § 12.3.

a) Simple Stem

16.2. This stem shows the three radicals in their simple form.
Variations in the vowel pattern relate to a distinction between
action and state. These variations are more clearly marked, as
regards their semantic relevance, in the South-West Semitic area
where, in the suffix-conjugation, the pattern *a-a-a* stands for an
action, *a-i-a* for a transient condition, and *a-u-a* for a lasting condition or state: e.g. Ar. *naẓara* "he looked at", *salima* "he was well",
ḥasuna "he was beautiful". The antiquity of this threefold vocalic
scheme in Arabic is confirmed by some of the oldest manifestations
in North-West Semitic, i.e. Amorite, Ugaritic, and the Tell Amarna
glosses. In the prefix-conjugation the variation in the second vowel
is at least partly paralleled: *u* or *i* corresponding to *a*, and *a* to *i*,
while *u* generally remains: e.g. Ar. *yanẓuru, yaslamu, yaḥsunu.*

In Akkadian the distinction between active and stative verbs is less pronounced as far as vowel variation is concerned, yet it remains generally identifiable. In stative verbs the distinctive vowel *i* predominates in the prefix-conjugations (pres. *ikabbit* "he becomes heavy", pret. *ikbit* "he became heavy"), while *a* is rarer—though ancient and attested in Old Akkadian and Old Babylonian (e.g. *iqrab* "he approached", later *iqrib*). In active verbs *a* is more common in the present tense and *u* in the preterite (e.g. pres. *išakkan* "he puts", pret. *iškun* "he put"); at times, however, *a* is found in the preterite as well (e.g. pres. *ilammad* "he learns", pret. *ilmad* "he learnt"); *i* appears in cases where the action of the verb is regarded as momentary (e.g. *idallip* "he disturbs") as well as in some verbs of motion (e.g. *ittiq* "he passes"); *u* occurs in all cases where the action is intransitive (e.g. *irappud* "he runs"). In the stative, which formally corresponds in Akkadian to the West Semitic suffix-conjugation (cf. § 16.38), active verbs have *i* as their second vowel (e.g. *šakin* "he is placed"), while stative verbs may have *a* or *u* as well, in accordance with the vowel of the corresponding adjective (e.g. *ḫalaq* "he is lost", alongside *ḫaliq*).

16.3. The passive is formed on the vowel pattern *u-i-a* in the suffix-conjugation; it is in full use in Arabic (e.g. *kataba* "he wrote", *kutiba* "it was written") where the prefix-conjugation in the passive has its own vowel scheme as well (e.g. *yaktubu* "he writes", *yuktabu* "it is written"). There is a purely formal coincidence here with the vowel distribution in the derived stem with prefix '-. Apart from Arabic, a passive of the simple stem exists in Ugaritic (where, in the prefix-conjugation, it cannot however be readily distinguished from the passive stem with prefix *n*-; cf. Gordon, UM, p. 65), in the Tell Amarna glosses, and in Hebrew, where in the suffix-conjugation it formally coincides with the stem with doubled second radical (**qubar* > *qubbar*; cf. § 10.8 d) and in the prefix-conjugation with the stem with prefix *h*- (*yoqbar*). It is also possible that there are some traces of this passive in the Aramaic of the Arpad inscriptions and in Biblical Aramaic where the second vowel is lengthened and the form thus coincides with that of the participle (e.g. *kətīb* "it was written" as well as "written"); but these forms may, in fact, be original participles whose functions have been extended by analogy. According to Petráček's recent studies on inner flexion (cf. § 11.3), the internal passive (which is wanting in Akkadian) is to be regarded as a secondary development of West Semitic.

b) Stem with Doubled Second Radical

16.4. This stem, which is attested over the whole Semitic area, seems to have a primarily "factitive" significance, i.e. as a causative in relation to a state or condition: e.g. Akk. *iblut* "he lived", *uballiṭ* "he made to live"; Syr. *ḥəsan* "he was strong", *ḥassen* "he strengthened". To this meaning-aspect must be added the denominative one (e.g. Syr. *kəlīlā* "crown", *kallel* "he crowned") and the intensive aspect (e.g. Ar. *kasara* "he broke", *kassara* "he shattered"; Akk. *ibtuq* "he cut", *ubattiq* "he cut to pieces").

16.5. Arabic possesses in this stem, too, a distinction between active and passive, brought about by a change of vowel pattern— in the same manner as shown in the simple stem: e.g. *qattala* "he massacred", *quttila* "he was massacred"; *yuqattilu* "he massacres", *yuqattalu* "he is massacred". The same passive exists in Hebrew— on the assumption that the Puʿal form (*qubbar*) owes the *a* of its second syllable to analogy with the prefix-conjugation (*yəqubbar*).

c) Stem with Lengthened First Vowel

16.6. This stem seems to have primarily reciprocal significance, i.e. to indicate an action accomplished together with another person: e.g. Ar. *kataba* "he wrote", *kātaba* "he corresponded". At times this stem also indicates an action directed towards an object as well as an attempt to accomplish something (conative): e.g. Ar. *qatala* "he killed", *qātala* "he fought" (= "tried to kill").

16.7. This stem is attested in Arabic and, though less frequently, in Ethiopic; in the latter the correlation between form and semantic value has been largely lost (e.g. *šāqaya* "he tormented", *wāḥaya* "he visited"). Traces of this stem in North-West Semitic are rather dubious (cf. the discussion in Garbini, SNO, pp. 126—34). It may therefore be concluded that this stem is typical of South Semitic.

16.8. Again, Arabic makes use of a variation in vowel pattern to express the distinction between active and passive—on the lines of the vocalization scheme applied to the previous stems, but with the first vowel long as the distinctive mark: e.g. *qābara*, pass. *qūbira; yuqābiru*, pass. *yuqābaru*.

16.9. A variant of the stem with long first vowel is that with a diphthong: this is a development of which there exist very few traces in North Semitic (e.g. Syr. *gawzel* "he set fire to") but more ample ones in Ethiopic (*qōbara*, *qēbara*: cf. Dillmann, EG, pp.146 to 147, § 78) and in Arabic, especially in modern Arabic (e.g. *ǧawraba* "he put on socks") in mainly denominal roots (cf. Brockelmann, GVG, I, pp. 514—15).

d) Stems with Prefixes *š-*, *h-*, *'-*

16.10. The Semitic languages present a series of stems with prefix *š-* or *h-* or *'-*, all sharing a causative connotation: e.g. Ug. *lhm* "to eat", *šlhm* "to cause to eat" = "to feed". The causative may refer to a state or condition, and in such cases it may coincide with the "factitive" of the stem with doubled second radical: the two themes are then used alongside each other without appreciable distinction (e.g. Akk. *kunnušu* and *šuknušu* "to subdue"). Another aspect of the causative is its declarative value (e.g. Heb. *hiṣdīq* "he pronounced just", from the root *ṣdq*, Eth. *'amsala* "he pronounced similar", from the root *msl*). Finally, the causative may have intransitive significance, i.e. in cases where the action remains attached to the subject (e.g. Akk. *šulburu* "to grow old", Heb. *hišmīn* "he grew fat", Ar. *'aqāma* "he remained"). South Semitic uses this stem widely for denominative verbs (Ar. *'aḥsana* "he did well" from *ḥasan* "beautiful", *'afṣaḥa* "he was eloquent" from *faṣīh* "eloquent"; Eth. *'asgala* "he divined" from *sagal* "divination", *'ab'ala* "he feasted" from *ba'āl* "feast").

16.11. Of the three stems, that with prefix *š-* (also found outside Semitic in Egyptian: e.g. *ś.nhn* "to bring up" from a root *nhn* "to be a child") occurs in Akkadian, in Ugaritic, and in the South Arabian dialects (here *s²* > *s¹*) with the exception of Sabaean: e.g. Akk. *ušamqit* "he caused to fall", from *mqt*; Ug. *ašhlk* "I cause to flow" from *hlk*; ESA *s¹ḏb* "he caused to place", from *ḏb*. The same prefix is attested in Aramaic (e.g. Bibl. Aram. *šaklilū* "they completed" from *kll*; Syr. *ša'bed* "he enslaved" from *'bd*); it appears also in Arabic and Ethiopic (as well as in Amorite and, in a few surviving traces, in other North-West Semitic languages) in combination with the infix *-t-* (cf. below, § 16.21).

16.12. The stem with prefix *h-* occurs in Amorite, in the Tell Amarna glosses (alongside the less frequent one with *š-*), in Hebrew, Moabite, Old Aramaic, Sabaean, and in the most ancient phases of Ṯamūdic and Liḥyānite: e.g. Heb. *hiqdīš* "he consecrated" from *qdš*; Bibl. Aram. *hanpēq* "he caused to go out" from *npq*; Sabaean *hḍr'* "he subdued" from *ḍr'*; Liḥ. *hawdaq* "he offered" from *wdq*. A few remnants of this prefix survive in classical Arabic (e.g. *harāqa* alongside *'arāqa* "he poured").

16.13. The stem with prefix *'-* appears in the most recent phase of Aramaic, in pre-Islamic North Arabic, in classical Arabic, and in Ethiopic: e.g. Syr. *'albeš* "he clad" from *lbš*; Liḥ. *'awdaq*, variant of *hawdaq* (cf. preceding paragraph); Ar. *'aqtala* "he caused to kill" from *qtl*; Eth. *'astaya* "he gave to drink" from *sty*. It is possible that this causative pattern might be detected in some disputed cases in Ugaritic (cf. Gordon, UM, p. 68). Developments in Aramaic and Arabic, together with the fact that the prefixes *h-* and *'-* are not found simultaneously in the various languages, suggest the possibility that both go back to one original theme whose prefix *h-* later became *'-*. There is evidence, moreover, of the existence of a fourth variant of the prefix, apparently of secondary origin, in the Phoenician form *yqbr* (suffix-conjugation): e.g. *yqdš* "he dedicated".

16.14. For the causative stem, too, Arabic possesses specific vowel patterns which relate to the distinction between active and passive (the vocalization is the same as in the preceding stems): *'aqbara*, pass. *'uqbira*; *yuqbiru*, pass. *yuqbaru*. The same pattern and meaning are represented by the Hebrew and Biblical Aramaic stem Hophal (*hoqbar*)—again on the assumption that the *a* of the second syllable is due, as it appears to be, to analogy with the prefix-conjugation (*yoqbar*); the *o* of the first syllable has to be explained in terms of § 10.8 e above.

e) Stem with Prefix *n-*

16.15. This stem has passive and reflexive meaning. It is attested over the entire Semitic area (with some traces in Egyptian) with the exception of Aramaic. In Ethiopic it is rare but occurs in some quadriradical verbs. Examples: Akk. *naprusu* "to be separated", root *prs*; Heb. *niš'al* "he was asked", root *š'l*; Ar. *'inqaṭa'a* "he was cut to pieces", root *qṭ'*. In Akkadian this theme adopts in part the vowel distribution of the simple stem (cf. § 16.2 and von Soden, GAG, p. 118); with stative verbs its meaning is predominantly ingressive: e.g. *ibašši* "he is", *ibbašši* "he becomes"; *našā'um* "to carry", *nanšūm* "to shoulder". In Ugaritic this stem is attested but the *n* is almost invariably assimilated to the following consonant (cf. however *nkbd* "honoured", root *kbd*). In Ethiopic—as has been mentioned—this stem appears with some quadriconsonantal verbs, e.g. *'anfar'aṣa* "he jumped"; from the semantic point of view, however, Ethiopic shows a development towards a causative connotation which is, perhaps, connected with the formal identity of the prefixes (Brockelmann, GVG, I, p. 536).

16.16. Arabic again has variations in the vowel scheme, but in the present case the expression of the passive becomes effective only in those instances where this aspect is absent in the normal theme: *'inqabara* and *'unqubira*, *yanqabiru* and *yunqabaru*.

f) Stems with Prefix (or Infix) *t-*

16.17. Of all the stems dealt with above under a to d, additional themes may be formed with the prefix (or infix) *t-*, producing reflexive, passive, and sometimes also reciprocal connotations (for further meaning variants in Akkadian cf. von Soden, GAG, p. 121).

16.18. *t-* is prefixed to the simple stem in the Aramaic languages (e.g. Syr. *'etqṭel* "he was killed", root *qṭl*) and in Ethiopic (e.g. *ta'asra* "he was bound", root *'sr*); it changes place with the first radical, and is thus infixed, in the other languages in which it is attested: in Akkadian (e.g. *mitḫuru* "to meet", root *mḫr*), in Amorite (cf. the proper name *Yabtaḫarna*), in Ugaritic (eg. *yrtḫṣ* "he washes himself", root *rḫṣ*), in Phoenician (e.g. *thtpk* "she is being overthrown", root *hpk*), in Moabite (e.g. *'lthm* "I am fighting", root *lhm*), and in Arabic (e.g. *'iqtatala* "he fought", root *qtl*).

16.19. In the stem with doubled second radical the metathesis of *t-* with the first radical takes place in Akkadian only: e.g. *uštallamū* "they are being kept safe", root *šlm*. In Hebrew and in Biblical Aramaic the initial *t* takes a further prefix *h-* in the suffix-conjugation, possibly by analogy with the causative with prefix *h-*: Heb. *hitqaddẹš* "he sanctified himself", root *qdš*; Bibl. Aram. *hitnaddabū* "they made a voluntary offering", root *ndb*. Examples in other languages: Syr. *'ethassan* "he was fortified", Ar. *takassara* "he was shattered", Eth. *taqaddasa* "he was sanctified". A notable phenomenon of Hebrew and Aramaic is the metathesis of the prefix *t-* before a dental or a palato-alveolar fricative (cf. § 9.22). Noteworthy in Akkadian is the Neo-Assyrian formation with reduplication of infixed *-ta-*: e.g. *uktataṣṣar* "he will be equipped".

16.20. The prefix *t-* produces a new stem in Arabic and Ethiopic when joined to the theme with first vowel lengthened: e.g. Ar. *taqātalū* "they fought together", root *qtl*; Eth. *tamāsalū* "they resembled each other", root *msl*.

16.21. The stem with prefix *š-* brings about the metathesis (cf. § 9.22) of this prefix with *t-*. The theme is common in Akkadian where it presents two types which differ in the forms of the present (*uštaqbar* and *uštaqabbar*—for *ušt-* > *ult-* cf. § 8.32); the type *uštaqbar* has the function of a passive of the *š-* stem (e.g. *uštalpat* "it will be destroyed", root *lpt*), while the type *uštaqabbar* has various and not yet fully explored connotations, including that of a causative of the simple theme with *t-* (e.g. *šutamḫuru* "to cause [numbers] to correspond with one another", root *mḫr*) and that of an inner passive of stative verbs (e.g. *šutamruṣu* "to endeavour", root *mrṣ*). This stem also exists in Arabic (e.g. *'istaqtala* "he exposed himself to death", root *qtl*) and in Ethiopic (e.g. *'astamḥara* "he showed himself merciful", root *mḥr*). It is also attested, though rarely and with certain doubts and reservations, in North-West Semitic (e.g. Ug. *tštḥwy* "she prostrates herself", Heb. *hištaḥăwā* "he prostrated himself", Syr. *'eštawdī* "he promised ‚confessed"; and already in Amorite proper names of the type *Šatašnī-'Il, Yištašnī-'Il*).

16.22. In the stem with prefix *'-* the combination with *t-* produces a special theme in Aramaic: e.g. Syr. *'ettrīm* "he was raised", root *rwm* (with assimilation *t'* > *tt*).

16.23. For all these stems (except the last which is attested in Aramaic only) Arabic has the usual variations in vowel pattern, but the effective expression of the passive is contingent on a formal and semantic contrast, i.e. it is realized only when the passive meaning is wanting in the ordinary form of the stem: *'iqtabara* and *'uqtubira*, *yaqtabiru* and *yuqtabaru*; *taqabbara* and *tuqubbira*, *yataqabbaru* and *yutaqabbaru*; *taqābara* and *tuqūbira*, *yataqābaru* and *yutaqābaru*; *'istaqbara* and *'ustuqbira*, *yastaqbiru* and *yustaqbaru*.

g) Other Stems

16.24. In addition to the basic stems set forth above, certain secondary and rarer types occur in the various languages. One such case is the theme classified as No. IX in Arabic, with a perfect of the type *'iqbarra* which is used for verbs indicating colours, physical defects, etc.: e.g. *'iṣfarra* "he was yellow", root *ṣfr*. A variant of theme IX is stem XI: *'iqbārra*. In the other Semitic languages, some forms corresponding to the stem with repeated third radical occur in Ethiopic (e.g. *bardada* "he covered with stones", *galbaba* "he wrapped"), in Syriac (e.g. *'abbed* "he enslaved") and perhaps in Akkadian (e.g. *utnennu* "to pray"—cf. Kienast's recent studies). There also exist a few cases where the first radical re-appears after the second (e.g. Ar. *ṭarṭaba* "he called [camels]", Syr. *qarqeš* "he shook"). Repetition of the second radical is a common feature in the modern Ethiopian languages, generally with iterative or intensive meaning (e.g. Amh. *sabābara* "he smashed", Tigriña *qatātala* "he slaughtered").

16.25. The extension of originally biradical roots gives rise in West Semitic, both Northern and Southern, to quadriliteral themes of the type *qabqab*, etc.: e.g. Heb. *gilgel* "he rolled", Syr. *balbel* "he confused", Ar. *zalzala* "he shook", Eth. *badbada* "he devastated".

16.26. It appears to be a characteristic tendency of Akkadian and Ethiopic to form further stems by a combination of those listed above. In Akkadian we have a series of additional forms with the infix *-tan-*, possessing iterative meaning, inserted in the simple theme (pres. *iqtanabbar*), in that with doubled second radical (pres. *uqtanabbar*), in that with prefix *š-* (pres. *uštanaqbar*), and in that with prefix *n-* (pres. *ittanaqbar*). An Old Aramaic form evidently due to Assyrian influence is *htn'bw*, a Hittanaphal of *y'b*(?), which appears in isolation in the inscription of Bar Rakib. Another

stem typical of Akkadian is that resulting from the combination
of the prefix *š*- and the doubling of the second radical (pres.
ušqabbar): this is a poetical form used for either of the two themes
which coalesce in it. As for Ethiopic, it forms a stem with doubled
second radical and one with lengthened first vowel from the theme
with prefix '- and from that with the (already compound) prefix *st*-;
the entire system in Ethiopic looks as follows:

I. 1. *qabara*	I. 2. *qabbara*	I. 3. *qābara*
II. 1. *'aqbara*	II. 2. *'aqabbara*	II. 3. *'aqābara*
III. 1. *taqab(a)ra*	III. 2. *taqabbara*	III. 3. *taqābara*
IV. 1. *'astaqbara*	IV. 2. *'astaqabbara*	IV. 3. *'astaqābara*

Finally, the combination of more than one stem is widely attested
in the modern Arabic and Ethiopian languages (cf. Brockelmann,
GVG, I, pp. 540—43).

h) Verbs with Four and Five Radicals

16.27. In all Semitic languages we encounter, to a greater or
lesser extent, a number of verbs with four radicals; in Ethiopic
there are also a few with five radicals. As there are virtually no
common Semitic roots among these verbs, we must consider them
innovations in the various languages. All verbs in this category
possess only a fraction of the stems and forms of the triradical
verb. The following principal types are attested:

a) In Akkadian alone we find verbs of the type with prefix *š*-:
šuqammumu "to be dead-silent", *šuparruru* "to expand", *šukēnu*
"to prostrate oneself". Their morphological structure is irregular;
there are no derived stems—apart from the *t*- stem.

b) In Akkadian and Ethiopic we find a group of verbs belonging
to the *n*- stem. The Akkadian verbs in this category all exhibit
either *l* or *r* as their second radical (e.g. *nabalkutu* "to pass over",
naparqudu "to lie on one's back"). The *n*- stem takes the place of
the simple stem, while the *š*- stem serves as causative; both of them
form iterative *tan*- stems (e.g. *ibbalakkat* "he passes", iterative
ittanablakkat; causative *ušbalakkat*, iterative *uštanablakkat*). The
Ethiopic verbs of this type do not form a causative, and a passive
with *t*- prefix occurs only rarely. Examples: *'anṣabraqa* "it shone",

'anzāhlala "he languished" (with "weak" second radical), 'anṣafṣafa "it dripped" (with reduplication).

c) Related to b are Arabic roots with *n* infix after the 2nd radical (e.g. 'ibranšaqa "he flourished") or with doubled 4th radical (e.g. 'išmaḥarra "he was very high").

d) Reduplicated roots (e.g. Ugaritic mǵmǵ "to mix", Hebrew gilgel "he rolled"); geminated roots (e.g. Syriac 'abded "he enslaved", Ugaritic ṣḥrr "to burn"); denominative verbs (e.g. Arabic basmala "he said bismillāhi"); original triradicals with added 2nd (mostly *l*, *r*, *n*) or 4th radical (e.g. Arabic ḥalbasa "he enticed"—cf. ḥalaba); verbs developed from causative stems (e.g. Syriac šaklel "he completed"—cf. Akkadian šuklulu). These verbs form reflexive-passive *t*- stems as well as inner passives in Arabic, Hebrew, and Old Aramaic, while 'a- causatives and causative-reflexive 'asta- stems are limited to Ethiopic (e.g. 'adangaṣa "he confused", 'astasanā'awa "he pacified").

e) Ethiopic verbs of five radicals are formed from triradicals by the repetition of the last two radicals (e.g. 'aḥmalmala "it became green", 'arsāḥsəḥa "he sullied").

2. The "Tenses"

16.28. The "tense" system presents one of the most complicated and disputed problems of Semitic linguistics. In the West Semitic area, Arabic and most of the other languages exhibit, according to the traditional approach, two conjugations which are usually called "tenses". But this nomenclature must be considered improper, as different temporal concepts converge in each of these two conjugations; it would be more appropriate to speak of "aspects". One of these conjugations uses prefixes (type yaqburu: the third person masculine singular is cited in accordance with accepted practice) and generally indicates an incomplete action which corresponds, according to circumstances, to our future, present, or imperfect. (The prefixes, which are the distinctive element of this conjugation, are in some instances supplemented by suffixes having the function of contrast and identification of the various persons.) The other conjugation employs suffixes (type qabara: qabarat, qabarta, etc.) and generally indicates a completed action which

corresponds, according to circumstances, to our past tenses. The
two conjugations are usually called "imperfect" and "perfect",
respectively, in the etymological sense of these terms.

16.29. East Semitic (Akkadian) presents a system of several
conjugations: one with prefixes for incomplete action (type *iqabbar*),
called "present"; another, also with prefixes, has a different vowel
and syllable distribution (inner morphemes) and connotes completed
action (type *iqbur*), called "preterite"; and a third one with suffixes
(type *qabir*), called "stative". This last type represents in essence
the conjugation of a noun and may constitute a verbal adjective
(e.g. *damiq* "he is good", *balṭāku* "I am alive") as well as a substantive (e.g. *zikarāku* "I am a man", from *zikaru* "man"). Finally,
there is the recent tendency (von Soden, GAG, pp. 104—105, and
before him Landsberger and other scholars) to detect in Akkadian
the existence of a fourth conjugation with infix *-ta-* (type *iqtabar*),
called "perfect", which expresses an action complete in itself but
still persisting in its effects (or subsequent to another completed
action). This conjugation must be regarded as an Akkadian
innovation.

16.30. Traditional Semitic grammar was inclined to consider the
Arabic situation as original and that in Akkadian as secondary.
More detailed study of the Semitic languages as well as Hamito-
Semitic comparisons have shown, however, that the position is
more complex: in several instances in West Semitic, both Northern
and Southern, we have discovered elements of a distinction between
two prefix-conjugations, and these findings have been corroborated
by evidence furnished by Hamitic languages, in particular by
Libyco-Berber. In Ugaritic the existence of two differentiated
conjugations on the consonantal pattern *yqbr* might be suggested
by the fact that the same pattern appears to indicate both completed
and incomplete action, while the *qbr* conjugation has notable points
of contact with the Akkadian stative (Goetze). In the Tell Amarna
glosses three conjugations have been identified: one of the *yiqbur*
type for completed action, one of the *yiqab(b)ar* type for incomplete
action, and a third form *qaba/i/ur* for completed action (corresponding to the stative?). In Hebrew the conjugation of the *yiqbor*
type is employed not only for incomplete but also for completed
action—as is shown particularly by the use of the conversive *w*.

Moreover, one cannot exclude the existence of forms of the type
yiqabbar (Meyer, Rössler), and, in fact, forms like *yəqabber*, usually
held to belong to the stem with doubled second radical, may
instead reflect a *yiqabbar* conjugation of the simple theme (Landsberger). In Ethiopic the conjugations *yəqabbər* and *yəqbər* (intrans.
yəqbar), which now relate to the distinction between indicative
and subjunctive, may originally have possessed a "tense" connotation not very different from the type of semantic contrast
observed in Akkadian. In addition Ethiopic has a suffix conjugation, the so-called "gerund", which is formed on the pattern
qabīr (cf. § 16.70) with pronominal suffixes—rather like the Akkadian stative. In Arabic, on the other hand, we are unable to pene-
trate to a stage preceding the considerable measure of systematization to which the language has been exposed. We have also insufficient data for Amorite where, formally at least, we encounter
the opposition *qabar*: *yaqbur*, yet we are not in a position to form
any reliable judgement as to the semantic significance of this
opposition. Finally, Hamitic languages present two distinct
prefix-conjugations, a "preterite" and a "present" (or "habitual"
form or "continuative") which reveal definite points of similarity
with the Akkadian verb: compare Akkadian *iprus* and *iparras*
with Libyan *ifres* and *ifarres* (Rössler).

16.31. These considerations have brought about a crisis in the
conventional conception of the primary character of the Arabic
system and have stimulated vigorous scholarly discussion (Brockelmann, Cohen, Driver, Fleisch, Klingenheben, Kurylowicz, Meyer,
Rössler, Rundgren, von Soden, Thacker, and others). Without
entering into the details of this debate, which is still unresolved
(cf. the bibliography), it now seems safe to say that the Arabic
"tense" system represents the result of a long process of evolution.
Proto-Semitic possessed almost certainly a nominal suffix-conjugation (surviving in the Akkadian stative and Ethiopic "gerund")
which in West Semitic has evolved into a verbal conjugation—yet
without differentiation of mood, which might well be a pointer
to its origin outside the verbal system; it is likely to have been the
function of this suffix-conjugation to record a state or condition
and to describe it as having been accomplished. As for the prefix-
conjugations, some scholars maintain that only one of them is

to be attributed to Proto-Semitic (Cohen). It might have had
the function of indicating action in contrast to state or condition—
without distinguishing between completed and incomplete action.
This latter distinction would have been realized only subsequently
in the historical development of individual Semitic languages—and
in a number of different ways. In West Semitic the prefix-conjugation appears to have been set apart for the designation of an
incomplete action in opposition to the suffix-conjugation which
developed into the expression of completed action. In East Semitic
(Akkadian) the prefix-conjugation might have continued in use for
both completed and incomplete action but subsequently evolving
into two types by means of vocalic and syllabic reconstitution
(*iqabbar* arises secondarily alongside *iqbur* by a functional re-
assignment of the intensive ?—thus Rundgren). The two different
aspects of action reside in the contrast between these two forms
which remain opposed, as a group, to the suffix-conjugation which
is retained for the designation of a state or condition. To postulate the existence of only one prefix-conjugation in Proto-
Semitic is considered by some scholars an inadequate solution—nor does its indeterminate character as regards tense
commend itself to them. This problem cannot be separated from
that of the moods (cf. §§ 16.32—36), because some have detected
in the West Semitic "jussive" *yaqbur* a development of the Akkadian preterite *iqbur*; conversely, the Akkadian subjunctive or
"relative" mood (*iqburu*) has recently been regarded as the ancestor
of the West Semitic prefix-conjugation *yaqburu* (Kienast). Mention
has already been made of the hypothesis claiming a secondary
origin of the Akkadian form *iqabbar* by means of a redesignation
of the stem with geminated second radical, but the view has also
been advanced that *iqabbar* was dropped or restricted in use in
West Semitic on account of its formal identity with the imperfect
of the geminated stem. A somewhat singular position in the reconstruction of the Semitic "tense" system is at present held by von
Soden who posits three prefix-conjugations: a preterite *yaqbur*,
a "momentary aspect" *yaqburu* and a durative present *yaqabbar*.

3. The Moods

16.32. A full range of moods in the "imperfect tense" (as regards
the "perfect" cf. the observations in the preceding paragraph)

is attested in Arabic, where the moods are being expressed by
means of differences in the endings: indicative *yaqbur-u*, subjunctive *yaqbur-a*, jussive *yaqbur*, energic *yaqbur-an(na)*. Whether
this range of moods could be attributed to Proto-Semitic, was rather difficult to determine when Brockelmann wrote on this
question (GVG, I, p. 554). Nowadays remarkable corroboration
of this modal variety has been furnished by Ugaritic which places
itself alongside Arabic with the same set of endings—recognizable
by the vocalisation of ' (though the severely defective spelling
leaves the distinction between the two forms of the energic in
doubt; some reservations have also been expressed as regards the
Ugaritic subjunctive in -*a*: cf. Garbini, SNO, p. 144). In other West
Semitic languages (as will be shown in the following paragraphs)
some remnants of moods have been discerned which agree wholly
or in part with the evidence furnished by Arabic and Ugaritic. As
will be seen in § 16.34, the North-West Semitic documentation
suggests a semantic development of the subjunctive into a cohortative; the differences vis-à-vis East-Semitic remain considerable.

16.33. In Akkadian the modal ·system shows a remarkable
divergence from West-Semitic. In the first place, the moods are
expressed not only in the imperfect but in all the "tenses". Secondly,
the endings differ from those in the other languages: the indicative
has none, and the subjunctive or "relative" mood (whose functions
are different from those of the subjunctive elsewhere: cf. von
Soden, GAG, p. 108) has -*u* (Assyrian -*ūni*); the other mood attested
is a so-called ventive in -*am*. It should be noted, however, that in
a group of Old Akkadian texts the suffix of the subjunctive appears
as -*a* (Gelb, OA, pp. 170—71) which would tally with the Arabic
and Ugaritic ending (but B. Kienast, in Or 29 [1960], pp. 152—53,
thinks that the supposed subjunctive in -*a* is, in fact, a ventive
without mimation).

16.34. In West Semitic, modal differentiation is limited to the
imperfect. In North-West Semitic (leaving aside Ugaritic—see
§ 16.32) Amorite presents *yaqbur* and *yaqburu*, but a modal distinction cannot be determined; in the Tell Amarna glosses we encounter
a volitive in -*a* and an energic in -*na*. The Hebrew documentation
is less relevant because the shedding of final vowels includes the
modal morphemes. In addition to the indicative there remains

a jussive which is characterized (but not in all cases) by vowel reduction: e.g. imperfect *yāqūm* "he rises", jussive (*way-*)*yāqom*. There also exists an energic or cohortative in -*ā*, used chiefly in the first person (e.g. *'eqṭəlā* "let me kill"). In the Dead Sea texts the forms with ending -*ā* are used for the simple indicative as well. The element *n* appears before suffixes, although it does not seem to carry energic value (e.g. *yiqqāḥennū* "he takes him"); it cannot, therefore, be identified with certainty as the same morpheme. In the consonantal spelling of Phoenician the distinction between indicative and subjunctive is expressed in the third person plural by the presence of -*n* in the indicative and its absence in the subjunctive. Modal differentiation may be said to have been entirely discarded in Syriac; but in more ancient Aramaic dialects, i.e. in Egyptian and Biblical Aramaic, we find—as in Phoenician—a distinction between indicative and jussive based on the presence or absence of -*n* in the third person plural; later on, the forms with -*n* predominate. The element *n*, which appears before suffixes and is attested in the late phases of Aramaic (except for a solitary instance in the Zkr inscription), seems unlikely to possess energic connotation (cf. Hebrew above).

16.35. In South-West Semitic the position of classical Arabic has already been dealt with. That of South Arabian and of pre-classical Arabic is probably similar, but the absence of vocalization allows only the identification of the energic morpheme -*n*. Ethiopic distinguishes two moods, the indicative and the subjunctive, by means of thematic variants: indicative *yəqabbər*, subjunctive *yəqbər*, subj. of intransitive verbs *yəqbar* (cf. § 16.30 for a comparison of the Ethiopic forms with the Akkadian prefix-conjugations).

16.36. Finally, all the Semitic languages have an imperative which, in the simple theme, has the vowel pattern characteristic of that stem (cf. § 16.2). The form of the imperative generally corresponds to that of the prefix-conjugation (short form) without its prefixes; any departure from this rule is due to the appearance of prosthesis or anaptyxis as a consequence of consonantal clusters in initial position (cf. §§ 9.14—17): e.g. Akk. prefix-conj. *iqbur*, imperative *qubur*, Heb. prefix-conj. *yiqbor*, imperative *qəbor* (but prefix-conj. *yikbad*, imperative *kəbad*), Eth. prefix-conj. (subjunctive) *yəqbər*, imperative *qəbər*, etc. In some North-West

Semitic languages (Ugaritic, Tell Amarna glosses, Hebrew) we also
find an imperative (masculine singular) with the further ending -*ā*
which is probably the cohortative element previously referred to
(§ 16.34).

4. Inflexion

a) Simple Stem: Suffix-Conjugation

16.37. Semitic verbal inflexion is effected by means of personal
prefixes and suffixes, probably of pronominal origin (as shown
by their external form). The suffix-conjugation of the simple
stem is inflected in the principal Semitic languages as shown
in table I. The following paragraphs offer some general observations
on this table:

I. Simple Stem: Suffix-Conjugation

		Akkadian	*Uga-* *ritic*	*Hebrew*	*Syriac*	*Arabic* (act.)	(pass.)	*Ethiopic*
Sing.	3 m.	qabir	qbr	qābar	qəbar	qabara	qubira	qabara
	f.	qabrat	qbrt	qābərā	qebrat	qabarat	etc.	qabarat
	2 m.	qabrāta	qbrt	qābartā	qəbart	qabarta		qabarka
	f.	qabrāti	qbrt	qābart	qəbart	qabarti		qabarkī
	1	qabrāku	qbrt	qābartī	qebret	qabartu		qabarkū
Pl.	3 m.	qabrū	qbr	qābərū	qəbar(ūn)	qabarū		qabarū
	f.	qabrā	qbr	qābərū	qəbar(ēn)	qabarna		qabarā
	2 m.	qabrātunu	qbrtm	qəbartem	qəbartōn	qabartum(ū)		qabarkəmmū
	f.	qabrātina	qbrtn	qəbarten	qəbartēn	qabartunna		qabarkən
	1	qabrānu		qābarnū	qəbarn(an)	qabarnā		qabarna
Du.	3 m.	(qabrā)	qbr			qabarā		
	f.	(qabirtā)	qbrt			qabaratā		
	2		qbrtm			qabartumā		
	1		qbrny					

16.38. a) The Akkadian stative (if account is taken of the connecting vowel -*ā*-, which characterizes its second and first persons,
and of the consistent suppression of the second vowel) corresponds
in its endings to the West Semitic perfect (see however below
apropos of each individual person). There are some noteworthy
Assyrian variants: *qabrāti* for *qabrāta* (which occurs also in Old
Babylonian) and *qabrāni* for *qabrānu*.

16.39. b) North-West Semitic of the first millennium has carried out consistently the characteristic changes connected with the incidence of stress (cf. §§ 10.8, 10.10). This has entailed, for Hebrew, the shedding of final short vowels (*qābar*), the lengthening of short vowels in pretonic open syllables (same example), the reduction to *ə* of short vowels in open unstressed syllables (*qābərā, qəbartem*); for Syriac, the apocope of both short and long final vowels, though the latter remain part of the graphic pattern (third plural masculine: *qəbar*, written *qbrw*; in verbs with "weak" third radical the pronunciation conforms to the spelling: e.g. *rəmaw* "they threw", *hədiw* "they rejoiced"), the reduction to *ə* or shedding of short vowels in open unstressed syllables (*qəbar, qebrat*), the change *a > e* in closed syllables (*qebrat*).

16.40. c) The personal endings do not vary in accordance with the internal vowel patterns (*qabara, qabira, qabura, qubira* are inflected with the same endings and are not, therefore, listed separately in the table).

16.41. d) The length of the final vowels, except for the third person where it is well established (and perhaps for the second and first persons dual), cannot be fixed with certainty for Proto-Semitic (this was also the case for the pronouns—cf. § 13.7); it will not, therefore, be indicated (traces of an originally long vocalization can be detected in some forms before pronominal suffixes: cf. §§ 16.137—42).

16.42. In the following, Proto-Semitic forms will be posited for each individual person (and later, in the same manner, for the other conjugations and stems). It is, however, well to insist from the outset on the hypothetical character of these reconstructions which are intended (and ought to be used) as working aids only. In many cases the reconstructions are subject to ambiguities and doubts; in others the developments which have been postulated may have been quite different. Finally, the proposed explanations often resolve the problems of only some of the Semitic languages.

16.43. While recalling the normal variations of vowel pattern (§§ 16.2—3) and bearing in mind the claims of the Akkadian stative (§ 16.31), we may propose, for the third person singular, the Proto-Semitic forms *qabar(a)* (masculine) and *qabarat* (feminine).

They appear as such in Arabic and in Ethiopic (as well as in Ugaritic and in the Tell Amarna glosses: e.g. *abadat* "she perished"). In Hebrew the final *-a* of the masculine reappears as a connecting vowel before pronominal suffixes (e.g. *qəbāranī*, with first person singular suffix); the *-ā* of the feminine seems to be formed on the analogy of the feminine morpheme of the noun, but the original ending *-at* reappears before pronominal suffixes (e.g. *qəbāratnī*, with first person singular suffix). Similarly, the ending *-t* of the feminine, which is otherwise dropped, is attested before pronominal suffixes in the consonantal spelling of Phoenician (e.g. *pꜥltn* "she made me", as against *pꜥl* "she made").

16.44. For the second person we may propose the Proto-Semitic forms *qabarta* (masculine) and *qabarti* (feminine) which appear as such in Arabic (probably also in Ugaritic). For the other languages (cf. §§ 16.38—41) note: a) in Hebrew, the Greek and Latin transcriptions almost invariably testify to a masculine suffix *-t*, so that the Masoretes appear to have adopted an archaic form, while for the feminine the Biblical *kətīb* reflects the older form with suffix *-tī*; b) in Ethiopic, the consonant of the suffix has become *k*, almost certainly by analogy with the first person singular; a similar process has taken place in the Neo-Assyrian variant forms *qabrāka* and *qabrāki*.

16.45. For the first person singular we may postulate a Proto-Semitic form *qabarku* which appears as such in Ethiopic (for the length of the final vowel cf. § 16.41) and, so far as the flexional suffix is concerned, in Akkadian (it should be recalled that the independent personal pronoun of the first person shows the consonantal element *k* as against *t* of the second person, cf. § 13.1). For the other languages (cf. §§ 16.38—41) note: a) the operation of analogy with the second person singular whereby, in North-West Semitic and in Arabic, the consonant of the ending becomes *t*; b) the phenomenon peculiar to Hebrew (though already attested in Amorite and the Tell Amarna glosses) where the vowel of the ending becomes *ī*, probably by analogy with the possessive suffix *-ī*.

16.46. For the third person plural we may propose the Proto-Semitic forms *qabarū* (masculine) and *qabarā* (feminine) which appear as such in Ethiopic (and probably also in Ugaritic). The

feminine ending -*ā* occurs also in Biblical, Targūmic, and Talmūdic
Aramaic. For the other languages (cf. §§ 16.38—41) note: a) in
Hebrew, as indeed already in the Tell Amarna glosses and later in
Nabataean, the feminine undergoes analogical adaptation to the
masculine; b) in Syriac, the supplementary suffixes -*ūn*, -*ēn* are
perhaps due to analogy with the personal pronouns '*attōn*, '*attēn*
and the suffixes -*hōn*, -*hēn* (the analogy is not perfect; in the prefix-
conjugation the feminine -*ān* departs from the analogy); c) in
Arabic, the feminine ending -*na* is probably due to analogy with
the corresponding ending of the prefix-conjugation.

16.47. For the second person plural we may posit the Proto-
Semitic forms *qabartumu* (masculine) and *qabartin(n)a* (feminine)
which seem to occur as such in Ugaritic. For the other languages
(cf. §§ 16.38—41) note: a) the Hebrew change $i > e$ in the feminine; the analogical formation (so far as the vowel is concerned)
of the masculine; and the stabilization of the original final vowel
attested in the Dead Sea documents by the *mater lectionis h* (cf.
similarly for the personal pronouns § 13.26); b) the Syriac vowel
changes $u > ō$ and $i > e$ (cf. § 10.10); and the formation of the
masculine on the analogy of the final consonant of the feminine
(a process begun in Egyptian Aramaic, which presents both *qbrtm*
and *qbrtn*, and completed in Biblical Aramaic, where we find
qəbartūn in the masculine and *qəbartēn* in the feminine); c) in
Ethiopic the change of the consonantal element of the suffix
into *k* by analogy with the corresponding person in the sing. (in
Akkadian we encounter the Neo-Assyrian variant form *qabrākunu*);
the merging of the short vowels *u, i* in *ə* (cf. § 8.96); and the shedding
of the final vowel in the feminine which reappears however before
pronominal suffixes (e.g. *qatalkənnāhū* "you killed him", with
the third person singular suffix).

16.48. For the first person plural we may propose the Proto-
Semitic form *qabarna* which appears as such in Arabic and in
Ethiopic. For the other languages (cf. §§ 16.38—41) note: a) in
Akkadian and Hebrew the final vowel is changed to *u*, probably
by analogy with the independent and suffixed personal pronouns
(Akk. *nīnu*, Heb. *naḥnū* and suffix-*nū*); b) in Syriac the subsidiary
ending -*an* is probably due to analogy with the ending -*an* of the
independent personal pronoun([*'ena*]*ḥnan*).

16.49. For the third person dual we suggest the Proto-Semitic forms *qabarā* (masculine) and *qabaratā* (feminine) which appear as such in Arabic (and probably also in Ugaritic). Of the other languages, Akkadian shows third person dual forms which are however used only in the Old Akkadian, Old Assyrian and Old Babylonian periods. In Akkadian the dual may occasionally be used also for three subjects (von Soden, GAG, p. 186).

16.50. For the second person dual we may propose the Proto-Semitic form *qabartumā* which appears as such in Arabic (and probably also in Ugaritic).

16.51. The first person dual is attested in Ugaritic only, and it has been doubted (Wagner) that such a form existed in Proto-Semitic. Hamito-Semitic comparisons, i.e. the presence in Old Egyptian of the first person dual ending *-ny* (coinciding with the Ugaritic morpheme) may possibly favour the assumption of such a form in Proto-Semitic. As regards its vocalization, we may perhaps propose a Proto-Semitic form *qabarnayā*.

b) Simple Stem: Prefix-Conjugation

16.52. The prefix-conjugation of the simple stem is inflected in the principal Semitic languages as shown in table II. The following paragraphs offer some general observations on this table:

16.53. a) The two prefix-conjugations of Akkadian ("present" and "preterite") and of Ethiopic (indicative and subjunctive) differ from each other formally and semantically, and their genetic connexion is not accepted by all scholars (cf. §§ 16.30, 16.35). The prefixes and suffixes attached to the two conjugations are, however, formally identical; they also agree with those of West Semitic generally—subject only to the observations in the following paragraphs. The Ethiopic subjunctive has two distinct patterns: transitive *yəqbər*, intransitive *yəqbar*.

16.54. b) North-West Semitic has put into effect, from the first millennium B.C., all the changes consequent upon the incidence of the stress-accent (cf. §§ 10.8, 10.10); this has entailed, for Hebrew, the shedding of final short vowels (**yaqburu > yiqbor*), the transition *u > o* of stressed short vowels (same example), the change *a > i* in closed unstressed syllables (same example;

II. Simple Stem: Prefix-Conjugation

	Akkadian (present)	Akkadian (preterite)	Ugaritic	Hebrew	Syriac	Arabic (active)	Arabic (passive)	Ethiopic (indicative)	Ethiopic (subjunctive) [transitive]
Sing. 3 m.	iqabbar	iqbur	yqbr	yiqbor	neqbor	yaqburu	yuqbaru	yeqabber	yeqber
f.	(taqabbar)	(taqbur)	tqbr	tiqbor	teqbor	taqburu	etc.	taqabber	teqber
2 m.	taqabbar	taqbur	tqbr	tiqbor	teqbor	taqburu		taqabber	teqber
f.	taqabbarī	taqburī	tqbrn	tiqborī	teqborīn	taqburīna		taqabrī	teqberī
1	aqabbar	aqbur	ảqbr	ʾeqbor	ʾeqbor	ʾaqburu		ʾaqabber	ʾeqber
Pl. 3 m.	iqabbarū	iqburū	y/tqbrū	yiqborū	neqborūn	yaqburūna		yeqabbrū	yeqberū
f.	iqabbarā	iqburā	tqbr(n)	tiqbornā	neqborān	yaqburna		yeqabbrā	yeqberā
2 m.	taqabbarā	taqburā	tqbrn	tiqborū	teqborūn	taqburūna		taqabrū	teqberū
f.	taqabbarā	taqburā	tqbrn	tiqbornā	teqborān	taqburna		taqabrā	teqberā
1	niqabbar	niqbur	nqbr	niqbor	neqbor	naqburu		neqabber	neqber
Du. 3 m.	(iqabbarā)	(iqburā)	y/tqbrn			yaqburāni			
f.	(iqabbarā)	(iqburā)	y/tqbrn			taqburāni			
2			tqbrn			taqburāni			

some scholars, however, regard the vowel *i* of the prefix as primary, alongside *a*, and as peculiar in origin to stative verbs), the reduction to *ə* of short vowels in open unstressed syllables (*yiqbərū*). In Syriac the same changes are operative—save for the process *a > e* which takes place in closed unstressed syllables (*neqbor*).

16.55. c) The variation of vowel pattern reflecting transitive or intransitive status (cf. § 16.2) has no effect on the form of the prefixes or suffixes, while the alteration of the vowel pattern in the passive (cf. § 16.3) brings about a change in the vowel of the prefix (*yu-* instead of *ya-*) which remains constant throughout the inflexion.

16.56. d) The differentiation of moods (cf. §§ 16.32—36) causes the addition of *-u* in the Akkadian subjunctive (Assyrian *-ūni*) for forms ending in a consonant, and the addition of *-am* in the ventive for forms ending in a consonant, of *-m* for those ending in *-i*, and of *-nim* for the others. In Arabic (and probably in Ugaritic) the subjunctive substitutes *-a* for the final vowel and drops the afformative *-na* or *-ni* when preceded by a vowel; the jussive drops the final vowel and *-na*, *-ni* when preceded by a vowel; the energic substitutes *-an* or *-anna* for the final vowel (*-ānni* in the dual and in the feminine plural) and drops *-na*, *-ni* when preceded by a vowel. These are the principles of modal distinctions; for details the reader is referred to the paradigms in the grammars of the various languages.

16.57. e) For the Akkadian "perfect" with infix *-ta-*, a type of conjugation which has to be regarded as an innovation confined to Akkadian (§ 16.29), the reader is referred to the paradigms in von Soden's GAG, both for the simple and the derived stems.

16.58. In the following survey we have to leave out of account the special thematic patterns of Akkadian and of Ethiopic, but we shall allow for the variations of vowel distribution dealt with in §§ 16.2—3. Turning to the individual forms we may propose, for the third person singular, Proto-Semitic *yaqburu* (masculine) and *taqburu* (feminine) which appear as such in Arabic (and probably also in Ugaritic). For the other languages (cf. §§ 16.53—56) note: a) in Akkadian the prefix has evolved: **ya- > *yi > i-* (cf. § 8.63); the same applies, of course, to the third person plural; b) in Syriac (third person sing and plural) the prefix *n-*, instead of *y-*, is characteristic; it is an innovation of East Aramaic (Old Aramaic and West Aramaic retain *y-*); c) *l-*, which occurs in Talmūdic Aramaic and occasionally in Mandaean as well as in Biblical Aramaic *leḥĕwē* "he is", may be considered a remnant of precative *l-* (cf. Brockelmann, GVG, I, p. 565).

16.59. For the second person singular we may propose Proto-Semitic forms *taqburu* (masculine) and *taqburī(na)* (feminine) which appear as such in Arabic (and probably also in Ugaritic). For the other languages (cf. §§ 16.53—56) note the omission of *-u* even in Akkadian and Ethiopic. This explanation rests on the assumption of a single conjugation *yaqburu* in Semitic; if, however, a distinction were to be made between the conjugation-patterns *yaqburu* and *yaqbur* (thus von Soden: cf. § 16.31) a different picture would emerge.

16.60. For the first person singular we may posit a Proto-Semitic form *'aqburu* which appears as such in Arabic (and probably also in Ugaritic). For the other languages (cf. §§ 16.53—56) note the shedding of *-u* even in Akkadian and Ethiopic. The concluding observations in the preceding paragraph are relevant also in the present context.

16.61. For the third person plural we may postulate Proto-Semitic forms *yaqburū(na)* (masculine) and *yaqburā/na* (feminine). Taking into account the general considerations set forth in §§ 16.53—56, these postulates agree broadly with the forms in Akkadian, Syriac (for the prefix *n-* cf. § 16.58), Arabic, and Ethiopic. For the other languages note: a) in Ugaritic, in Hebrew, and in the only Palmyrene occurrence the consonantal prefix is *t-* instead of *y-* in the feminine (in Ugaritic and the Tell Amarna glosses it may be *t-* in the masculine as well), by analogy with the second person plural and the third singular feminine; b) in the Hebrew of the Dead Sea texts the ending *-ūn* instead of *-ū* has been attested, probably owing to Aramaic influence; c) in Syriac the feminine ending *-ān* has been adapted, in part, to conform with the masc. *-ūn*.

16.62. For the second person plural we may propose the Proto-Semitic forms *taqburū(na)* (masculine) and *taqburā/na* (feminine) which are broadly reflected in Arabic and Ethiopic (and probably also in Ugaritic). For the other languages (cf. §§ 16.53—56) note: a) in Akkadian the feminine ending -*ā* takes the place of the masculine ending -*ū*; b) in Syriac the feminine ending -*ān* has again been adapted in part to tally with the masculine -*ūn*.

16.63. For the first person plural we would posit a Proto-Semitic form *naqburu* which appears as such in Arabic (and probably also in Ugaritic). For the other languages (cf. §§ 16.53—56) note the Akkadian prefix *ni-* which may be the result of analogy with the prefix *i-* of the third person.

16.64. For the third person dual we may propose a Proto-Semitic form *yaqburā(ni)*—in which case the Arabic feminine with prefix *t-* and the fluctuating use of *y-/t-* in Ugaritic are to be attributed to analogy with the second person dual; or else a Proto-Semitic feminine *taqburā(ni)* might be suggested—in which case the Akkadian feminine with prefix *i-* would be due to analogy with the masculine.

16.65. For the second person dual Arabic and Ugaritic postulate a Proto-Semitic form *taqburā(ni)*.

c) Simple Stem: Imperative

16.66. The imperative of the simple stem is inflected in the principal Semitic languages as shown in table III.

III. Simple Stem: Imperative

		Akkadian	Ugaritic	Hebrew	Syriac	Arabic	Ethiopic
Sing. 2	m.	qubur	qbr	qəbor	qəbor	'uqbur	qəbər
	f.	qubrī	qbr	qibrī	qəbor	'uqburī	qəb(ə)rī
Pl. 2	m.	qubrā	qbr	qibrū	qəbor(ūn)	'uqburū	qəb(ə)rū
	f.	qubrā	qbr	qəbornā	qəbor(ēn)	'uqburna	qəb(ə)rā
Du. 2						'uqburā	

Taking into consideration the merging of short *u*, *i* into *ə* in Ethiopic (cf. § 8.96), we may propose the Proto-Semitic endings (cf. § 16.36):

	Singular	Plural	Dual
2 m.	—	-*ū*	} -*ā*
f.	-*ī*	-*ā*/*na*	

16.67. Note: a) in Akkadian the feminine ending -$\bar{a}$ takes the place of the masculine ending -$\bar{u}$; b) the Syriac auxiliary endings -$\bar{u}n$, -$\bar{e}n$ might possibly be the result of analogy with the suffix-conjugation (the element -n occurs already in the masculine plural of the imperative in the Arpad inscriptions).

d) Simple Stem: Nominal Forms

16.68. The active participle of the simple stem (table IV) goes back to a Proto-Semitic form *qābir* which appears as such in Akkadian, Amorite, Ethiopic, and Arabic (and probably also in Ugaritic). In Hebrew we have *qōbēr*, owing to the changes $\bar{a} > \bar{o}$ (cf. § 8.83) and $i > \bar{e}$ (cf. § 10.8c). Syriac has *qāber* as a result of the change $i > e$ (cf. § 10.10d). The Ethiopic pattern *qābər* (for $i > ə$ cf. § 8.96) can no longer be formed at will, but it is still used for some substantives and adjectives (e.g. *wārəs* "heir", *ṣādəq* "just"), while another participial form (or *nomen agentis*?) assumes the theme *qabāri*.

IV. Simple Stem: Participle

	Akkadian	Ugaritic	Hebrew	Syriac	Arabic	Ethiopic
Active	qābiru	qbr	qōbēr	qāber	qābir	(qabāri, qābər)
Passive			qābūr	qəbir	maqbūr	qəbūr

16.69. The passive participle of the simple stem exhibits the widely used nominal patterns *qabir* and *qabūr*. Both coexist in Amorite and occur, though rarely, in Akkadian (von Soden, GAG, p. 60) where the function of the passive participle is normally assumed by the verbal adjective. Hebrew *qābūr* seems to presuppose an original *qabur*, while Syriac *qəbir* is to be referred back to *qabir* (already the most ancient Aramaic inscriptions present the consonantal spelling *qbyr*); and Ethiopic *qəbūr* may possibly derive from an original *qabūr*. Arabic adds the prefix *m-* (*maqbūr*), probably by analogy with the participial forms of the derived stems, and the Nabataean *mqbwr* is almost certainly the result of Arabic influence. However, *qabir* and *qabūr* are also used in Arabic: e.g. *nasīǧ* "fabric" (= "woven"), *naḥir* "slaughtered", *rasūl* "envoy" (= "sent"), etc.

16.70. The verbal noun or infinitive has a variety of forms in the simple stem; they generally merge with the wide range of nominal patterns. Among these is the common theme *qabār* which occurs in Akkadian (*qabāru*), in Hebrew (*qābōr*, with the change *ā* > *ō*—cf. § 8.83), and sporadically elsewhere. The "construct" infinitive of Hebrew may be the phonetic result of a different theme (**qubur* > *qəbor*). While the most ancient Aramaic inscriptions exhibit the radical consonants only, Egyptian Aramaic has the prefix *m-* which recurs in Biblical Aramaic (*miqbar*) and later in Syriac (*meqbar*). Syriac also makes extensive use of *qabār* (e.g. *'əbādā* "action", *qərābā* "battle") which in the Modern Aramaic dialects appears as the regular form of the infinitive. In Ethiopic the forms *qabīr* and *qabīrōt* predominate, but *qəbrat*, *məqbar*, etc., also exist (and may belong to an older phase of the language). For the Ethiopic "gerund", cf. §§ 16.30—31.

e) Derived Stems: Suffix-Conjugation

16.71. In the other stems the inflexional suffixes and prefixes remain unaffected and, for that reason, will not be dealt with in the following; nor will the variations of vowel pattern connected with the passive. The ensuing analysis will, therefore, be directed towards a comparison of the stems in the various languages and a conjectural reconstruction of common forms (the basis, as usual, will be the third person singular masculine; cf. table V). It will be seen that the Akkadian stative differs in vowel pattern from the West Semitic suffix-conjugation and will therefore be left aside for our present purposes. The following comparative treatment refers therefore to the West Semitic area where certain common themes can be detected. In East Semitic some important divergent features persist, but this does not imply that they are secondary (cf. §§ 16.31 and 16.43).

16.72. For the stem with doubled second radical we would propose the common form *qabbara* which appears as such in Arabic and in Ethiopic (and probably also in Ugaritic). In Hebrew we have *qibbar* or *qibbẹr*: the change *a* > *i* in the first vowel conforms to the requirements of § 10.8e, while the change *a* > *ẹ* in the second vowel may be due to analogy with the vowel of the imperfect (*yəqabbẹr*). In Syriac *qabber* the change *a* > *e* in the second vowel might be accounted for in the same way as in Hebrew (imperfect *nəqabber*).

V. Derived Stems

a) Stem with Doubled Second Radical

	Akkadian	Ugaritic	Hebrew (active)	(passive)	Syriac (active)	(passive)	Arabic (active)	(passive)	Ethiopic
Suff.-Conj.	qubbur	qbr	qibba/er	qubbar	qabber		qabbara	qubbira	qabbara
Pref.-Conj.	{uqabbar / uqabbir}	yqbr	yəqabber	yəqubbar	nəqabber		yuqabbiru	yuqabbaru	{yəqēbber / yəqabber}
Imperative	qubbir	qbr	qabber		qabber		qabbir		qabber
Participle	muqabbiru	mqbr	məqabbēr	məqubbār	məqabber	məqabbar	muqabbir	muqabbar	(maqabber)
Infinitive	qubburu		qabbōr (cstr. qabber)	qubbōr (cstr. qubbar)	məqabbārū		taqbīr		qabbərō(t)

b) Stem with Lengthened First Vowel

	Arabic (active)	(passive)	Ethiopic
Suff.-Conj.	qābara	qūbira	qābara
Pref.-Conj.	yuqābiru	yuqābaru	yəqābər
Imperative	qābir		qābər
Participle	muqābir	muqābar	(maqābər)
Infinitive	qibār		qābərō(t)

c) Stem with Prefix š-

	Akkadian	Ugaritic
Suff.-Conj.	šuqbur	šqbr
Pref.-Conj.	ušaqbar / ušaqbir	yšqbr
Imperative	šuqbir	šqbr
Participle	mušaqbiru	mšqbr
Infinitive	šuqburu	

d) Stems with Prefix h-, '-

	Hebrew (active)	Hebrew (passive)	Syriac ('active)	Syriac (passive)	Arabic (active)	Arabic (passive)	Ethiopic
Suff.-Conj.	hiqbîr	hoqbar	'aqber		'aqbara	'uqbira	'aqbara
Pref.-Conj.	yaqbîr	yoqbar	naqber		yuqbiru	yuqbaru	yāqabar / yāqbar
Imperative	haqbēr		'aqber		'aqbir		'aqber
Participle	maqbîr	moqbār	maqber	maqbar	muqbir	muqbar	(maqbar)
Infinitive	haqbēr (estr. haqbîr)	hoqbēr	maqbārū		'iqbār		'aqbərō(t)

e) Stem with Prefix n-

	Akkadian	Ugaritic	Hebrew	Arabic (active)	Arabic (passive)	Ethiopic
Suff.-Conj.	naqbur		niqbar	'inqabara	'unqubira	taqabra
Pref.-Conj.	iqqabbar / iqqabir	yqbr	yiqqāḇēr	yanqabiru	yunqabaru	yətqabar
Imperative	naqbir		hiqqāḇēr	'inqabir		taqabar
Participle	muqqabru		niqbār	munqabir	munqabar	
Infinitive	naqburu		hiqqāḇōr, niqḇōr (ostr. hiqqāḇēr)	'inqibār		taqab(ə)rō(t)

f) Simple Stem with t-

	Akkadian	Ugaritic	Syriac	Arabic (active)	Arabic (passive)
Suff.-Conj.	qitbur		'etqəber	'iqtabara	'uqtubira
Pref.-Conj.	iqtabbar / iqtabar	yqtbr	netqəber	yaqtabiru	yuqtabaru
Imperative	qitbar	iqtbr	'etqabr	'iqtabir	
Participle	muqtabru		metqəber	muqtabir	muqtabar
Infinitive	qitburu		metqəbārū	'iqtibār	

g) Stem with Doubled Second Radical with t-

	Akkadian	Hebrew	Syriac	Arabic (active)	Arabic (passive)	Ethiopic
Suff.-Conj.	uqtabbar	hitqabba/er	'etqabbar	taqabbara	tuqubbira	taqabbara
Pref.-Conj.	uqtabbir	yitqabber	netqabbar	yataqabbaru	yutaqabbaru	yətqēbbar / yətqabbar
Imperative	qutabbir	hitqabber	'etqabbar	taqabbar		taqabbar
Participle	muqtabbiru	mitqabber	metqabbar	mutaqabbir	mutaqabbar	
Infinitive	qutabburu	hitqabber	metqabbārū	taqabbur		taqabbarō(t)

h) Stem with Lengthened First Vowel with t-

	Arabic (active)	Arabic (passive)	Ethiopic
Suff.-Conj.	taqābara	tuqūbira	taqābara
Pref.-Conj.	yataqābara	yutaqābaru	yətqābar
Imperative	taqābar		taqābar
Participle	mutaqābir	mutaqābar	
Infinitive	taqābur		taqāberō(t)

i) Stem with Prefix *š-* with *t-*

	Akkadian	Arabic (active)	Arabic (passive)	Ethiopic
Suff.-Conj.	*šutaqbur*	*'istaqbara*	*'ustuqbira*	*'astaqbara*
Pref.-Conj.	{ *uštaqbar, uštaqabbar* / *uštaqbir* }	*yastaqbiru*	*yustaqbaru*	{ *yāstaqabar* / *yāstaqber* }
Imperative	*šutaqbir*	*'istaqbir*		*'astaqber*
Participle	*muštaqbiru*	*mustaqbir*	*mustaqbar*	
Infinitive	*šutaqburu*	*'istiqbār*		*'astaqberō(t)*

j) Stem with Prefix *h-*, *'-* with *t-*

	Syriac
Suff.-Conj.	*'ettaqbar*
Pref.-Conj.	*nettaqbar*
Imperative	*'ettaqbar*
Participle	*mettaqbar*
Infinitive	*mettaqbārū*

16.73. For the stem with first vowel lengthened we may propose the common form *qābara* which appears as such in the languages in which this stem is attested (Arabic and Ethiopic).

16.74. For the stems with prefix *š-*, *h-*, *'-* we may posit the common forms *šaqbara*, *haqbara*, *'aqbara* with which the Arabic and Ethiopic documentation conforms (and thus probably also in Ugaritic). In Hebrew we have *hiqbīr*: the change $a > i$ in the first vowel is a result of the rule stated in § 10.8e, while the transition $a > ī$ in the second vowel may be due to analogy with the vowel of the imperfect *yaqbīr* (cf. § 16.83). In Syriac *'aqber* the change $a > e$ in the second vowel might be accounted for in the same way as in Hebrew (imperfect *naqber*).

16.75. For the stem with prefix *n-* we may tentatively suggest, by analogy with the forms in the preceding paragraph, the common element *naqbara*, but no language actually exhibits this form. In Hebrew we have *niqbar*, with the customary change $a > i$ (cf. § 10.8e); Arabic has *'inqabara*, with prosthetic *'i-* and a syllabic distribution which may have been influenced by the imperfect *yanqabiru*.

16.76. For the simple stem with *t-* we may perhaps propose, by analogy with the forms in the preceding paragraphs, a common element *taqbara* of which, however, the only possible relic might be seen in the Ethiopic *tanšə'a* "he rose" alongside *tanaš'a* "he was raised up". Apart from such a remnant the form *taqbara* has been driven out by analogical formations: in Ethiopic we have *taqabra*, probably by analogy with the simple stative *qabra*, as well as *taqabara*. Syriac has *'etqəber*, perhaps on the pattern of the imperfect *netqəber*. Elsewhere we encounter metathesis between the *t* and the first radical of the verb (cf. § 16.18): thus, in addition to Akkadian, the Arabic *'iqtabara*, with prosthetic *'i*; the thematic pattern might again be the result of analogy with the imperfect *yaqtabiru*.

16.77. For the stem with *t-* and doubled second radical we postulate the common form *taqabbara* which appears as such in Arabic and in Ethiopic. In Hebrew we have *hitqabbar* or *hitqabbẹr*: the prefix *h-* may result from analogy with the Hiphil, and the form as a whole seems to follow the pattern of the imperfect (*yitqabbẹr*).

Syriac *'etqabbar* is probably again influenced by the imperfect *netqabbar*.

16.78. For the stem with *t-* and first vowel lengthened we may take as a basis the form *taqābara* which appears as such in Arabic and in Ethiopic. It was probably a general South Semitic feature, but the purely consonantal South Arabian script does not allow us to arrive at firm conclusions.

16.79. For the stem with prefix *š-* and *t-* we may take as a basis the form *'astaqbara*—attested as such in Ethiopic. Arabic *'istaqbara* is formed with prosthetic *'i-* on the analogy of the stem with prefix *n-* and the simple stem with *t-* (cf. §§ 16.75—76).

16.80. The stem with prefix *'-* and *t-* is found in Aramaic only: Syriac *'ettaqbar* is formed by the assimilation *t'* > *tt* (cf. § 16.22) and on the analogy of the imperfect (*nettaqbar*).

f) Derived Stems: Prefix-Conjugation

16.81. For the stem with doubled second radical we may propose a Proto-Semitic form *yuqabbir(u)* which appears as such in Arabic; Amorite and Ugaritic, however, have *a* instead of *u* in the prefix (*yaqabbir*). In the Akkadian preterite *uqabbir* the initial *y* has been dropped (cf. § 8.63). In Hebrew *yəqabbẹr* we see reduction to *ə* of the prefix-vowel in the open unstressed syllable as well as the change *i* > *ẹ* of the short stressed vowel (cf. § 10.8g, c). In Syriac we find *nəqabber*, with reduction to *ə* of the prefix-vowel in the unstressed open syllable and the change *i* > *e* in the closed syllable (cf. § 10.10c, d). The Ethiopic subjunctive *yəqabbər* presents the merging of Proto-Semitic *u, i* in *ə* (cf. § 8.96).

16.82. For the stem with first vowel lengthened we may take as a basis the form *yuqābir(u)*, attested in South Semitic only; it appears as such in Arabic, while the Ethiopic *yəqābər* again shows the common transition of *u, i* into *ə* (cf. § 8.96).

16.83. For the stems with prefix *š-, h-, '-* we may posit the Proto-Semitic forms *yušaqbir(u)*, *yuhaqbir(u)*, *yu'aqbir(u)*. The first seems to be represented by Ugaritic *yšqbr*, though the vowel of the prefix is different (*yašaqbir*), and by the Akkadian preterite *ušaqbir* where the initial *y-* has been dropped (cf. § 8.63). In

Hebrew we have $*yə'aqbir > *yaqbir > yaqbīr$ (the change $i > ī$ in the stressed syllable, instead of $i > ẹ̄$ [cf. § 10.8c], might conceivably be the result of analogy with the imperfect of verbs with medial w/y [$yāqīm$]). Syriac has $*nə'aqbir > *naqbir > naqber$, with the change $i > e$ in the closed syllable (cf. § 10.10d). The Arabic development is $*yu'aqbiru > yuqbiru$. The Ethiopic subjunctive shows $*yə'aqbər$ (for u, $i > ə$ cf. § 8.96) $> yāqbər$.

16.84. For the stem with prefix n- we may postulate a Proto-Semitic form $yanqabir(u)$ which appears as such in Arabic (but cf. Amorite $yinqabir$). The Akkadian preterite $iqqabir$ embodies the change $ya- > i-$ (cf. § 8.63) and assimilation of n to the first radical. Ugaritic $yqbr$, too, appears to show assimilation of n to the first radical. In Hebrew $yiqqabẹr$ we observe the change $a > i$ in the initial closed unstressed syllable (cf. § 10.8e), assimilation of n to the first radical, and the development $i > ẹ$ in the stressed vowel of the final syllable (cf. § 10.8c).

16.85. For the simple stem with t- we may propose a Proto-Semitic form $yatqabi/ar(u)$. Akkadian has $iqtabar$ in the preterite, with the change $ya- > i-$ (cf. § 8.63) and metathesis between t and the first radical. Ugaritic $yqtbr$ shows metathesis and a different vowel in the prefix ($yiqtabir$). Syriac $netqəber$ exhibits the usual reduction to $ə$ of the short vowel in the unstressed open syllable (cf. § 10.10c) and the change $a > e$ ($i > e$) of the two short vowels in closed syllables (cf. § 10.10d). In Arabic $yaqtabiru$ metathesis takes place. Ethiopic has $yətqabar$: the prefix $yə-$ is probably due to analogy with the other preformatives of derived stems.

16.86. For the stem with t- and doubled second radical we may postulate the Proto-Semitic form $yat(a)qabbi/ar(u)$ with which the Arabic $yataqabbaru$ agrees. In the Akkadian preterite we have $uqtabbir$, with initial $u-$ by analogy with other derived stems, and metathesis between t and the first radical (cf. § 16.19). Hebrew $yitqabbẹr$ shows the change $a > i$ in the initial closed unstressed syllable (cf. § 10.8e) and the change $i > ẹ$ of the short stressed vowel in the final syllable (cf. § 10.8c). Syriac $netqabbar$ has the customary transition $a > e$ in the initial closed syllable (cf. § 10.10d). In the Ethiopic subjunctive $yətqabbar$ the prefix $yə-$ is probably the result of analogy with the other derived stems.

16.87. For the stem with *t-* and lengthened first vowel we may take as a basis the form *yat(a)qābar(u)* which is attested in South Semitic only: Arabic *yataqābaru* corresponds to this form, while in Ethiopic *yətqābar* the prefix *yə-* is formed as in the other derived stems.

16.88. For the stem with prefix *š-* and *t-* we may posit a Proto-Semitic *yaštaqbiru* to which the Arabic form corresponds—apart from the normal change *š > s* (cf. however Amorite *yištaqbir*). In the Akkadian preterite *uštaqbir* the initial *u-* is the result of analogy with the other derived stems. The Ethiopic prefix-conj. *yāstaqbər* reveals the transition $a > ā$ in the initial syllable by analogy with the stem with prefix '- as well as the change $i > ə$ in the final syllable (cf. § 8.96).

16.89. The stem with prefix '- and *t-* occurs in Aramaic only: derived from a conjectural *ya'taqbar(u)* is the Syriac *nettaqbar*, with the change $a > e$ in the initial closed syllable (cf. § 10.10d) and the assimilation of '.

g) Derived Stems: Imperative

16.90. In West Semitic, both Northern and Southern, the forms of the imperative in the derived stems generally correspond to those of the imperfect without its prefixes: any departure from this rule (which will be examined presently) is almost invariably due to the appearance of prosthetic vowels (cf. §§ 9.14—15). In East Semitic some Assyrian variant forms (*qabbir* for *qubbir* in the stem with doubled second radical, *šaqbir* for *šuqbir* in the stem with prefix *š-*) suggest a situation that was originally similar, i.e. correspondence with the forms of the preterite without its prefixes. The Akkadian development is, however, of some complexity, and the reader is referred to the paradigms; the following treatment is confined to variant formations in West Semitic.

16.91. In the stems with prefix *h-*, '- Hebrew *haqbẹr* shows the evolution **yuhaqbiru > *yəhaqbẹr* (§ 10.8) to *haqbẹr*. Arabic *'aqbir* represents **yu'aqbir* (§ 16.83) to *'aqbir*.

16.92. In the stem with prefix *n-* Hebrew prefixes prosthetic *hi-*, and Arabic prosthetic *'i-* (cf. § 9.15).

16.93. In the simple stem with *t*- Ugaritic and Arabic add a prosthetic *'i*- (cf. § 9.15). In Syriac retraction of the vowel and stress produces the form *'etqabr* instead of **'etqǝber*. In Ethiopic *taqabar* shows the insertion of a vowel after the first radical (cf. § 9.14), i.e. either as an anaptyctic vowel *ǝ* subjected to vowel harmony or by analogy with the stems with *t*- and second radical doubled and with first vowel lengthened (*taqabbar, taqābar*).

16.94. In the stem with *t* and second radical doubled Hebrew adds prosthetic *hi*- (cf. § 9.15).

16.95. In the stem with prefix *š*- and *t*- Arabic adds prosthetic *'i*- (cf. § 9.15).

h) Derived Stems: Participle

16.96. For the participles of the derived stems we may propose Proto-Semitic forms characterized by the prefix *mu*- and the vowel *i* after the second radical in the active, and by the same prefix *mu*- and the vowel *a* after the second radical in the passive. These forms have been reconstructed on the basis of Akkadian, Amorite, and Arabic. However, Hebrew and Syriac (causative stems) and Ethiopic have *a* as the vowel of the prefix. Apart from these characteristics, the participles correspond structurally to the imperfect (in Akkadian to the preterite). For the Ethiopic forms see § 16.101.

16.97. Akkadian, which presents active forms only (but the function of the passive participle is often assumed by the verbal adjective: cf. § 16.69), follows the general principles set forth in the preceding paragraph. The only exceptions are the stem with prefix *n*- (participle [**munqabru* >] *muqqabru*) and the simple stem with *t*- (participle *muqtabru*) in which the vowel *i* is dropped owing to the succession of short syllables (von Soden, GAG, p. 14).

16.98. In Ugaritic the only participles attested are those of the stems with second radical doubled and with prefix *š*- in the active: the consonantal structure (*mqbr* and *mšqbr*, respectively) does not indicate the vowel quality of the prefix.

16.99. In Hebrew the prefix *ma*- is reduced, in accordance with the conditions affecting short vowels in unstressed open syllables

(§ 10.8 g), to *mə-*; *mə-*, in its turn, is contracted with the prefixes of the various stems—thus producing, in the stem with *h-*, the forms (**məhaqbīr* >) *maqbīr* and (**məhoqbar* >) *moqbār*, in the stem with *t-* and geminated second radical the form (**məhitqabbęr* >) *mitqabbęr*. An unusual form of participle occurs in Hebrew (also in Phoenician, so far as the consonantal spelling indicates) in the stem with *n-*: *niqbār*, formed by analogy with the suffix-conj.; cf. also Ugaritic *nkbd*.

16.100. In Syriac the prefix *ma-* is reduced, in accordance with the principles governing short vowels in open unstressed syllables (§ 10.10 c), to *mə-*; and *mə-*, in its turn, is contracted with the prefix '- producing the form (**mə'aqber* >) *maqber*, while in the remaining stems the change *a > e* (cf. § 10.10 d) takes place (*metqəber*, *metqabbar*, *mettaqbar*).

16.101. In Ethiopic the prefix is stabilized in the form *ma-*. The active use of the participle is, however, greatly restricted, and the form *qabāri* of the simple stem gives rise to analogical formations in the derived stems (*qabbāri*, *'aqbāri*, etc.). In fact, the participle in Ethiopic has become a lexical item rather than a regular morphological feature.

i) Derived Stems: Infinitive

16.102. The infinitives of the derived stems have a number of forms which can more suitably be examined in each of the languages; we shall confine ourselves to the observation of certain common features.

16.103. In Akkadian the infinitive coincides with the stative followed by the nominal morpheme (stative *qubbur*, infinitive *qubburu*; stative *šuqbur*, infinitive *šuqburu*; etc.).

16.104. In Hebrew the infinitive is formed on the pattern of the imperfect without its prefixes and thus coincides with the imperative. By analogy with the absolute infinitive *qābōr* of the simple stem Hebrew also forms absolute infinitives of various derived stems with final vowel *ō* (*qabbōr*, *qubbōr*, *hiqqābōr*, *niqbōr*). The absolute infinitive is, however, rarely used in Hebrew, while the slightly different construct forms are widespread.

16.105. In Biblical Aramaic the ending -*ā* of the st. abs. fem. is characteristic of the infinitive of the derived stems (cf. § 16.70). In Syriac the infinitive retains the prefix *m-* of the simple stem, the second radical receiving the vowel *ā* and the third the (abstract) ending -*ū(t)* (the final -*t*, which does not occur in the absolute state, appears before suffixes): *məqabbārū, maqbārū, metqəbārū*, etc.

16.106. In Arabic the infinitive possesses several patterns, some of which reveal similar schemes and may be grouped together (*'iqbār, 'inqibār, 'iqtibār, 'istiqbār; taqabbur, taqābur*); apart from these, we have the infinitives of the stem with doubled second radical (*taqbīr*), with lengthened first vowel ([*qíbār >*] *qibār*), and others.

16.107. In Ethiopic the infinitive is formed on the same pattern as the imperative; to this is added the ending -*ō(t)*: *qabbərō(t), qābərō(t), 'aqbərō(t)*, etc.

5. The so-called "Weak" Verbs

16.108. The following chapters will be concerned with an examination of some types of verbs which differ from the regular pattern. These verbs contain either pharyngals and laryngals (in particular '), or the alveolar nasal *n*, or semivowels (*w, y*), or their second and third radicals are identical. In traditional Semitic grammar (cf. Brockelmann, GVG, I, pp. 584—638; also Gray, SCL, pp. 110—18) these groups of verbs are usually lumped together under the term "weak verbs". Their forms are regarded as explicable on a basis of triradical roots, either by means of phonetic changes characteristic of the consonants concerned or by the operation of analogy. More advanced linguistic study has shown, however, that those principles suffice for the explanation of only a limited number of these verbal forms, i.e. those with pharyngals and laryngals and those with (original) initial *y-* (though not without some reservations). In the remaining groups it may be shown that we are dealing, for the most part, with biconsonantal roots, the third radical having arisen secondarily in a process of integration with the predominant triradical system. This is confirmed by the fact (already referred to in §§ 11.5—9) that many "weak" verbs appear in several forms which have in common two

radicals and a basic range of meaning—but differ in the third
radical. If this explanation reflects the linguistic reality accurately,
then we must consider as mere working aids those theories which
have been applied, especially to Arabic grammar (cf. Fleisch, TPA,
pp. 118—38), in order to account for all the forms of these verbs
in terms of the triconsonantal system. The ensuing treatment has
purely descriptive aims and restricts the term "weak" to verbs
of probable biradical origin; it will call attention to certain facts
of fundamental importance to the study of comparative Semitic
grammar. For detailed information about independent developments in the various languages the reader is referred to the relevant
grammars. The fact that we are dealing with trends pulling in
opposite directions (the reduction of triradical roots and the expansion of biradical ones) as well as the complex nature of certain
phenomena will leave a wide margin of uncertainty which can be
reduced only by specific advance in the study of this branch of
comparative Semitic grammar.

6. Verbs with Pharyngals and Laryngals

16.109. The verbs with pharyngals and laryngals exhibit certain
specific peculiarities. These are connected, for the most part, with
the characteristics inherent in these consonants (cf. particularly
§ 9.6); in some cases, however, they are occasioned by analogy
with the "weak" verbs (cf. below). The glottal stop ' occupies a
special position which gives rise to phenomena not shared by other
consonants: the verbs with ' will, therefore, be dealt with separately.
It should also be recalled in this context that in Akkadian all the
consonants of the pharyngal and laryngal series are reduced to '
(§§ 8.53—54); hence Akkadian will only be considered in connexion
with the verbs containing the glottal stop: the change $a > e$
caused by ' derived from h and ', and sometimes also from $ġ$ and h
(cf. § 8.54), has produced two verbal classes (with a and with e),
even though there are considerable fluctuations between them.

16.110. Verbs with pharyngals and laryngals (in Hebrew and
Syriac also those with r: cf. § 8.25) are characterized by the tendency to change into a vowels contiguous to those consonants,
no doubt as an aspect of assimilation. In Hebrew this tendency
is the rule (e.g. *$yišloh$ "he sends" $> yišlah$); the question arises,

however, whether in some cases this phenomenon does not, in fact, represent the preservation of an original *a* (e.g. in *yaḥšob* "he thinks", where the *a* of the prefix reflects the vowel of the Proto-Semitic *yaqburu*). In Hebrew a subsidiary vowel of the *a* type establishes itself after ʿ and *ḥ* (rarely *h*) when the consonant would otherwise be without vowel at the close of a syllable: e.g. *yaʿmod "he stands" > *yaʿămod*; *yaʿmədū "they stand" > *yaʿamdū* (but *yaḥmol* "he shows compassion"). Moreover, a "liaison" *a* is inserted into the articulation between the long vowels of other timbres and a following pharyngal or laryngal: e.g. *hišmī "he caused to hear" > *hišmīăʿ* (cf. § 9.6). In Syriac the tendency to change into *a* vowels contiguous to pharyngals or laryngals is somewhat sporadic: e.g. *nebʿaṭ* alongside *nebʿoṭ* "he pushes", *nedkor "he remembers" > *nedkar*; the change is regular, however, in cases in which *e* would occur before a pharyngal or laryngal in final position: e.g. *ʾetdəker "he remembered" > *ʾettəkar* (cf. Brockelmann, SG, pp. 86—87, § 186). The phenomenon is fairly rare in Arabic (e.g. *yaftuḥu "he opens" > *yaftaḥu*). In Ethiopic the change *ə* > *a* occurs in the prefixes of verbal forms whose first radical has a laryngal followed by *a* (by way of vowel harmony): *yəḥawwər "he goes" > *yaḥawwər*. The opposite process *a* > *ə* takes place when a laryngal is followed by a vowel other than *a*: *našaʾū "they raised" > *našəʾū*. Finally, Ethiopic lengthens *a* before a vowelless laryngal: *samaʿku "I have heard" > *samāʿku* (cf. Praetorius, *Grammatica Aethiopica*, pp. 16—18, § 16; Ullendorff, SLE, pp. 212—14).

16.111. A characteristic feature of Hebrew, as presented to us by the Masoretic tradition, is its inability to double pharyngals and laryngals—with consequent compensatory vowel lengthening: e.g. *baʿʿer "he consumed" > *bāʿer*. Biblical Aramaic shares the same inability in the tradition of the Masoretes (including also *r*): but while in the case of ʾ, *r* and sometimes ʿ there is compensatory vowel lengthening (e.g. *barrik "he blessed" > *bārik*), it is absent in connexion with *h*, *ḥ*. Moreover, there are indications that at certain times and in certain areas the consonant was doubled (e.g. the dissimilation *haʿʿel "cause to enter!" > *hanʿel*). The accurate phonetic notation of the Masoretes rejects simple *šəwā* with pharyngals and laryngals and uses instead a compound *šəwā*, chiefly with *a* (cf. § 16.110) but also with other vowels: e.g. *yeḥĕzaq* "he is strong". In this example, as well as in the previously cited *ya'ămod*, we have a typical instance of vowel harmony in Hebrew.

16.112. The first characteristic of verbs with ' is the elision of postvocalic ', with consequent lengthening of the preceding vowel in the North Semitic area: e.g. from the root *'ḫd* "to seize", Proto-Semitic **ya'ḫudu*, Akk. *īḫuz*, Heb. *yōḥēz*, Syr. *nēḥod*; but Ar. *ya'ḫuḏu*, Eth. *yə'əḥəz* (as well as *ya'aḥaz*). In Akkadian, *i'* produces *ī* in Babylonian, *ē* in Assyrian: e.g. **i'kul* "he ate" > Bab. *īkul*, Ass. *ēkul*. In Hebrew, the form *yōḥēz* is the result of an evolution which may be represented as follows: **ya'ḫudu* > **yāḫuz* > **yōḫoz* > *yōḥēz* (by dissimilation). This development is, however, confined to a few verbs with ' as first radical (*'bd* "to perish", *'by* "to want", *'kl* "to eat", *'mr* "to say", *'py* "to bake"); their inflection is regarded as "weak" by contrast to the others. There is, however, a good deal of contamination and interference between "weak" verbs and others of this type (cf. Beer-Meyer, Hebräische Grammatik, II, pp. 46—47). In South Semitic, where this phenomenon does not as a rule occur, we encounter in Arabic a type of dissimilation of two ' in the same syllable: e.g. **a'ḫudu* "I take" > *'āḫuḏu*, **a'mana* "he believed" > *'āmana*.

16.113. In Akkadian some verbal forms with first radical ' show syncope of intervocalic ', followed by contraction in which the vowel of the prefix prevails: e.g. **i'akkal* "he eats" > *ikkal*, **u'arrak* "he lengthens" > *urrak*. Another characteristic of Akkadian is the assimilatory complex *nn*, commoner than '', resulting from a meeting of *n* and ' in the verbal stem with prefix *n-*: e.g. *innabbit* "he flees" alongside *i''abbat* "he is destroyed" (cf. von Soden, GAG, pp. 126—29). Syriac has some verbs with first radical ' which are formed by analogy with those with first radical *w/y* (e.g. *'awkel* "he caused to eat", from the root *'kl*); and similarly in Arabic (e.g. **i'taḫaḏa* "he took" > *'ittaḫaḏa* by analogy with e.g. **iwta'ada* "he promised" > *'itta'ada*). Some imperative forms which drop initial ' (e.g. Syr. *zel* "go!" from *'zl*, Ar. *ḫuḏ* "take!" from *'ḫd*) are analogous with those of verbs with first radical *w/y*.

16.114. In verbs with third radical ' the characteristic elision of postvocalic ' in North Semitic (cf. § 16.112) brings about coalescence with the verbs with third radical *y* as far as the resulting vowel is concerned (cf. § 16.121): e.g. Proto-Semitic *mali'a "it was full", Akk. (stative) mali, Heb. *mālē̆*, Syr. məlī (beside məlā); but Ar. mali'a, Eth. malə'a (mal'a). In Hebrew, ' is preserved at the beginning of a syllable, probably by analogy (or perhaps restored by the Masoretes ?): e.g. mālə'ū "they were full". Finally, a small group of Akkadian verbs (e.g. pr' "to cut") treats final ' as a normal radical (von Soden, GAG, p. 133).

16.115. The peculiarities of the verbs with ', outlined in the preceding paragraphs, do not apply to verbs with second radical ', for they follow the general pattern of pharyngals and laryngals (cf. §§ 16.109—111). In Akkadian, however, these verbs are sometimes inflected by analogy with those of second radical w/y: thus alongside ida''im "it becomes dark" išāl "he asks" (but in Assyrian sometimes iša''al; cf. von Soden, GAG, pp. 130—33). In Syriac, neš'al "he asks" > nešal (cf. Nöldeke, Kurzgefaßte Syrische Grammatik, p. 108, § 171) shows syncope of '. (Note the imperative sal of the corresponding Arabic verb s'l.)

7. Verbs with First Radical n

16.116. In North Semitic vowelless n is generally assimilated to the following consonant: e.g. Akk. *indin "he gave" > iddin; Ug. *ynpl "he falls" > ypl; Heb. *yinṣor "he guards" > yiṣṣor; Syr. *nenṭor "he guards" > neṭṭor. This assimilation does not take place in Hebrew before consonants of the pharyngal and laryngal group, as these consonants cannot be geminated (cf. § 16.111): e.g. Heb. yinḥal "he inherits". In Biblical Aramaic the n is frequently maintained in these circumstances (e.g. yintənūn "they give"), but this is probably due to secondary dissimilation of the doubled consonant—as may be shown by several cases in which n cannot be held to be original (e.g. tinda' "thou wilt know" < *tidda', from the root yd': cf. Rosenthal, Grammar of Biblical Aramaic, pp. 16—17, 47). In Syriac, the assimilation of n becomes inoperative in several verbs with second radical h: e.g. nenhar "it shines", root nhr. The North Semitic imperative is formed without n: e.g. Heb. gaš "approach!" from ngš, Syr. ṭor "guard!" from nṭr; Hebrew verbs with second vowel o, on the other hand, retain their initial n: e.g. nəṣor "guard!". In Akkadian the imperative of these verbs generally presents a prosthetic vowel

11*

(*idin* "give!" from *ndn, uqur* "destroy!" from *nqr*), but in Old
Akkadian and in Assyrian forms without prosthesis do occur (e.g.
din "give!").

16.117. In South Semitic, *n* is not subject to such special treatment—except for some cases in South Arabian: e.g. **stnṣr* "he
asked for help" > *stṣr*.

8. Verbs with *w*, *y*

16.118. For the verbs with *w*, *y* it is well to recall the phonetic
laws about semivowels (cf. §§ 8.61—65, 10.3, 9.7—8, 9.11, 9.13,
9.20) as well as the working of analogy affecting "regular" and
"weak" verbs; they are particularly exposed to the operation of
Systemzwang by which originally biradical verbs are integrated
within the triconsonantal system.

16.119. Verbs with first radical *w* and *y* constitute, in origin,
distinct categories; only those with first radical *w* (and they are
the more numerous group) seem to be genuinely "weak". Reciprocal
influences between the two categories and the passage of verbs
from one group to the other are, however, so common that it is
well to deal with them together. In the first place, we note the
characteristic change in North-West Semitic of *w* > *y* when in
initial position (cf. § 8.64): e.g. Akk. Ar. Eth. *wld* "to bear", Ug.
Heb. Syr. *yld*. The original distinction between these two categories of verbs emerges once more in various forms of the derived
stems: e.g. in the Hebrew verb *yšb* "to sit" the first radical is
originally *w*—as is demonstrated by the stem with prefix *h*-:
hōšīb, whereas in *ytb* "to be good" the *y* is primary—as is proved
by the form *hēṭīb*. Over the entire Semitic area initial *w* is absent in
the imperative: e.g. from the root *wld* Akk. *lidī*, Heb. *ləđī*, Ar.
lidī, Eth. *ladī* "give birth!" (but *wəṣar* "go out!"). Syriac *ilad* is
exceptional (by analogy with the verbs *primae y*), but forms like
teb "sit!" and *hab* "give!", etc., agree with their counterparts in
the other languages. Initial *w* does not appear in the imperfect:
from the same root *wld*, Heb. *yēləđ*, Syr. *nēlad*, Ar. *yalidu*, Eth.
(subjunctive) *yəlad* (Akkadian forms a partial exception: *ūlid*;
note in Hebrew and Syriac the vowel lengthening in the prefix).
Finally, certain West Semitic languages have infinitives without *w*

and with "feminine" ending: Heb. *ledet*, Ar. *lidat*, Eth. *lǝdat*
(Akkadian has *walādu* or *alādu* by reduction of initial *w* according
to § 8.63; but cf. the noun *šubtu* from the root *wšb*). For the complex
forms of the verbal stem with *š* in Akkadian, cf. von Soden, GAG,
pp. 141—42.

16.120. In the verbs with medial radical *w, y* the imperative
exhibits the appropriate long vowel between the first and third
radicals: e.g. Akk. *kūn* "be steady!", Heb. Syr. Eth. *qūm* "rise!"
(Ar. *qum* owing to the reduction of the long vowel in the closed
syllable); Akk. *šīm*, Heb. *śīm*, Syr. *sīm*, Eth. *šīm* "put!" (Ar.
šim for the same reason as above). A medial vowel *ā* is rare: e.g.
Akk. *bāš* "be ashamed!" (cf. Heb. *bōš*). The characteristic vowel
remains and is long (also in Arabic) in the prefix-conjugation: thus
Akk. preterite *ikūn*, Heb. *yāqūm*, Syr. *nǝqūm*, Ar. *yaqūmu*, Eth.
(subjunctive) *yǝqūm*; Akk. preterite *išīm*, Heb. *yāśīm*, Syr. *nǝsīm*,
Ar. *yašīmu*, Eth. (subjunctive) *yǝšīm*. In the Ethiopic forms, imperative as well as prefix-conjugation, the vowels are marked long
on etymological grounds; this does not necessarily reflect actual
pronunciation. In the suffix-conjugation West Semitic presents
Heb. *qām*, Syr. *qām*, Ar. *qāma*, Eth. *qōma* (in the Ethiopic form
the vowel *ō* is derived from the diphthong *aw*; it is noteworthy that
the usual Hebrew change *ā* > *ō* does not take place in this case,
though there are traces of it in the form *nuḫti* "I am quiet" of
the Tell Amarna glosses and in the Latin transcription *chon* "he
was" in Phoenician-Punic); Heb. *śām* (but also *bīn* "he understood"),
Syr. *sām* (but *mīt* "he died"), Ar. *šāma*, Eth. *šēma*. Interference
between the two classes is not unusual and is confirmed by the
Akkadian stative *kīn* and *šīm* (Assyrian *kēn* and *šēm*); in the prefix-
conjugation this interference was only sporadic (e.g. Heb. *yāśūm*
alongside the usual *yāśīm*). The inflexion of the Arabic perfect
shows the reappearance of the characteristic vowel: *qāma, qumta*;
šāma, šimta. In the derived stem with doubled second radical,
some languages present forms which correspond to those of the
"regular" verbs (Ar. *qawwama*, Eth. *qawwama*, Syr. *qayyem*), while
Hebrew has formations on the pattern of the verbs with doubled
second radical (*qōmēm*). Akkadian (which has gemination of the
second radical also in the present of the simple stem) exhibits
instead the doubling of the third radical, provided it is followed

by a vowel (e.g. *idukkū* "they kill", *išimmū* "they place", against the singulars *idūak* > *idāk* and *išīam*). The stem with *š* is formed similarly: e.g. *ušmāt* "he kills", *ušmattū* "they kill"; *ušmīt* "he killed", *ušmittū* "they killed". Formations by analogy with other "weak" verbs occur in Hebrew (e.g. *yūmat* "he is being killed", on the pattern of the verbs with first radical *w*).

16.121. It is characteristic of the verbs with third radical *w*, *y* (with which coalesce those with third radical ') that *y* predominates over *w* in North Semitic. Example of a verb with original *y* (the prefix- and suffix-conjugations are indicated): root *bky*, Akk. *baki* (stative), *ibki* (preterite), Heb. *bākā*, *yibkē*, Syr. *bəkā*, *nebkē*, Ar. *bakā*, *yabkī*, Eth. *bakaya*, *yəbkī* (subjunctive). Example of a verb with original *w*: root *dlw*, Ar. *dalā*, *yadlū*, Eth. *dalawa*, *yədlū* (subjunctive), but Akk. *idlu*, Heb. *dālā*, *yidlē*, Syr. *dəlā*, *nedlē*. These examples show: a) there are in Akkadian various exceptions to the North Semitic predominance of the type with *y* over that with *w* (e.g. *imnu* "he counted", *iḫdu* "he rejoiced"); b) the Ethiopic forms *bakaya* and *dalawa* agree with the regular pattern and appear to favour the conception of these verbs as original triradicals; this assumption is scarcely set aside by certain changes *awa* > *ō* (e.g. *halawa* and *halō* "he was"); c) the triradical origin is also supported by certain Ugaritic forms which keep *w* and *y* (e.g. *åtwt* "she came"); d) some interesting fluctuations between *w* and *y* are exhibited by South Arabian: from the root *rḍw* "to be content" the prefix-conjugation of the stem with *h*- has *yhrḍwn* and *yhrḍyn*. The greater part of these verbal forms can be explained by syncope of *w*, *y* between vowels and subsequent contraction of those vowels. This process is of some consequence in the historical development of the Semitic languages generally (e.g. Akk. *ibanniū* "they build", later *ibannū*). Noteworthy is also the tendency to shorten or even to drop final vowels resulting from contraction: thus Akk. *ibni* "he built" for *ibnī*.

9. Verbs with Identical Second and Third Radicals

16.122. In the verbs with identical second and third radicals, commonly called *verba mediae geminatae*, the probable biconsonantal origin is particularly evident; integration within the triconsonantal system demonstrates the force of analogy.

16.123. In Akkadian the verbs of this group are completely adapted to the regular pattern. A biradical form is presented by the stative of the verbs which indicate a condition (e.g. *dān* "he is strong", *sār* "he is false"); this form (which is standard in Old Babylonian) is paralleled in Neo-Babylonian by those corresponding to regular verbs (e.g. *elil* "he is pure"). A small group of verbs with second radical *l* or *r* forms a special durative type with *n*: e.g. *na'arruru* "to come to the rescue", *naparruru* "to disband", etc. In the inflexion of these verbs gemination of the third radical frequently occurs before vocalic suffixes: e.g. *lin'arirru* "let them help".

16.124. In Hebrew the perfect of the simple stem is integrated with the regular pattern (type *sābab*), but stative verbs have biradical forms (type *ham*); the imperfect and imperative also have biradical elements (type *yāsob, sob*). Some forms with doubled first radical are attributed to Aramaic influence: e.g. *yissob* alongside *yāsob* (cf. § 16.125). Before vocalic suffixes the second radical is geminated: e.g. *yāsobbū*; before consonantal suffixes a connecting vowel is introduced: *ō* in the perfect and *ē* in the imperfect, e.g. *sabbōtī, təsubbēnā* (cf. the similar formation of verbs with third radical *w/y*: e.g. *tiglēnā*). In the derived stems metaplastic formations are common: Polel, Polal, Hithpolel; others are inflected by analogy with the "weak" verbs: e.g. the Hophal *yōsab* modelled on verbs with first radical *w* (*yōšab*).

16.125. In Syriac biradical forms are widely attested: the perfect of the simple stem is *baz, bezzat*, while in the imperfect the first radical is doubled, by analogy with the verbs primae *n* (type *nebboz*). The masculine singular participle is formed on the pattern of the verbs mediae *w* (type *bā'ez*): this analogy does not extend to the feminine and the plural (in contrast to Jewish Aramaic and Mandaean). In the derived stems forms on the model of the "regular" verbs are widespread, e.g. *'etbəzez*, etc.

16.126. In Arabic, the verbs of this type appear in the forms *farra*, perfect, *yafirru*, imperfect; and in the derived stems *fārra, yufārru*; *'afarra, yufirru*, etc. When the last radical has no vowel, analogy with the "regular" verbs operates: e.g. *'afrarta*, etc.

16.127. In Ethiopic, integration with the "regular" verb is prevalent (perfect *ḥašaša*, imperfect *yəḥaššəš*). In the perfect

of stative verbs (type *ḥamma*) and in the simple stem with *t-*
(type *tanabba*) biradical forms are attested. In the imperative
and the imperfect the shortened forms exist alongside those
fashioned on the analogy of the "regular" verbs.

10. Doubly Irregular or Defective Verbs

16.128. All the Semitic languages have doubly irregular verbs,
i.e. verbs which combine two of the categories discussed in the
foregoing: e.g. Akk. *'wr* "to be awake" (first radical *'* and second *w*),
Heb. *nś'* "to carry" (first radical *n* and third *'*), Syr. *lwy* "to
accompany" (second radical *w* and third *y*), Ar. *wqy* "to take care"
(first radical *w* and third *y*), Eth. *whb* "to give" (first radical *w* and
second *h*), etc. In these verbs the inflexion takes account of the
characteristics of both categories concerned. Much rarer are verbs
in which all three radicals are "weak": e.g. Akk. **awū* "to speak",
ewū "to become", etc.

16.129. There also exist a number of defective verbs whose forms
diverge from the general patterns hitherto discussed. For such
verbs the reader is referred to the grammars of the individual
languages. In general these anomalies can be resolved artificially by
subsuming such verbal forms under categories to which in essence
they do not belong: thus Hebrew *lqḥ* "to take" behaves like a verb
of first radical *n* (imperfect *yiqqaḥ*) and *hlk* "to go" like a verb of
first radical *w* (imperfect *yēlek*); Syriac *'zl* "to go" assimilates its *l*
in certain circumstances (first person singular perfect: *'ezzet*) and *slq*
"to go up" assimilates the *l* and has forms like a verb with first
radical *n* (imperfect *nessaq*); Arabic *r'y* "to see" presents shortened
forms (imperfect *yarā*); Akkadian verbs such as *izuzzu* "to stand"
and *itūlu* "to lie" exhibit forms that may be referred to several
different categories (first radical *n*, medial radical *w/y*, etc.); cf. von
Soden, GAG, pp. 154—56.

11. Semantic Categories in "Weak" Verbs

16.130. B. Landsberger (*Islamica* 2 [1926], pp. 362 ff.) was the
first to recognize that there existed a measure of correlation
between several types of "weak" verbs (cf. § 6.116 ff.) and certain
semantic categories. While details have not yet been worked out,
the most important categories—according to von Soden—are:

16.131. Verbs *primae n*: a) verbs whose biradical basis, without the element *n*, connotes a noise, e.g. Sem. *nbḥ/ḫ* "to bark" (i.e. "to say *buḥ*"), *npḫ* "to blow" (i.e. "to sound *puḫ*"); b) verbs in which the element *n* has locative meaning, e.g. Sem. *nś'* "to lift up", Akk. *ndy* "to throw down", Heb. *npl* "to fall down", Arab. *nzl* "to descend", Eth. *nbr* "to sit down".

16.132. Verbs *primae w, y*: a) verbs which describe certain involuntary actions, e.g. Sem. *wld* "to give birth", Arab. *wǧd* "to find", Eth. *wdq* "to fall"; b) verbs which connote the aim or target of a motion, e.g. Sem. *wrd* "to go down", Eth. *wsd* "to lead to".

16.133. Verbs *mediae w*: a) verbs which describe a change of condition or transition from one situation to the opposite one, e.g. Sem. *mwt* "to die", West Sem. *qwm* "to get up"; b) verbs which refer to types of motion, e.g. Akk. *dwl* "to go to and fro", Heb. and Eth. *rwṣ* "to run".

16.134. Verbs *mediae y*: a) verbs which describe a physiological function, e.g. Sem. *šyn* "to urinate"; b) verbs connoting a definite outcome or result, e.g. Sem. *śym* "to place, fix", Akk. Ar. Eth. *ḫyr* "to elect".

16.135. Verbs *ultimae w, y*: a) (only ultimae *y*) verbs of terminative meaning, e.g. Sem. (except Eth.) *bny* "to build", Heb. Aram. *gly* "to reveal"; b) verbs which describe durative actions, e.g. West Sem. *r'y* "to see", Akk. Heb. Aram. *mnw* "to count".

16.136. Verbs *mediae geminatae*: especially verbs which connote a number of individual actions ("Kettendurative"), e.g. Akk. *šll*, Syr. *bzz* "to plunder", Arab. *'dd* "to count", etc. For the change of categories cf. e.g. Heb. *šgg* and *šgy* "to err", Ar. *frr* and *nfr* "to flee".

12. Verbs with Pronominal Suffixes

16.137. Before pronominal suffixes we often witness the reappearance of Proto-Semitic elements which have undergone considerable development in the forms without suffixes. Certain alterations of morphemes and endings also occur, and some connecting vowels are inserted. Some scattered information on these points has already been given in various places in this book.

16.138. In Akkadian the pronominal suffixes are appended to verbal forms without alteration; some endings take the ventive morpheme -*an* before the suffixes—and this fact has a certain comparative interest.

16.139. In Hebrew the Proto-Semitic endings of the perfect reappear before suffixes: third singular masculine -*a*, third singular feminine -*at*, second singular feminine -*tī*. In the second person plural masculine we have *tū* instead of *tem*, probably as a result of shortening of the Proto-Semitic -*tumū*. The suffix-pronouns can be appended directly to the forms of the imperfect in the case of the second person only (type *yiqborkā*); for the suffixes of the other persons a connecting vowel is inserted on the model of the verbs with third radical *y* (type *yiqbərēnī*); the same occurs in the imperative (type *qobrēnī*). For forms with -*an* before the suffixes (like *yiqqāḥennū*) cf. § 16.34.

16.140. In Syriac the Proto-Semitic endings of the perfect reappear before suffixes: third singular masculine -*a*, second singular masculine -*tā*, second singular feminine -*tī*, third plural feminine -*ā*, first plural -*nā*; likewise in the imperative: second plural masculine -*ū*, second plural feminine -*ā*. In those persons of the imperfect which have no afformatives a connecting vowel *i* appears (type *neqbəriw*) which may occur also in the imperative. Finally, Old Aramaic may insert -*an* (cf. §§ 16.138—39) before the suffixes: e.g. Eg. Aram. *yəśīminnāk* "he puts thee".

16.141. In Arabic long final vowels appear in the perfect endings in the second singular feminine (type *qabartīnī* beside *qabartinī*) and in the second plural masculine (type *qabartumūnī*).

16.142. In Ethiopic long final vowels are substituted in the perfect endings of the second singular masculine (-*kā*) and in the first person plural (-*nā*). In the second plural feminine the full ending -*kənnā* appears which is more often shortened to -*kā*. Dissimilation is the cause of the change -*ī* > *ə* in the second singular feminine before the suffix pronoun -*nī*. For further details cf. §§ 13.14, 13.27.

Bibliography

The following bibliography includes works published up to the end of 1962; in the text, however, only works which appeared up to the end of 1961 have been considered. The bibliography is selective and, except in cases of special importance, does not include works published before 1908 (the date of Vol. I of Brockelmann's *Grundriß*... and of his *Kurzgefaßte vergleichende Grammatik*...). Inclusion of a work in this bibliography does not necessarily connote agreement with its theses.

The abbreviations used in the bibliography are those of the *Bibliographie sémitique* published periodically in *Orientalia*, with the addition of: AIOK XXIV = *Akten des XXIV. Internationalen Orientalisten-Kongresses* (Wiesbaden 1959); SOLDV = *Studi orientalistici in onore di G. Levi Della Vida*, 2 vol. (Roma 1956); ZS = *Zeitschrift für Semitistik*.

I. The Semitic Languages

A. Scope of the Survey

Barth, J., *Sprachwissenschaftliche Untersuchungen zum Semitischen* (Leipzig 1907—11).

Bergsträsser, G., *Einführung in die semitischen Sprachen* (München 1928).

Bibliographie sémitique, in Or 16 (1947), 103—29; 17 (1948), 91—103; 19 (1950), 445—78; 22 (1953), 1*—38*; 26 (1957), 50*—115*; 28 (1959), 59*—90*; 30 (1961), 42*—61*.

Blake, F. R., *Studies in Semitic Grammar*, in JAOS 35 (1917), 375—85; 62 (1942), 109—18; 65 (1945), 111—16; 66 (1946), 212—18; 73 (1953), 7—16.

Brockelmann, C., *Grundriß der vergleichenden Grammatik der semitischen Sprachen*, 2 vol. (Berlin 1908—13).

—, *Kurzgefaßte vergleichende Grammatik der semitischen Sprachen. Elemente der Laut- und Formenlehre* (Berlin 1908).

—, *Précis de linguistique sémitique* (Paris 1910).

—, *Semitische Sprachwissenschaft*, 2. Aufl. (Leipzig 1916).

de Lacy O'Leary, *Comparative Grammar of the Semitic Languages* (London 1923).

Dhorme, P., *Langues et écritures sémitiques* (Paris 1930).

Fleisch, H., *Introduction à l'étude des langues sémitiques* (Paris 1947).

Fronzaroli, P., *Prospettive di metodo statistico nella classificazione delle lingue semitiche*, in ANLR Ser. 8, 16 (1961), 348—80.

Gray, L. H., *Introduction to Semitic Comparative Linguistics* (New York 1934).

Handbuch der Orientalistik, hrsg. von B. Spuler, III. Semitistik (Leiden 1953—54).

Kramers, J. H., *De semietische talen* (Leiden 1949).

Langues et écritures sémitiques, in Dictionnaire de la Bible, Supplément, V (Paris 1957), 257—334.

Levi Della Vida, G. (and others), *Linguistica semitica: presente e futuro* (Roma 1961).

Nöldeke, Th., *Beiträge zur semitischen Sprachwissenschaft* (Strasbourg 1904).

—, *Die semitischen Sprachen*, 2. Aufl. (Leipzig 1899).

—, *Neue Beiträge zur semitischen Sprachwissenschaft* (Strasbourg 1910).

Pedersen, J., *Semiten (Sprache)*, in Reallexikon der Vorgeschichte, XII (Berlin 1928), 14—50.

Renan, E., *Histoire générale et système comparé des langues sémitiques*, 1, 3ème éd. (Paris 1863).

Rinaldi, G., *Le lingue semitiche* (Torino 1954).

Segert, S., *Considerations on Semitic Comparative Lexicography*, in ArOr 28 (1960), 470—87.

—, *Semitistische Marginalien*, in ArOr 29 (1961), 80—118.

Ullendorff, E., *What is a Semitic Language ?*, in Or 28 (1958), 66—75.

von Soden, W., *Zur Einteilung der semitischen Sprachen*, in WZKM 56 (1960), 177—91.

Wright, W., *Lectures on the Comparative Grammar of the Semitic Languages* (Cambridge 1890).

Zimmern, H., *Vergleichende Grammatik der semitischen Sprachen* (Berlin 1898).

B. North-East Semitic

Aro, J., *Studien zur mittelbabylonischen Grammatik* (Helsinki 1955).

de Meyer, L., *L'accadien des contrats de Suse* (Leiden 1962).

Finet, A., *L'accadien des lettres de Mari* (Bruxelles 1956).

Gelb, I. J., *Morphology of Akkadian* (Chicago 1952).

—, *Old Akkadian Writing and Grammar* (Chicago 1961).

Salonen, E., *Untersuchungen zur Schrift und Sprache des Altbabylonischen von Susa* (Helsinki 1962).

Ungnad, A., *Grammatik des Akkadischen*, 3. Aufl. (München 1949).

von Soden, W., *Der hymnisch-epische Dialekt des Akkadischen*, in ZA 40 (1932), 163—227; 41 (1933), 90—183, 236.

—, *Grundriß der akkadischen Grammatik* (Roma 1952).

C. North-West Semitic

Aistleitner, J., *Studien zur Frage der Sprachverwandtschaft des Ugaritischen*, in Acta Orientalia 7 (1957), 251—307; 8 (1958), 51—98.

—, *Untersuchungen zur Grammatik des Ugaritischen* (Berlin 1954).

Albright, W. F., *The Early Alphabetic Inscriptions from Sinai and their Decipherment*, in BASOR 110 (1948), 6—22.

Altheim, F. und Stiehl, R., *Die aramäische Sprache unter den Achaimeniden* (Frankfurt 1960 ff.).

Bauer, H. und Leander, P., *Grammatik des Biblisch-Aramäischen* (Halle 1927).

Bauer, H. und Leander, P., *Historische Grammatik der hebräischen Sprache* (Halle 1922).

Beer, G. und Meyer, R., *Hebräische Grammatik*, 2 vol. (Berlin 1952—55).

Birkeland, H., *The Language of Jesus* (Oslo 1954).

Böhl, F. M. T., *Die Sprache der Amarnabriefe mit besonderer Berücksichtigung der Kanaanismen* (Leipzig 1909).

Brockelmann, C., *Syrische Grammatik*, 7. Aufl. (Leipzig 1955).

Burchardt, M., *Die altkanaanäischen Fremdworte und Eigennamen im Ägyptischen* (Leipzig 1909—10).

Cantineau, J., *Grammaire du palmyrénien épigraphique* (Le Caire 1935).

—, *Le nabatéen*, 2 vol. (Paris 1930—32).

Dahood, M., *The Linguistic Position of Ugaritic in the Light of Recent Discoveries*, in *Sacra Pagina*, I (Paris-Gembloux 1959), 269—79.

Dalman, G., *Grammatik des jüdisch-palästinischen Aramäisch*, 2. Aufl. (Leipzig 1905).

Dammron, A., *Grammaire de l'araméen biblique* (Strasbourg 1961).

Dhorme, É., *Déchiffrement des inscriptions pseudo-hiéroglyphiques de Byblos*, in *Syria* 25 (1946—48), 1—35.

—, *La langue de Canaan*, in RB 22 (1913), 369—93; 23 (1914), 37—59, 344—72.

Ebeling, E., *Das Verbum der El-Amarna-Briefe* (Leipzig 1910).

Epstein, J. N., *A Grammar of Babylonian Aramaic* (Jerusalem 1960).

Friedrich, J., *Kanaanäisch und Westsemitisch*, in *Scientia* 84 (1949), 220—23.

—, *Phönizisch-punische Grammatik* (Roma 1951).

Garbini, G., *Il semitico di nord-ovest* (Napoli 1960).

—, *L'aramaico antico* (ANLM, ser. 8, vol. 7, fasc. 5) (Roma 1956).

—, *Nuovo materiale per la grammatica dell'aramaico antico*, in RSO 34 (1959), 41—54.

Gardiner, A. H., *Once again the Proto-Sinaitic Inscriptions*, in JEA 48 (1962), 45—48.

Gelb, I. J., *La lingua degli Amoriti*, in ANLR ser. 8, 13 (1958), 143—64.

Gesenius, W. und Bergsträsser, G., *Hebräische Grammatik*, 29. Aufl. (Leipzig 1918—29).

Ginsberg, H. L., *The Classification of the North-West Semitic Languages*, in AIOK XXIV, 256—67.

Goetze, A., *Is Ugaritic a Canaanite Dialect?*, in *Language* 17 (1941), 127—38.

Gordon, C. H., *Ugaritic Manual* (Roma 1955).

Goshen-Gottstein, M. H., *Linguistic Structure and Tradition in the Qumran Documents* (Jerusalem 1958).

Harris, Z. S., *A Grammar of the Phoenician Language* (New Haven 1936).

—, *Development of the Canaanite Dialects* (New Haven 1939).

Janssens, G., *Contribution au déchiffrement des inscriptions pseudo-hiéroglyphiques de Byblos*, in *La nouvelle Clio* 7—9 (1955—57), 361—77

Joüon, P., *Grammaire de l'hébreu biblique*, 2ème éd. (Rome 1947).

Kutscher, E. Y., *Studies in Galilean Aramaic* (Jerusalem 1952).

—, *The Study of the Aramaic Grammar of the Babylonian Talmud*, in *Leshonenu* 26 (1962), 149—83.

Leander, P., *Laut- und Formenlehre des Ägyptisch-Aramäischen* (Göteborg 1928).

Margolis, M. L., *Lehrbuch der aramäischen Sprache des babylonischen Talmuds* (München 1910).

Martin, M., *A Preliminary Report after Re-Examination of the Byblian Inscriptions*, in Or 30 (1961), 46—78.

—, *Revision and Reclassification of the Proto-Byblian Signs*, in Or 31 (1962), 250—71, 339—83.

Moran, W. L., *The Hebrew Language in its Northwest Semitic Background*, in *The Bible and the Ancient Near East* (London 1961), 54—72.

Moscati, S., *Il semitico di nord-ovest*, in SOLDV II, 202—21.

—, *Sulla posizione linguistica del semitico nord-occidentale*, in RSO 31 (1956), 229—34.

Nöldeke, Th., *Kurzgefaßte Syrische Grammatik*, 2. Aufl. (Leipzig 1898).

—, *Mandäische Grammatik* (Halle 1875).

Petermann, J. H., *Brevis Linguae Samaritanae grammatica, litteratura, chrestomathia cum glossario* (Berlin 1873).

Polotsky, J. H., *Studies in Modern Syriac*, in JSS 6 (1961), 1—32.

Rosenthal, F., *A Grammar of Biblical Aramaic* (Wiesbaden 1961).

—, *Die aramaistische Forschung seit Th. Nöldeke's Veröffentlichungen* (Leiden 1939).

—, *Die Sprache der palmyrenischen Inschriften und ihre Stellung innerhalb des Aramäischen* (Leipzig 1936).

Rossell, W. H., *A Handbook of Aramaic Magical Texts* (Ringwood Borough 1953).

Rowley, H. H., *The Aramaic of the Old Testament* (London 1929).

Schulthess, F., *Grammatik des christlich-palästinischen Aramäisch* (Tübingen 1924).

Segal, M. H., *A Grammar of Mishnaic Hebrew*, 2nd ed. (Oxford 1958).

Segert, S., *Die Sprache der moabitischen Königsinschrift*, in ArOr 29 (1961), 197—268.

Sobelmann, H., *The Proto-Byblian Inscriptions: a Fresh Approach*, in JSS 6 (1961), 226—45.

Stevenson, W. B., *Grammar of Palestinian Jewish Aramaic* (Oxford 1924).

Ullendorff, E., *The Position of Ugaritic within the Framework of the Semitic Languages*, in *Tarbiz* 24 (1954—55), 121—25.

—, *Ugaritic Marginalia*, in Or 20 (1951), 270—74.

—, *Ugaritic Marginalia II*, in JSS 7 (1962), 339—51.

van den Branden, A., *Anciennes inscriptions sémitiques*, in BO 17 (1960), 218—22.

—, *Le déchiffrement des inscriptions protosinaïtiques*, in al-Machriq 52 (1958), 361—95.

—, *Les inscriptions protosinaïtiques*, in OrAn 1 (1962), 197—214.

D. South-West Semitic

Beeston, A. F. L., *A Descriptive Grammar of Epigraphic South Arabian* (London 1962).

Brockelmann, C., *Arabische Grammatik*, 14. Aufl. (Leipzig 1960).

Cantineau, *Accadien et sudarabique*, in BSLP 33 (1932), 175—204.

Caskel, W., *Lihyan und Lihyanisch* (Köln-Opladen 1954).

Cohen, D., *Le vocabulaire de base sémitique et le classement des dialectes méridionaux*, in Sem 11 (1961), 55—84.

Dillmann, A., *Grammatik der Äthiopischen Sprache*, 2. Aufl. von C. Bezold (Leipzig 1899), Engl. transl. by J. A. Crichton (London 1907).

Fleisch, H., *L'arabe classique. Esquisse d'une structure linguistique* (Beyrouth 1956).

—, *Traité de philologie arabe*, I (Beyrouth 1961).

Fück, J., '*Arabīya. Untersuchungen zur arabischen Sprach- und Stilgeschichte* (Berlin 1950), French transl. by Cl. Denizeau (Paris 1955).

Gaudefroy-Demombynes, M. et Blachère, R., *Grammaire de l'arabe classique*, 3ème éd. (Paris 1952).

Höfner, M., *Altsüdarabische Grammatik* (Leipzig 1943).

Leslau, W., *South-East Semitic (Ethiopic and South-Arabic)*, in JAOS 63 (1943), 4—14.

—, *The Position of Ethiopic in Semitic: Akkadian and Ethiopic*, in AIOK XXIV, 251—53.

Littmann, E., *Syria. IV. Semitic Inscriptions C. Safaïtic Inscriptions* (Leyden 1943).

Moscati, S., *Nordarabico, sudarabico, etiopico*, in RSO 34 (1959), 33—39.

Praetorius, F., *Grammatica Aethiopica* (Karlsruhe-Leipzig 1886).

Petráček, K., *A Study in the Structure of Arabic*, in *Orientalia Pragensia* 1 (1960), 23—38.

Rabin, C., *Ancient West Arabian* (London 1951).

Ullendorff, E., *The Ethiopian Languages and their Contribution to Semitic Studies*, in *Africa* 25 (1955), 154—60.

van den Branden, A., *Les inscriptions thamoudéennes* (Louvain 1950).

—, *Les textes thamoudéens de Philby*, 2 vol. (Louvain 1956).

E. Proto-Semitic, Hamito-Semitic, Indo-European

Cohen, M., *Essai comparatif sur le vocabulaire et la phonétique du chamito-sémitique* (Paris 1947).

—, *Langues chamito-sémitiques*, in *Les langues du monde*, 2ème éd. (Paris 1952), 81—181.

Cuny, A., *Invitation à l'étude comparative des langues indoeuropéennes et des langues chamito-sémitiques* (Bordeaux 1946).

—, *Recherches sur le vocalisme, le consonantisme et la formation des racines en «Nostratique», ancêtre de l'Indo-Européen et du Chamito-Sémitique* (Paris 1943).

Greenberg, J. H., *The Afro-Asiatic (Hamito-Semitic) Present*, in JAOS 72 (1952), 1—9.

Heilmann, L., *Camito-semitico e indoeuropeo* (Bologna 1949).

Klingenheben, A., *Die Präfix- und die Suffixkonjugationen im Hamitosemitischen*, in MIOF 4 (1956), 211—77.

Mayer, M. L., *Ricerche sul problema dei rapporti fra lingue indouropee e lingue semitiche*, in *Acme* 13 (1960), 77—100.

Moscati, S., *Sulla più antica storia delle lingue semitiche*, in RANL ser. 8, 15 (1960), 79—101.

—, *Sulla ricostruzione del protosemitico*, in RSO 35 (1960), 1—10.

Pilszczikowa, N., *Le haoussa et le chamito-sémitique à la lumière de l'Essai comparatif de Marcel Cohen*, in *Rocznik Orientalistyczny* 24 (1960), 97—130.

Reinisch, L., *Das persönliche Fürwort und die Verbalflexion in den chamitosemitischen Sprachen* (Wien 1909).

Rössler, O., *Akkadisches und libysches Verbum*, in Or 20 (1951), 101—107, 366—73.

—, *Der semitische Charakter der libyschen Sprache*, in ZA 50 (1952), 121—50.

—, *Verbalbau und Verbalflexion in den semitohamitischen Sprachen*, in ZDMG 100 (1950), 461—514.

Thacker, T. W., *The Relationship of the Semitic and Egyptian Verbal Systems* (Oxford 1954).

Ungnad, A., *Das Wesen des Ursemitischen* (Leipzig 1925).

Vycichl, W., *Gedanken zur ägyptisch-semitischen Sprachverwandtschaft*, in Mus 73 (1960), 173—76.

—, *Is Egyptian a Semitic Language?*, in *Kush* 7 (1959), 27—44.

—, *Nouveaux aspects de la langue égyptienne*, in BIFAO 58 (1959), 49—72.

F. Language and Script

Cohen, M., *La grande invention de l'écriture et son évolution*, 3 vol. (Paris 1958).

Diringer, D., *The Alphabet. A Key to the History of Mankind* (London 1948).

—, *Writing* (London 1962).

Driver, G. R., *Semitic Writing from Pictograph to Alphabet*, Rev. ed. (London 1954).

Février, J. G., *Histoire de l'écriture*, Nouv. éd. (Paris 1959).

Gelb, I. J., *A Study of Writing* (London 1952).

Ullendorff, E., *Studies in the Ethiopic Syllabary*, in *Africa* 21 (1951), 207—17.

van den Branden, A., *L'origine des alphabets protosinaïtique, arabes préislamiques et phénicien*, in BO 19 (1962), 198—206.

von Soden, W., *Das akkadische Syllabar* (Rom 1948).

II. Phonology

A. Preliminaries

Mittwoch, G., *Die traditionelle Aussprache des Äthiopischen* (Berlin 1926).

Pfeiffer, R., *Clues to the Pronounciation of Ancient Languages*, in SOLDV II, 338—49.

Sperber, A., *Hebrew Based Upon Greek and Latin Transliterations*, in HUCA 12—13 (1937—38), 103—274.

—, *Hebrew Grammar: a New Approach*, in JBL 62 (1943), 137—262.

B. The Phonological System

Aro, J., *Die semitischen Zischlaute (ṭ), š, ś und s und ihre Vertretung im Akkadischen*, in Or 28 (1959), 321—35.

Bauer, H., *Wechsel von p, m, b mit u im Aramäischen und Arabischen, in* ZS 10 (1935), 11—13.

Beeston, A. F. L., *Arabian Sibilants*, in JSS 7 (1962), 222—33.

—, *Phonology of the Epigraphic South Arabian Unvoiced Sibilants*, in *Transactions of the Philological Society*, 1951, 1—26.

Birkeland, H., *The Syriac Phonematic Vowel System*, in *Festskrift til Prof. O. Broch* (Oslo 1947), 13—39.

Blake, F. R., *The Apparent Interchange between a and i in Hebrew*, in JNES 9 (1950), 76—83.

Cantineau, J., *Cours de phonétique arabe* (Paris 1960).

—, *Esquisse d'une phonologie de l'arabe classique*, in BSLP 43 (1946), 93—140.

—, *Essai d'une phonologie de l'hébreu biblique*, in BSLP 46 (1950), 82—122.

—, *La «mutation des sifflantes» en sudarabique*, in *Mélanges Gaudefroy-Demombynes* (Le Caire 1935—45), 313—23.

—, *Le consonantisme du sémitique*, in Sem 4 (1953), 79—94.

Ferguson, C. A., *The Emphatic l in Arabic*, in *Language* 32 (1956), 446—52.

Fischer, W., *K > Š in den südlichen semitischen Sprachen*, in *Münchener Studien zur Sprachwissenschaft* 8 (1956), 25—38.

Fleisch, H., *Études de phonétique arabe*, in MUSJ 28 (1949—50), 225—85.

Fronzaroli, P., *La fonetica ugaritica* (Roma 1955).

Goetze, A., *The Sibilants of Old Babylonian*, in RA 52 (1958), 137—49.

Knudsen, E. E., *Cases of Free Variants in the Akkadian q Phoneme*, in JCS 15 (1961), 84—90.

LaSor, W. S., *The Sibilants in Old South Arabic*, in JQR 48 (1957), 161—73.

Martinet, A., *La palatalisation «spontanée» de g en arabe*, in BSLP 54 (1959), 90—102.

—, *Remarques sur le consonantisme sémitique*, in BSLP 49 (1953), 67—78.

Morag, S., *The Vocalization Systems of Arabic, Hebrew, and Aramaic* ('s Gravenhage 1962).

Moscati, S., *Il sistema consonantico delle lingue semitiche* (Roma 1954).

—, *Preistoria e storia del consonantismo ebraico antico* (ANLM, ser. 8, vol. 5, fasc. 8) (Roma 1954).

Petráček, K., *Der doppelte phonologische Charakter des Ghain im klassischen Arabisch*, in ArOr 21 (1953), 240—62.

—, *Die Struktur der semitischen Wurzelmorpheme und der Übergang 'ain > ġain und 'ain > r im Arabischen*, in ArOr 23 (1955), 475—78.

—, *Zur Artikulation des sogenannten emphatischen l im Arabischen*, in ArOr 20 (1952), 509—23.

Polotsky, H. J., *Études de grammaire gouragué*, in BSLP 39 (1938), 137—75.

Rabin, C., *The Hebrew Development of Proto-Semitic ā*, in *Tarbiz* 30 (1960), 99—111.

Reif, J. A., *The Loss of Consonantal Aleph in Ugaritic*, in JSS 4 (1959), 16—20.

Rosén, H. B., *A Marginal Note on Biblical Hebrew Phonology*, in JNES 20 (1961), 124—26.

—, *ha-'Ibrīt še-lānū* (Tel Aviv 1956).

Rössler, O., *Ghain im Ugaritischen*, in ZA 54 (1961), 158—72.

—, *Zur Frage der Vertretung der gemeinsemitischen Laryngale im Akkadischen* (ʿ ḫ = ġ), in AIOK XXIV, 129—32.

Růžička, R., *La question de l'existence du ġ dans les langues sémitiques en général et dans la langue ugaritienne en particulier*, in ArOr 22 (1954), 176—237.

Stehle, D., *Sibilants and Emphatics in South Arabic*, in JAOS 60 (1940), 507—43.

Ullendorff, E., *The Semitic Languages of Ethiopia. A Comparative Phonology* (London 1955).

Vilenčik, Y., *Welchen Lautwert hatte ḍ im Ursemitischen?*, in OLZ 33 (1930), 89—98.

von Soden, W., *Aramäisches ḫ erscheint im Spätbabylonischen vor m auch als g*, in AfO 19 (1959—60), 149.

—, *Vokalfärbungen im Akkadischen*, in JCS 2 (1948), 291—303.

C. Conditioned Phonetic Changes

Bravmann, M. M., *Some Aspects of the Development of Semitic Diphtongs*, in Or 8 (1939), 244—53; 9 (1940), 45—60.

Cowan, W., *Arabic Evidence for Proto-Semitic */awa/ and */ō/*, in *Language* 36 (1960), 60—62.

Růžička, R., *Konsonantische Dissimilation in den semitischen Sprachen* (Leipzig 1909).

Speiser, E. A., *Secondary Developments in Semitic Phonology. An Application of the Principle of Sonority*, in AJSL 42 (1926), 145—69.

Spitaler, A., *Zur Frage der Geminatendissimilation im Semitischen*, in Zeitschrift für Indogermanische Forschungen 61 (1954), 257—66.

D. Syllable and Accent

Birkeland, H., *Akzent und Vokalismus im Althebräischen* (Oslo 1940).

—, *Altarabische Pausalformen* (Oslo 1940).

—, *Stress Patterns in Arabic* (Oslo 1954).

Blake, F. R., *Pretonic Vowels in Hebrew*, in JNES 10 (1951), 243—55.

Brockelmann, C., *Neuere Theorien zur Geschichte des Akzents und des Vokalismus im Hebräischen und Aramäischen*, in ZDMG 94 (1940), 332—71.

Brønno, E., *Studien über hebräische Morphologie und Vokalismus* (Leipzig 1943).

Bush, F. W., *Evidence from Milḥamah and the Masoretic Text for a Penultimate Accent in Hebrew Verbal Forms*, in *Revue de Qumran* 2 (1959—60), 501—14.

Cantineau, J., *De la place de l'accent de mot en hébreu et en araméen biblique*, in *Bulletin d'études orientales* 1 (1931), 81—98.

—, *Élimination des syllabes brèves en hébreu et en araméen biblique*, in *Bulletin d'études orientales* 2 (1932), 125—44.

Goetze, A., *Accent and Vocalism in Hebrew*, in JAOS 59 (1939), 431—59.

Sarauw, C., *Über Akzent und Silbenbildung in den älteren semitischen Sprachen* (Kopenhagen 1939).

Segal, J. B., *The Diacritical Point and the Accents in Syriac* (London 1953).

III. Morphology

A. Preliminaries

Botterweck, G. J., *Der Triliterismus im Semitischen* (Bonn 1952).

Brockelmann, C., *Semitische Keimwortbildungen*, in ZS 5 (1927), 6—38.

Greenberg, J. H., *The Patterning of Root Morphemes in Semitic*, in *Word* 6 (1950), 162—81.

Heller, J., *Neuere Literatur zur Biliterismus-Frage*, in ArOr 27 (1959), 678—82.

Huizinga, A. H., *Analogy in the Semitic Languages* (Baltimore 1901).

Hurwitz, S. T. H., *Root-Determinatives in Semitic Speech* (New York 1913).

Kuryłowicz, J., *L'apophonie en sémitique* (Warszawa 1961).

Moscati, S., *Il biconsonantismo nelle lingue semitiche*, in Bibl 28 (1947), 113—35.

Petráček, K., *Die innere Flexion in den semitischen Sprachen*, in ArOr 28 (1960), 547—606; 29 (1961), 513—45; 30 (1962), 361—408 (wird fortgesetzt).

B. The Noun

Aartun, K., *Zur Frage des bestimmten Artikels im Aramäischen*, in *Acta Orientalia* 24 (1959), 5—14.

Barth, J., *Die Nominalbildung in den semitischen Sprachen*, 2. Aufl. (Leipzig 1894).

Baumgartner, W., *Das hebräische Nominalpräfix mi-*, in ThZ 9 (1953), 154—57.

Bravmann, M. M., *Genetic Aspects of the Genitive in the Semitic Languages*, in JAOS 81 (1961), 386—94.

—, *On a Case of Quantitative Ablaut in Semitic*, in Or 22 (1953), 1—24.

—, *The Plural Ending -ūt- of Masculine Attributive Adjectives in Akkadian*, in JCS 1 (1947), 343.

Brockelmann, C., *Diminutiv und Augmentativ im Semitischen*, in ZS 6 (1928), 109—34.

Cantineau, J., *La notion de schème et son altération dans diverses langues sémitiques*, in Sem 3 (1950), 73—83.

Cazelles, H., *La mimation nominale en Ouest-Sémitique*, in GLECS 5 (1951), 79—81.

Christian, V., *Die Entstehung der semitischen Kasusendungen*, in ZS 3 (1924), 17—26.

Cohen, M., *Noms d'animaux et de plantes à préfixe n en éthiopien*, in GLECS 5 (1951), 85—87.

Entretiens sur la détermination et l'indétermination, in GLECS 5 (1948—51), 73—76, 78, 81—82, 88—96, 98.

Féghali, M. et Cuny, A., *Du genre grammatical en sémitique* (Paris 1924).

Fleisch, H., *Le nom d'agent faʿal*, in MUSJ 32 (1955), 165—72.

Friedrich, J., *Der Schwund kurzer Endvokale im Nordwestsemitischen*, in ZS 1 (1922), 3—14.

Gelb, I., *La mimazione e la nunazione nelle lingue semitiche*, in RSO 12 (1930), 217—65.

Goetze, A., *The Akkadian Masculine Plural in -ānū/ī and its Semitic Background*, in *Language* 22 (1946), 121—30.

Kuryłowicz, J., *La mimation et l'article en arabe*, in ArOr 18, 1—2 (1950), 323—28.

Lagarde, P. de, *Übersicht über die im Aramäischen, Arabischen und Hebräischen übliche Bildung der Nomina* (Göttingen 1889).

Lemoine, E., *Théorie de l'emphase hébraïque* (Paris 1951).

Leslau, W., *Ethiopic Denominatives with Nominal Morphemes*, in Mus 75 (1962), 139—75.

Loretz, O., *Die hebräische Nominalform qattāl*, in Bibl 41 (1960), 411—16.

Matouš, L., *Zum sog. inneren Plural im Arabischen*, in ArOr 24 (1956), 626—30.

Moscati, S., *Il plurale esterno maschile nelle lingue semitiche*, in RSO 29 (1954), 28—52.

—, *Lo stato assoluto dell'aramaico orientale*, in AION 4 (1962), 79—83.

—, *On Semitic Case-Endings*, in JNES 17 (1958), 142—44.

—, *Plurali interni in ugaritico?*, in RSO 32 (1957), 339—52.

Nyberg, H. S., *Wortbildung mit Präfixen in den semitischen Sprachen*, in *Le monde oriental* 14 (1920), 177—289.

Rin, S., *The Termination -ē in the Plural Absolute*, in Leshonenu 25 (1961), 17—19.

Speiser, E. A., *The "Elative" in West-Semitic and Akkadian*, in JCS 6 (1952), 81—92.

—, *Studies in Semitic Formatives*, in JAOS 56 (1936), 22—46.

—, *The Terminative-Adverbial in Canaanite-Ugaritic and Akkadian*, in IEJ 4 (1954), 108—15.

Tagliavini, C., *Alcune osservazioni sul primitivo valore della mimazione e nunazione nelle lingue semitiche*, in *Donum natalicium Schrijnen* (Chartres 1929), 240—90.

Torczyner, H., *Die Entstehung des semitischen Sprachtypus*, I (Wien 1916).

Troupeau, G., *Le schème de pluriel Fuʿlān en arabe classique*, in GLECS 7 (1955), 65—66.

von Soden, W., *Status rectus-Formen vor dem Genitiv im Akkadischen und die sogenannte uneigentliche Annexion im Arabischen*, in JNES 19 (1960), 163—71.

Wagner, E., *Die erste Person Dualis im Semitischen*, in ZDMG 102 (1952), 229—33.

Wehr, H., *Der arabische Elativ* (Wiesbaden 1953).
Young, E. J., *Adverbial -u in Semitic*, in *Westminster Theological Journal*
  13, 2 (1951), 151—54.

C. The Pronoun

Barth, J., *Die Pronominalbildung in den semitischen Sprachen* (Leipzig 1913).
Bravmann, M. M., *Hebrew štayim in the Light of Syriac and Turkic*, in
  Proceedings of the American Society for Jewish Research 21 (1952), 1—2.
Caspari, W., *Zum hebräischen Demonstrativ*, in ZS 7 (1931), 41—52.
Castellino, G., *Observations on the Akkadian Personal Pronouns in the Light
  of Semitic and Hamitic*, in MIOF 5 (1957), 185—218.
—, *The Akkadian Personal Pronouns and Verbal System in the Light of
  Semitic and Hamitic* (Leiden 1962).
Greenberg, H., *An Afro-Asiatic Pattern of Gender and Number Agreement*, in
  JAOS 80 (1960), 317—21.
Kienast, B., *Das Personalpronomen der 2. Person im Semitischen*, in AIOK
  XXIV, 253—55.
—, *Erwägungen zu einer neueren Studie über semitische Demonstrativa*, in
  Or 26 (1957), 257—68.
Loewenstamm, S. E., *On Ugaritic Pronouns in the Light of Canaanitic*, in
  Leshonenu 23 (1958—59), 72—84.
Rosén, H.B., *Zur Vorgeschichte des Relativsatzes im Nordwestsemitischen*, in
  ArOr 27 (1959), 186—98.
Rundgren, F., *Über Bildungen mit (š)- und n-t-Demonstrativen im Semi-
  tischen* (Uppsala 1955).
Trager, G. L. and Rice, F. A., *The Personal Pronoun System of Classical
  Arabic*, in *Language* 30 (1954), 224—29.

D. The Numeral

Barth, J., *Zur Flexion der semitischen Zahlwörter*, in ZDMG 66 (1912),
  94—102.
Bauer, H., *Noch einmal die semitischen Zahlwörter*, in ZDMG 66 (1912),
  267—70.
Cantineau, J., *Le nom de nombre « six » dans les langues sémitiques*, in *Bulletin
  des études arabes* 13 (1943), 72.
Loewenstamm, S. E., *The Development of the Term "First" in the Semitic
  Languages*, in *Tarbiz* 24 (1954—55), 249—51.
Reckendorf, H., *Der Bau der semitischen Zahlwörter*, in ZDMG 65 (1911),
  550—59.
von Soden, W., *Die Zahlen 20—90 im Semitischen und der Status absolutus*,
  in WZKM 57 (1961), 24—28.

E. The Particles

Eitan, I., *Hebrew and Semitic Particles*, in AJSL 44 (1928), 177—205, 254—60;
  45 (1929), 48—63, 130—45, 197—211; 46 (1930), 22—50.
Garbini, G., *La congiunzione semitica *pa-*, in Bibl 38 (1957), 419—27.

Guidi, I., *Particelle interrogative e negative nelle lingue semitiche*, in *A Volume of Studies presented to E. G. Browne* (Cambridge 1922), 175—78.

Sarna, N. M., *The Interchange of the Prepositions beth and min in Biblical Hebrew*, in JBL 78 (1959), 310—16.

F. The Verb

Ahrens, K., *Der Stamm der schwachen Verba in den semitischen Sprachen*, in ZDMG 64 (1910), 161—94.

Bauer, H., *Die Tempora im Semitischen* (Berlin 1910).

Blake, F. R., *A Resurvey of Hebrew Tenses* (Roma 1951).

Bravmann, M. M., *Notes on the Forms of the Imperative in Hebrew and Arabic*, in JQR 42 (1961), 51—56.

Brockelmann, C., *Die „Tempora" des Semitischen*, in Zeitschrift für Phonetik 5 (1951), 133—54.

Brzuski, W. K., *Note sur les thèmes à seconde radicale graphiquement redoublée en sudarabique épigraphique*, in *Rocznik Orientalistyczny* 25 (1961), 127—31.

Christian, V., *Das Wesen der semitischen Tempora*, in ZDMG 81 (1927), 232—58.

Cohen, M., *Le système verbal sémitique et l'expression du temps* (Paris 1924).

Dahood, M., *Some Aphel Causatives in Ugaritic*, in Bibl 38 (1957), 62—73.

Dombrowski, B. W. W., *Some Remarks on the Hebrew Hitpaʿel and Inversative -t- in the Semitic Languages*, in JNES 21 (1962), 220—23.

Driver, G. R., *Problems of the Hebrew Verbal System* (Edinburgh 1936).

Fleisch, H., *Les verbes à allongement vocalique interne en sémitique* (Paris 1944).

—, *Sur le système verbal du sémitique commun et son évolution dans les langues sémitiques anciennes*, in MUSJ 27 (1947—48), 39—60.

Goetze, A., *The So-Called Intensive of the Semitic Languages*, in JAOS 62 (1942), 1—8.

—, *The Tenses of Ugaritic*, in JAOS 58 (1938), 266—309.

Hammershaimb, E., *Das Verbum im Dialekt von Ras Schamra* (Kopenhagen 1941).

Heidel, A., *The System of the Quadriliteral Verb in Akkadian* (Chicago 1940).

Janssens, G., *De werkwoordelijke „Tijden" in het semietisch, en in het bizonder in het hebreeuws*, in JEOL 15 (1957—58), 97—103.

Jirku, A., *Eine 'Afʿel-Form im Ugaritischen?*, in AfO 18 (1957), 129—30.

Kienast, B., *Das Punktualthema *yaprus und seine Modi*, in Or 29 (1960), 151—67.

—, *Verbalformen mit Reduplikation im Akkadischen*, in Or 26 (1957), 44—50.

—, *Weiteres zum R-Stamm des Akkadischen*, in JCS 15 (1961), 59—61.

Kuryłowicz, J., *Esquisse d'une théorie de l'apophonie en sémitique*, in BSLP 53 (1957—58), 1—38.

—, *Le système verbal du sémitique*, in BSLP 45 (1949), 47—56.

Leslau, W., *Le thème verbal fréquentatif dans les langues éthiopiennes*, in RES 1939, 15—31.

—, *Le type verbal qatälä en éthiopien méridional*, in MUSJ 31 (1954), 15—98.

Martin, W. J., *Some Notes on the Imperative in the Semitic Languages*, in RSO 32 (1957), 315—19.

Meyer, R., *Das hebräische Verbalsystem im Lichte der gegenwärtigen Forschung*, in *Congress Volume Oxford 1959* (Leiden 1960), 309—17.

—, *Spuren eines westsemitischen Präsens-Futur in den Texten von Chirbet Qumran*, in *Von Ugarit nach Qumran* (Berlin 1958), 118—26.

—, *Zur Geschichte des hebräischen Verbums*, in VT 3 (1953), 225—35.

Moran, W. L., *Early Canaanite yaqtula*, in Or 29 (1960), 1—19.

Moscati, S., *Il participio passivo in semitico*, in RSO 37 (1962), 51—57.

Müller, W. W., *Die Wurzeln Mediae und Tertiae y/w im Altsüdarabischen* (Tübingen 1962).

Praetorius, F., *Zur Kausativbildung im Semitischen*, in ZS 5 (1927), 39—42.

Rössler, O., *Die Präfixkonjugation Qal der Verba I^{ae} Nûn im Althebräischen und das Problem der sogenannten Tempora*, in ZAW 74 (1962), 125—41.

—, *Eine bisher unbekannte Tempusform im Althebräischen*, in ZDMG 111 (1961), 445—51.

Rowton, M. B., *The Use of Permansive in Classic Babylonian*, in JNES 21 (1962), 233—303.

Rundgren, F., *Das althebräische Verbum. Abriß der Aspektlehre* (Uppsala 1961).

—, *Das altsyrische Verbalsystem*, in *Språkvetenskapliga Sällskapets i Uppsala Forhandliger 1958—60*, 49—75.

—, *Der aspektuelle Charakter des altsemitischen Injunktivs*, in *Orientalia Suecana* 9 (1960), 75—101.

—, *Intensiv und Aspekt-Korrelation. Studien zur äthiopischen und akkadischen Verbalstammbildung* (Uppsala-Wiesbaden 1959).

Saydon, P. P., *The Conative Imperfect in Hebrew*, in VT 12 (1962), 124—26.

Solá-Solé, J. M., *L'infinitif sémitique* (Paris 1961).

Speiser, E. A., *The Durative Hithpaʿel: a tan-Form*, in JAOS 75 (1955), 118—21.

Stinespring, W. F., *The Active Infinitive with Passive Meaning in Biblical Aramaic*, in JBL 81 (1962), 391—94.

Vycichl, W., *Ein passives Partizip qatīl im Ägyptischen und Semitischen*, in ZDMG 109 (1959), 253—57.

von Soden, W., *Tempus und Modus im Semitischen*, in AIOK XXIV, 263—65.

—, *Unregelmäßige Verben im Akkadischen*, in ZA 16 (1952), 163—81.

Wernberg-Møller, P., *Observations on the Hebrew Participle*, in ZAW 71 (1959), 54—67.

Lexicography

A. North-East Semitic (Akkadian)

Delitzsch, Fr., *Assyrisches Handwörterbuch* (Leipzig 1896).

Gelb, I. J., *Glossary of Old Akkadian* (Chicago 1957).

Muss-Arnold, W., *A Concise Dictionary of the Assyrian Language. Assyrisch-Englisch-Deutsches Handwörterbuch*, 2 vol. (Berlin 1894—1905).

von Soden, W., *Akkadisches Handwörterbuch, unter Benutzung des lexikalischen Nachlasses von Bruno Meißner bearbeitet* (Wiesbaden 1959 ff.).

The Assyrian Dictionary of the University of Chicago. Editorial Board J. Gelb, Th. Jacobsen, B. Landsberger, A. L. Oppenheim (Chicago 1956 ff.).

B. North-West Semitic

Brockelmann, C., *Lexicon Syriacum*, ed. ṣecunda (Halis Saxon. 1928).

Brown, F., Driver, S. R., Briggs, C. A., *A Hebrew and English Lexicon of the Old Testament* (Oxford 1906).

Dalman, G., *Aramäisch-Neuhebräisches Handwörterbuch zu Targum, Talmud und Midrasch*, 2. Aufl. (Frankfurt 1922, Reprint 1938).

Gesenius, W., *Hebräisches und Aramäisches Handwörterbuch über das Alte Testament*, bearb. von Frants Buhl. Unveränderter Neudruck der 1915 erschienenen 17. Auflage (Berlin-Göttingen-Heidelberg 1950).

Jean, Ch. F. et Hoftijzer, J., *Dictionnaire des inscriptions sémitiques de l'Ouest* (Leiden 1960 ff.).

Koehler, L. et Baumgartner, W., *Lexicon in Veteris Testamenti libros* (Leiden 1953).

—, *Supplementum ad Lexicon in Veteris Testamenti libros* (Leiden 1958).

Levy, J., *Neuhebräisches und Chaldäisches Wörterbuch*, 4. vol. (Leipzig 1876—89).

Margoliouth, G. P., *Supplement to the Thesaurus Syriacus of R. Payne Smith* (Oxford 1927).

Payne Smith, R., *Thesaurus Syriacus*, 2 vol. (Oxon. 1868—97).

Schulthess, Fr., *Lexicon Syropalaestinum* (Berlin 1903).

Zorell, F., *Lexicon Hebraicum et Aramaicum Veteris Testamenti* (Roma 1940 ff.).

C. South-West Semitic

Belot, J. B., *Vocabulaire arabe-français à l'usage des étudiants* (Beyrouth 1883, many reprints).

Conti Rossini, C., *Chrestomathia Arabica Meridionalis Epigraphica* (Roma 1931), 99—261.

Dillmann, A., *Lexicon Linguae Aethiopicae* (Lipsiae 1865, Reprint New York 1954).

Freytag, G. W., *Lexicon Arabico-Latinum*, 4 vol. (Halis Saxon. 1830—37).

Grébaut, S., *Supplément au Lexicon Linguae Aethiopicae de A. Dillmann et édition du Lexique de Juste d'Urbin (1850—1855)* (Paris 1952).

Lane, E. W., *Arabic-English Lexicon*, 8 vol. (London 1863—1893, Reprint 1955).

Wehr, H., *A Dictionary of Modern Written Arabic*, ed. by J. Milton Cowan (Wiesbaden 1961).

Wörterbuch der Klassischen Arabischen Sprache. Auf Grund der Sammlungen von A. Fischer, Th. Nöldeke, H. Reckendorf u. a. Quellen hrsg. durch die Deutsche Morgenländische Gesellschaft (Wiesbaden 1957ff.).

List of Abbreviations used in the Text

The abbreviations used for reviews are those of the *Bibliographie sémitique* of *Orientalia*. Those used for books are as follows:

Brockelmann, SG = Brockelmann, C., *Syrische Grammatik*, 7. Aufl. (Leipzig 1955).

Brockelmann, GVG = Brockelmann, C., *Grundriß der vergleichenden Grammatik der semitischen Sprachen*, 2 vol. (Berlin 1908—13).

Dillmann, EG = Dillmann, A., *Ethiopic Grammar*, 2nd ed. (London 1907):

Fleisch, TPA = Fleisch, H., *Traité de philologie arabe*, I (Beyrouth 1961).

Garbini, SNO = Garbini, G., *Il semitico di nord-ovest* (Napoli 1960).

Gelb, OA = Gelb, I. J., *Old Akkadian Writing and Grammar* (Chicago 1952).

Gordon, UM = Gordon, C. H., *Ugaritic Manual* (Roma 1955).

Gray, SCL = Gray, L. H., *Introduction to Semitic Comparative Linguistics* (New York 1934).

Rabin, WA = Rabin, C., *Ancient West Arabian* (London 1951).

Ullendorff, SLE = Ullendorff, E., *The Semitic Languages of Ethiopia. A Comparative Phonology* (London 1955).

von Soden, GAG = von Soden, W., *Grundriß der akkadischen Grammatik* (Roma 1952).

WILHELM BRANDENSTEIN — MANFRED MAYRHOFER

Handbuch des Altpersischen

1964. XII, 160 Seiten, broschiert DM 26,—

Das Altpersische — als sprachliches Medium der Achämeniden-Großkönige von ebensolcher Bedeutung für die Althistorie, wie als eine der beiden erhaltenen altiranischen Sprachen für mehrere philologisch-linguistische Disziplinen — ist zur Zeit nur in einer monumentalen Gesamtdarstellung R. G. Kents (²1953) zugänglich; es fehlt an noch erhältlichen kurzen Einführungen in einer geläufigen Sprache. Das vorliegende Handbuch soll diese Lücke schließen; es bietet, nach einer Einleitung, die Grundtatsachen der vergleichenden Laut- und Formenlehre, eine größere Anzahl von Texten und ein Glossar. Dieses soll einerseits die Textlektüre — auch für Nichtphilologen — ermöglichen, andererseits aber auch den gesamten etymologisch trennbaren altpersischen Wortschatz enthalten. Über R. G. Kent wird durch kritische Überprüfung seiner linguistischen Wertungen, durch Erfassung der neueren Fachliteratur, v. a. aber durch die Einbeziehung der „Nebenüberlieferung" altpersischer Wörter (in elamischen, aramäischen, griechischen u. a. Quellen) hinausgestrebt. — Das in spanischer Sprache erschienene kleine Werk der beiden Autoren, „Antiguo Persa" (1958) bildet zwar den Ausgangspunkt, doch ist das „Handbuch des Altpersischen" völlig neu abgefaßt worden.

HENRIK SAMUEL NYBERG

A Manual of Pahlavi

Part I: Texts, Alphabets, Index, Paradigms, Notes and an Introduction

1964. XXVIII, 184 Seiten, broschiert ca. DM 24,—

Das Hilfsbuch des Pehlevi, das in einer begrenzten Auflage in den Jahren 1929 bis 1931 in Uppsala veröffentlicht wurde und seit Jahrzehnten vergriffen ist, erscheint jetzt in einer durchgreifenden Neubearbeitung unter dem Titel „A Manual of Pahlavi". Das Englische wurde diesmal als Sprache gewählt, um das Buch den des Deutschen wenig kundigen Parsen in Indien zugänglich zu machen. Der 1. Band umfaßt die Texte, die Schriftlehre, den Index der Pahlavi-Wörter, Verbparadigmen, einen textkritischen Apparat und eine Einleitung über die benutzten Ausgaben und den Handschriftenbestand. Ganz neu ist die Aufnahme von Proben der sassanidischen Inschriften und des Turfan-Psalters.
Der 2. Band, für den das Material teilweise verarbeitet ist, wird das Glossar und einen Abriß der Grammatik enthalten.

OTTO HARRASSOWITZ · WIESBADEN